"The Kids in the Hall were groun[d] and much bolder than anything an[.] the time. I watched them religiously and always laughed my ass off." —Judd Apatow

"I'll openly admit that the Kids in the Hall were a direct influence on *Portlandia*. We definitely took ideas from them, and I know I've said out loud 'How would the Kids in the Hall end this sketch? How would they do it?'" —Fred Armisen

"They were the step after *Saturday Night Live*. This was something new." —Lorne Michaels

"They were just so fucking good." —Patton Oswalt

"The Kids in the Hall were fresh and sharp and funny and cool. They were constantly moving forward. When all the cylinders are firing at a Kids in the Hall show, it reaches the level of comedy art." —Mike Myers

"I love those guys, they're the best. Anybody who meets them likes them. They're my kind of humour." —Bob Odenkirk

"The fact that people are still going to see the Kids in the Hall when they tour speaks to their legacy. Their stuff holds up, you know?" —David Cross

"All of us in *The State* knew who they were, and I think we all felt like, 'Oh, these fuckers. We need to compete with these assholes.' And of course, in our minds, they were fuckers and assholes because they were successful."

—Michael Ian Black

"Comedic milestones—when comedy takes a step forward—are the moments that, as a comedy person, you live for. The Kids in the Hall were one of them. Modern sketch comedy owes them the hugest debt of gratitude."

—Paul Feig

"The Kids were my eye-opening 'Sex Pistols' moment. When I watched them I said, 'Wait, I can do this too!'"

—Jonah Ray

"There are only a few sketch comedy groups that survive the test of time. The Kids in the Hall were so bold, so imaginative, and so brilliant, that they will go down on the very top of that list, next to *Monty Python's Flying Circus*. Their work is as perfect today as it was the day they released it."

—Thomas Lennon

"The Kids in the Hall quoted to an acquaintance is the litmus test for friendship. Silly, subversive, intelligent comedy delivered with heart. They have no parallel."

—Bobcat Goldthwait

"The Kids in the Hall set the tone for what sketch comedy could be. They showed that cultural impact was as important as comedy, and I don't think there's ever been a comedy troupe that's been able to pull that off since."
— George Stroumboulopoulos

"Individually and collectively, the Kids in the Hall are some of the funniest people to ever do a sketch show, and Paul Myers is the perfect guy to write a book about them."
— Frank Conniff

"Everything they did was done with truth. And it was so refreshing, too. The Kids in the Hall was what people call 'smart comedy.' It fed your brain."   — Steve Higgins

"The Kids in the Hall are spectacular! They're a continuation and a combination of what we did in Second City, and what Monty Python was doing for us at the time. They were all so gifted, and their storytelling was very cool and sophisticated."   — David Steinberg

"The Kids in the Hall are easily the most influential comedians of my generation and one of the greatest sketch troupes of all time."
— Kliph Nesteroff, author of *The Comedians: Drunks, Thieves, Scoundrels and the History of American Comedy*

Also by Paul Myers

A Wizard a True Star: Todd Rundgren in the Studio

*It Ain't Easy: Long John Baldry and the
Birth of the British Blues*

Barenaked Ladies: Public Stunts, Private Stories

THE KIDS
IN THE HALL

One Dumb Guy

PAUL MYERS

FOREWORD BY SETH MEYERS

ANANSI

Copyright © 2018 Paul Myers

Published in Canada in 2018 and the USA in 2018 by
House of Anansi Press Inc.
www.houseofanansi.com

The script excerpted from the Kids in the Hall sketch "Reg"
on pages 121–122 is provided courtesy of The Broadway Video Group, Inc.

House of Anansi Press is committed to protecting our natural
environment. As part of our efforts, the interior of this book is printed on
paper that contains 100% post-consumer recycled fibres, is acid-free,
and is processed chlorine-free.

22 21 20 19 18   2 3 4 5 6

Library and Archives Canada Cataloguing in Publication

Myers, Paul, 1960–, author
The Kids in the Hall : one dumb guy / Paul Myers.

Issued in print and electronic formats.
ISBN 978-1-4870-0183-4 (softcover).—ISBN 978-1-4870-0185-8 (Kindle).
—ISBN 978-1-4870-0184-1 (EPUB)

1. Kids in the Hall (Comedy group)—Biography. 2. Comedians—
Canada—Biography. I. Title.

PN2307.M94 2017   791.45092'2   C2016-907270-3
                          C2016-907271-1

Library of Congress Control Number: 2017953508

Book design: Alysia Shewchuk

 Canada Council   Conseil des Arts   ONTARIO ARTS COUNCIL
for the Arts   du Canada   CONSEIL DES ARTS DE L'ONTARIO
                                                           an Ontario government agency
                                                           un organisme du gouvernement de l'Ontario

*We acknowledge for their financial support of our publishing program the
Canada Council for the Arts, the Ontario Arts Council, and the Government
of Canada.*

Printed and bound in Canada

For Liza Algar, who inspires me and coconspires with me every step of the way

CONTENTS

FOREWORD

In 1995, the summer between my junior and senior years of college, I worked in New York City as an intern for Comedy Central. On the first day, my boss led me into a closet cluttered with VHS tapes and told me I had eight weeks to organize and catalogue it. For the first few weeks I was committed to the job and well on track to complete it as instructed, but then I stumbled upon the complete *The Kids in the Hall* and it all went to hell.

You see, I grew up in a household without cable. I loved *Saturday Night Live* and had heard tale of this other edgier Lorne Michaels show that aired on HBO, but had only caught glimpses of it at sleepovers or off bootleg tapes that fellow comedy nerds had brought to campus. And now, here I was with full access and I was resolved to take advantage of it. Each day, I would do the bare minimum of work to not draw attention to myself, and in the spaces in between I watched every episode of every season of this wonderful show.

I fell in love. If *SNL* was the Rolling Stones playing arenas, *The Kids in the Hall* was an indie band playing a low-ceilinged rock club full of adoring fans. The lo-fi opening credits alone let you know this was something grittier than you were used to. Sweeping shots of New York City were replaced with Canadian suburbia and parking lots. And while Lorne kept the device of actors finding the lens while their names bounced underneath them, there was no Don Pardo bellowing their identities. You had to read them, like liner notes on the back of an album.

And soon, you learned each of their styles. For precise character work, Mark McKinney was your guy. If you loved foreign films, Bruce McCulloch had the eye of an auteur. Scott Thompson was the open book, sharing himself via monologues unlike anything you'd ever seen. And for sharply written premises, it was Kevin McDonald and Dave Foley. Their differing skill sets fit together perfectly. For years, I've thought of the five of them like a perfectly constructed basketball team and just now I'm realizing it should have been hockey. It's not like they never mentioned the Maple Leafs.

They were so funny, but beyond that they were so decent. When they played women, it was done with integrity and never for a cheap laugh. When they spoke of gay culture, it was as something to be proud of rather than a comic stereotype. In later years, when I found myself writing sketches for a living, I often turned to them as a standard for what I wanted to accomplish.

When my summer as a Comedy Central intern ended, I went to my boss for my employee evaluation. He told me that he'd been impressed early on, but that he couldn't help but notice how my efforts flagged in the second half of my time there. While he had once considered offering me a job when I graduated, he couldn't in good conscience say that he would now. I admitted that I'd allowed myself to become distracted. He asked me what by and when I told him *The Kids in the Hall*, he said, "There are worse things to throw an opportunity away for."

I don't regret it.

Enjoy this book.

Seth Meyers

Here Come the Brides

On a Sunday evening in May 2015, I entered San Francisco's prestigious Warfield Theatre to catch up with my old friends, the legendary comedy troupe the Kids in the Hall. As longtime stage director Jim Millan ushered me backstage, I found the Kids distractedly immersed in their various preshow rituals. As usual, it fell to Kevin McDonald to greet me, offering drinks and snacks before walking me over to a large round table where Mark McKinney nodded hello from behind a newspaper and Bruce McCulloch broke briefly from a conversation with his wife, Tracy, to raise an eyebrow in lieu of a verbal greeting. A jittery Scott Thompson darted in and out of the room, seeming to have misplaced something important, while Dave Foley offered me a warm handshake with one hand while nursing a soft drink in the other, having recently gone on the wagon. By this point, I had known the troupe for over thirty years, but while these five middle-aged men had long since outgrown their childlike name, very little else seemed to have changed about them since the day we met. While a sense of imminent fun hung over the backstage area, this was not a party; these men were about to go to work at the job they had created for themselves back on the streets of Toronto in the early '80s. As showtime approached, Millan politely asked all visitors to clear the room and take their seats, affording me my first glimpse of the 2,300+ fans in the sold-out house. Surprisingly, it wasn't all silver foxes like myself. It seemed to me that roughly half the house was comprised of millennials or younger; a large cross section of these people hadn't even been born when *The Kids in the Hall* TV series originally aired on network television in the late '80s. It was entirely possible that, for many, this was their first time at a Kids in the Hall live show. As the houselights dimmed, a recording of Shadowy Men on a Shadowy Planet's "Having an Average Weekend"—the official theme for the Kids' TV series—echoed through the auditorium to cheers of instant recognition. The air was electric. As nostalgia washed over me, I realized that the Kids and I had come a long way—some thirty years and 4,239 km (2,634 miles) to be precise. My mind raced back to Toronto in the winter of 1985, to the small club show where I had first realized that maybe, just maybe, these guys had something special.

As in all the best stories, ours opens on a dark and stormy night, when an especially nasty blizzard was heaping obscene amounts of snow upon the city of Toronto. TTC streetcars were backed up all along Queen Street and most major surface routes, and you couldn't get a cab to save your life. Frankly, if you had nothing better to do, you were best advised to stay home under a blanket, preferably near a space heater.

Yet some of us daring comedy aficionados *did* have something better to do, we who had bravely trudged through six-foot snowdrifts, past cars that wouldn't be dug out until morning, just to get to a tiny cabaret bar called the Rivoli, where a photocopied poster stapled to a telephone pole out front beckoned, "Man the Laff Boats, it's the Kids in the Hall." Once safely inside the warm confines of the Riv, we bought our drinks from the bartender and talent booker, Carson, and took our seats just as Dave, Kevin, Bruce, Mark, and Scott commandeered two cramped but functional stages and went about the hilarious business of fulfilling their weekly residency. Earlier that afternoon, the five Kids had huddled backstage to mull over whether they should even play the show at all, operating on the assumption that nobody would make it through the storm or feel much like laughing if they did. Thankfully, they opted to do the show anyway—for themselves—whether anyone showed up or not.

"The show went on," remembers McDonald, "and this became the first night that we had a lineup around the block; we even had to turn people away. After that night, we always had a great audience at the Rivoli."

The troupe had been honing their act for months, and I had been laughing along with their uniquely suburban take on social justice, big-city life, and institutional hypocrisy.

Week after week, I witnessed them creating fresh material out of the ether, developing new characters, and forging a unique comedy aesthetic. While clearly informed by *Monty Python's Flying Circus*, *SCTV*, and *Saturday Night Live*, their highly disruptive comedy was as anarchic as any punk rock show playing in the neighbouring bars of the Queen Street strip. Sure, they were all white males, but in the early '80s, just having one of those white males be openly gay—and not always playing it for laughs—seemed downright revolutionary. While the Kids played all the female roles themselves, it never seemed like a campy drag act, and their "ladies" were frequently the heroes of their scenes. While their name was already age inappropriate—even then, they were all in their early to mid-twenties—it announced them as perennial outsiders, the punks in the corridor, ready to break into the big room by any means necessary.

I discovered the Kids early on and by kismet. After my younger brother, the sketch comedian and writer Mike Myers, had flourished at the Second City Theatre's comedy workshops, I found myself following him to class where soon I too was learning the ways and history of improv comedy alongside fellow students Kevin McDonald and Dave Foley. I quickly became friends with Kevin and Dave, who told me their troupe had been doing some shows and that I should come to see them. As fate would have it, my girlfriend at the time mentioned a comedy troupe she'd heard about that featured a fellow student at York University named Scott. All roads led to the Rivoli.

Over the coming months, as Toronto thawed out and warmed up, so too did the buzz around the Kids in the Hall.

Eventually, that buzz translated into a career in television, and I became a regular member of the studio audience for their live tapings. Soon, our secret was out, and their name spread across the country and beyond. Just as *SCTV* had put Canadian comedy on the map, *The Kids in the Hall* updated it and made it even cooler. As they moved into film and theatre tours, various tensions within the troupe would at times threaten their fragile union, but like any thirty-year marriage, they have somehow made it work.

As the curtain opened at the Warfield in 2015, the marriage analogy was underlined by the sight of all five Kids in bridal gowns, symbolically reaffirming their vows through classic sketches, while offering new material, just as they had back in those chilly Rivoli days.

After the show, Kevin told me that while these five strong-willed individuals would probably always find something to fight over, this same tension was also the secret to their longevity. Just like their fictional garage rock band, Rod Torfulson's Armada featuring Herman Menderchuk, there have been times in the Kids' career when they questioned if they were going to make it. It wasn't easy, and it wasn't always fun. As a troupe, they've often made risky artistic choices, and probably shot themselves in the foot more than once. But according to McDonald, the state of their union is as strong as ever. "We create most of our own problems," he tells me, "then we're sad about it. But later on we can see the humour. I think it helps us write better sketches. I always say that individually, we're all smart guys, but collectively, we're really just one dumb guy."

These pages constitute the inside story of how that One Dumb Guy managed to create some of the funniest sketch comedy ever performed, and inspired their peers and subsequent generations of sketch comedians to create programs such as *Mr. Show with Bob & David, The State, The Ben Stiller Show, Portlandia, Key & Peele,* and most recently, *Baroness von Sketch Show.*

Today, the Kids in the Hall still make me laugh whenever I see them or their work, and despite cheating death and worse, they're still here. The story of just how they *got* here begins in earnest in the province of Alberta, when a young drunk punk named Bruce McCulloch met a well-travelled diplomat's son named Mark McKinney.

ONE

Mark and Bruce Cut Loose at the Moose

Bruce Ian McCulloch was born on May 12, 1961, in Edmonton, Alberta, where, like many future comedians, he got his first laughs in his first-grade classroom. "My teacher would say something like 'I told you umpteen times not to do that,'" McCulloch recalls, "so I said, 'Yes, but you didn't tell me how many umpteen was.' She actually laughed, and then the whole class laughed, and I was like, 'Oh, that's what it feels like to make a joke and be funny.'"

His middle name came from his father, Ian McCulloch, a hard-drinking travelling salesman who, despite being a mean drunk, was also something of a bohemian possessed of a sharp sense of humour and a healthy respect for the arts—comedy in particular. "My dad was kind of a Willy Loman figure," says McCulloch, "but he also played the bass in clubs, and loved jazz and weird comedy records. I remember liking *The Button-Down Mind of Bob Newhart* and

Woody Allen's *Standup Comic*, and my dad telling me how fortunate he felt to have seen Lenny Bruce in concert one time in Montreal."

A bright kid, McCulloch began to cultivate his own sense of humour as a coping mechanism to process his father's frequent bouts of drunken rage and other exploits, including one time when he crashed the family car. It was not unusual for young Bruce to lie awake in bed while his dad blasted out his Dave Brubeck records downstairs at all hours of the morning. Poetically, he remembers this time as a "beige wasteland of cigarette smoke and complacency where nothing was really going on for me."

Things changed radically when he was eight years old, and his mother, June Hicks, filed for divorce, leaving Bruce and his sister, Heather, to follow their dad to Winnipeg, Manitoba, to live with their new stepmother, Connie Buchanan. It would be nearly two years before Bruce saw his biological mother again. "My parents had an old-fashioned '60s divorce," says McCulloch, "where I wasn't allowed to mention my mom's name, or even have a picture of her in my room. When I was entering junior high, we moved to Calgary and my life kind of started."

Always a clever student, Bruce's grades began to suffer after the divorce and relocation. By now his comedy coping mechanism was second nature, and he found that being funny and weird helped him to navigate a confusing emotional landscape. Only now he had discovered that athletics were a great way to work off some of the teen angst, and he showed genuine promise as a competitive power lifter and a star athlete, albeit a quirky one. "My nickname was

Power Jerk," says McCulloch, "because I was both power-ful and a jerk."

McCulloch would remain obsessed with sports until he was fourteen years old, when fate introduced him to a sixteen-year-old aspiring musician named Reid Diamond. The two became fast friends, and Diamond, already possessed of his own sense of style, mentored McCulloch in the counterculture, steering him away from athletics and introducing him to the joys of alcohol and exotic British rock records. "For a while I gave up football," says McCulloch, "because the guys that did sports were kind of losers. But I soon got back into wrestling, power lifting, and taking solo bike trips; all that stuff. It's funny, I've been distance running since I was eleven, and even when we'd all party all night, I'd wake up and go for a run. All my rock friends thought I was a fag, but I did it anyway."

In a futile effort to fit in and be a cool kid, McCulloch attempted to keep his sense of humour to himself. When Diamond heard that McCulloch was funny, he confronted him about it. "Reid said, 'Hey, I just met someone who says you're funny. You're not funny,'" McCulloch remembers. "Up until then, I had kept my comic side hidden from him, but it became harder and harder to hide because, in that very clichéd way, I had discovered that being funny could get me out of trouble in school."

Still, it would be a few years before McCulloch found an outlet for his funny side, and in the meantime, he plunged deeper into a pattern of drinking, fighting, and rock 'n' roll. He remembers feeling "rudderless" and uncertain much of the time, fearing that he might end up just another funny guy at some factory somewhere, riffing around the snack machine at break time.

"I never thought that there was a possibility to pursue the arts in my life," says McCulloch. "When you read the autobiographies of Bob Dylan or Patti Smith, they both say they had no idea what they were going to do with their creativity; they were just wandering around. I was like that too. I had absolutely no thought that my individuality or my weird worldview could get me anywhere. Reid and I just did weird and elaborate things."

When he was fifteen, he would try out gags on his girl-friend. "One time, I waited twenty-five minutes for her to come over while wearing a paper bag on my head with 'Welcome' written on it," McCulloch recalls. "Another time, I sent her a dead fish through the mail with a note-card saying 'Don't worry, there's not a dead fish in here.' I remember it really made her mom mad at me."

Most weekends in the mid-1970s, your average teenager could be found huddled around a television set late at night, cracking up over the latest revolution in comedy, *Saturday Night Live*. McCulloch, on the other hand, preferred to stay out late on the weekends seeing bands, crashing parties, drinking, and sometimes fighting. "Watching TV was for losers," he recalls. "Even later on, when people said they wanted to go to a movie on the weekend, I thought, 'You fucking loser.'"

One day, Diamond introduced Bruce to another musi-cian friend of his who lived out in Calgary's Braeside dis-trict, guitarist and budding illustrator Brian Connelly. Diamond and Connelly were dead set on starting a band,

and their sheer confidence made a lasting impression on McCulloch. But he was not a musician and remembers feeling left out. "These guys were my world at the time," says McCulloch. "They knew what they wanted, but I didn't know what I was going to do, so I was doubly lost. Even though I knew I had a special brain, I began to carry this sadness, like I was destined to be a loser."

At the time, Calgary offered few opportunities for a young artist to nurture and cultivate his sensitive soul. The oil boomtown was still mostly rural, populated by tough manual labourers, stiff-suited oil executives, and actual Stetson-wearing cowboys ripping up the main drag in their loud-ass pickup trucks. For McCulloch, this was a lonely place to be. "There were some pretty girls, but there were very few kind girls, and certainly no artistic girls that I knew of. If you went to a bar and you didn't look like a cowboy, you'd get beat up. If you used words with too many syllables, you were 'gay.'"

During his final year at high school, McCulloch's estranged mother asked him to move in with her, and for a time her basement offered him a pleasant sanctuary. June had become a real estate agent and was frequently out showing properties, so McCulloch had the run of the place, inviting his weight-lifting friends over after their meets. But things changed drastically after what he now refers to as "Tequila-Fest," an infamous "competitive drinking event" wherein he and his fellow lifters attempted to consume their own weight in alcohol. The morning after the gathering, June returned home to find her son passed out on the front yard, curled up in the fetal position, and encased

in a cocoon of Silly String and vomit. What she saw inside
the house was even worse: broken furniture, vomit-stained
carpets, and more passed-out teens. She was so shocked
by the carnage, McCulloch remembers, that she staggered
back to the front yard and suffered a heart attack right there
on her own front steps. During the slow recovery period
that followed, June saw her commission-based sales dry up,
leading to the bank foreclosing on her home. When June
moved in with his sister, Heather, McCulloch was told he
was unwelcome. At just nineteen years old, Bruce found
himself homeless, with no money, no prospects, and no idea
of what to do next. As he later wrote in his memoir, *Let's
Start a Riot*, he came to the profound realization that we are
all only "three bad breaks away from living in a cardboard
fort." For the first time in his young life, Bruce McCulloch
was truly on his own.

In search of financial security, Bruce struggled through
a succession of odd jobs that included handing out fliers
and hawking Ginsu steak knives. He was growing up fast,
and realized that he had to step off the treadmill before it
crushed him entirely. He opted to go back to school, enrol-
ling in business and public relations courses at Calgary's
Mount Royal Community College. Bruce assumed it would
be easy to suppress his true nature if it could lead him to a
normal and lucrative career as a "suit," but it was not to be.

"I tried very hard to stuff down my personality and get
into the world of business," says McCulloch. "It didn't suit
me at all. I hated it."

Inevitably, his personality would leak out in subtly subversive acts of creative rebellion, such as wearing pyjamas

to class or adopting eccentric social personas. His fear of the antiseptic "straight" life pushed him toward creative outlets such as comedy and writing for the college paper. Viewed in the context of his tortured adolescence, it is hardly surprising that McCulloch gravitated toward the microscopic Calgary punk rock scene. He and Diamond spent many nights at The Calgarian, a local music venue that was a favourite roadhouse for touring punk bands from out of town, including D.O.A. from British Columbia, Hüsker Dü from Minnesota, and Black Flag from Southern California. Watching their tour buses pull out of town, McCulloch began harbouring dreams of his own escape from Calgary while he actively pursued his own performance career around town.

"I did a little comedy music," says McCulloch. "I played my bass and a drum machine, and I'd sing some songs I'd written, like 'Girl Trouble' or an ode to shoes. Calgary was a small and rough little upstart scene; really, it was just a handful of guys at the time."

Diamond and Connelly soon left Calgary to pursue their punk rock dream in Toronto, and before long they began urging McCulloch to join them. If he wanted to make it, they told him, Toronto was the place to be. With a standing invitation to crash with Diamond and Connelly at their Toronto rooming house, McCulloch made his first visits to check out the city for himself. "In those days, you could fly on half a ticket, the return portion of someone else's flight, with no questions asked," says McCulloch. "Of course, you could never do that today, but in those days, I would answer someone's want ad and pay, say, $60 to some nervous guy selling his unused seat. Then I'd fly to Toronto on someone else's name. It was a different time."

Compared to Calgary, Toronto was practically New York City. With its wider selection of punk bars and record stores, he could pick up the latest Viletones single or check out the Toronto and New York bands who played seminal clubs like The Edge, The Turning Point, or Larry's Hideaway, every night of the week. "Toronto was super-influential on me," says McCulloch, "and I'd always go home with my mind blown."

After a few of these trips, the Calgary punk scene began to feel claustrophobic, and a little too violent for his budding artistic sensibilities. "In some ways I'm tough," McCulloch admits, "but I'm also a little soft. I wasn't so into that whole Black Flag thing. I didn't want to shave my head and jump off a stage. If there'd been emo back then, I might have been caught up in that. I was as much into the New York Dolls and T. Rex as I was into the Sex Pistols."

Up until this point, Bruce had been equally fascinated by both comedy and rock 'n' roll. He knew he would have to pick one, and eventually concluded that only under the banner of comedy could he have the freedom and flexibility to convey the breadth of his passions. He admits that his reasoning was informed by the arrogance of youth. "I naïvely thought I was the smartest and funniest guy in the world, but once I made the decision to pursue comedy, all of my art, including my songs, were in a comedy vein."

A few months later, Bruce made the significant decision to accompany a few of his friends to watch an evening of improvised Theatresports sketch comedy. Sitting in the audience at Calgary's Loose Moose Theatre, McCulloch says, he instantly felt at home there. The sports half of Theatresports intrigued him; improv teams competed and worked their way up a house league bracket, while a panel of judges would blow their whistles from the sidelines when a sketch was dead on arrival. The audience was also part of the show and encouraged to throw foam "boo-bricks" at the stage when a scene failed. It was competitive and sometimes cruel, but the performers seemed fearless, if a little crazy. Bruce thought the improvisers—among them Frank and Tony Totino, Jim Curry, Kathleen Foreman, and Dennis Cahill—were the coolest people he had ever seen. This, he thought, was a form of comedy that promised both the structure to build upon and the freedom to move comedically within it.

"It was exhilarating," McCulloch recalls. "I just stared up at that stage. I had found my place, and even though I had no idea how to get up there, I literally told myself, 'This is what I'm going to do with my life.'"

Fortuitously, McCulloch chanced upon the Totino brothers enjoying a little post-show cheesecake at a café on 4th Street. Offstage, they seemed less like rock stars. Stammering, Bruce approached them and asked how he could get into Theatresports. The next day, he took their advice and enrolled in the Loose Moose workshop program, studying scene work and learning the comedy systems of their founder, the influential British sketch comedy guru, Keith Johnstone. "You could tell that Keith was not from here," says McCulloch, "mostly because he wore Ski-doo boots well into May."

Johnstone's improvisation ethos was exemplified by the motto "Don't be prepared," and most of the improvised scene work on the Loose Moose stage drew on instinct coupled with an aggressive, athletic approach to finding authentic, yet comedic, stage interactions.

"Keith was always at the periphery in the workshops," says McCulloch, "but most of my actual classes were with Jim Curry or the Totino brothers. Keith's advice was simple: just make things up, try not to be boring, but don't try to be interesting either. At first, I wasn't very good at it, and I can still remember walking up those stairs to the theatre, panicking, and thinking, 'Oh my god, I have to be funny.' It was intense, and after each session, I'd just go home and think all week about what happened in class."

In a relatively short time, McCulloch was invited to test his newly acquired skills in front of a paying crowd on the Loose Moose stage. With no choice but to sink or swim, he quickly became conversant in the basics of sketch comedy and, as his confidence grew, he waded into solo pieces and even performed five minutes of nascent stand-up comedy that relied less on "jokes" and more on beat poetry and obtuse observational monologues. "I went out with weird stuff," admits McCulloch, "and I refused to do relatable things like complaining about airline food. It was this sort of bizarro performance art, but I discovered that I was a natural. Still, my monologues were secondary to the sketch stuff, and I'd only do a couple minutes and then go back to sketches."

Even if he'd wanted to pursue stand-up, Calgary had nowhere for him to do it. During his next visit to Toronto, early in 1981, Bruce checked out Mark Breslin's legendary stand-up venue, Yuk Yuk's, but left feeling unsatisfied. "It was so gross," says McCulloch. "I mean, eventually I saw some great guys there, but not on those first few nights." Similarly, a trip to Toronto's Second City left him underwhelmed by what he saw as "corny piano music" accompaniment to predictable topical sketches employing "those fuckin' wooden chairs."

"There were probably some great minds at Second City," says McCulloch, "but they were hidden under the architecture of the institution it had become."

Back at Theatresports, McCulloch was part of a two-man team called Jerry's Kids with future DreamWorks animator Andrew Pearce. While they did well, week after week, things kicked into high gear when Jerry's Kids was drafted into what was then the hottest team at the Loose Moose, The Audience. According to McCulloch, The Audience seemed to be going places. "They'd even made up little buttons that said 'The Audience,' which blew my mind. I was a little younger than them, so I just looked up to those guys; I thought they were so great. In actual fact, they weren't particularly skilled at the time, but they were naturals." The Audience at one time or another included Bill Gemmil, Garry Campbell, Norm Hiscock, Frank van Keeken, and a particularly intense performer named Mark McKinney.

"One of my first memories of Mark," says McCulloch, "was him rehearsing for too long on the stage with the piano guy for some piano thing. And I'm sitting there heckling them, going, 'How fuckin' long are you going to be rehearsing? You've been onstage for half our rehearsal.'"

Despite the initial tension, the two hit it off, if tentatively, and began a friendship based on mutual admiration and begrudging respect. "We weren't like the best friends in the world," says McCulloch, "but we each looked across the room and saw another guy playing an instrument really well, and figured maybe we could both play our instruments really well together. But it wasn't like two high-school buddies who go on to form a band. It was about the work; we had a chemistry."

Mark Douglas Brown McKinney's path to the Loose Moose had been anything but predictable. His father, Russell McKinney, was a Canadian diplomat who had relocated to Ottawa after World War II on the Canadian equivalent of the GI Bill. After diplomatic postings in such exotic locations as Indonesia, Russell and Chloe McKinney's second child, Mark, was born at Ottawa General Hospital, on June 26, 1959. Russell had stayed behind, while Chloe rushed home to have the baby in Canada. Three years earlier, they had had a daughter, Jayne, and it would be six years before they had another son, Nick.

Living the rootless life of a diplomat's family meant the McKinneys were never in one place long enough to make lasting friendships, and like McCulloch, Mark discovered humour was a quick way to connect with an ever-changing cast of school chums. His secret weapon was the ability to pry a laugh from boarding school bullies, which was also a valuable mechanism of survival. "In grade nine I caught a couple of the older kids who were probably very stoned,"

McKinney recalls. "I just started doing voices and stuff and I had them rolling. I just remember thinking, 'Muahaha! Something's here!' My nomadic existence, and a constantly changing cultural landscape, left me forever feeling like the odd man out, which became a crucible that forged my comedy. People drifted away, but on the other hand, I also had so many unique experiences and absorbed a wide variety of cultures that it opened up my senses."

McKinney describes his mother as a "culturally voracious" woman who instilled in her son a love and respect for comedy, exposing him to the films of Woody Allen and other humourists of the day. "She took me to see *Bananas* and *Play It Again, Sam*," says McKinney, "and from then on I'd see all of Woody's movies as they came out; *Sleeper*, *Love and Death*, and then *Annie Hall*. By then, of course, I'd discovered *Monty Python's Flying Circus*, which proved to be deeply influential on me."

Travel trained his ear for dialects and broadened his mind culturally. After two years in Denmark, where, McKinney says, he learned to speak Danish before fully acquiring English, the family was whisked away to Port of Spain, Trinidad and Tobago, where he became deeply immersed in West Indian culture. "It was fantastic," recalls McKinney. "I didn't wear shoes for three years, although the whole time in Trinidad I was barely able to see my hand in front of my face."

Born with weak eyesight, McKinney says he overcompensated by listening more attentively to the local patois. "I developed a pretty good ear, so I ended up taking in the world in a different way."

While there was very little drama in McKinney's home life, the constant moving brought with it a sense of alienation and isolation that would be with him for his entire life. "None of my school friendships lasted very long," says McKinney. "One day, they'd just be gone or we'd move away. I'd ask my parents, 'Where is that nice older woman who used to take care of me when I'd smash my face falling off rocks in Trinidad?' Gone."

When he was ten, home was Paris, France, where he mastered French while attending school with Brigitte Bardot's son, became a fan of the French satirist Thierry Le Luron, from whom he cribbed his first comic impression of France's then finance minister (soon to be prime minister), Valéry Giscard d'Estaing. He also became playmates with his downstairs neighbour, Monique Giroux, the daughter of Claude Giroux, the charismatic French-Canadian producer of the classic Claude Lelouch film *A Man and a Woman*. Sensing his "fervid but unfocused interest" in film, Giroux took 12-year-old Mark to his first film set.

"I got to meet the star, the legendary Jean Gabin," says McKinney, "and he later went on to produce *The Story of O* and *Emmanuelle* and sent me racy production stills from the S&M classic, signed by the star to me, at boarding school. Claude and his opera singer wife, Maureen McNally, had five exotic daughters. Monique and I actually started dating during the 1985–86 season of *SNL* when I was a writer there. I invited her to a taping where my Tom Hanks sketch was bombing until his mustache started falling off."

While Mr. McKinney was stationed in D.C., Mark was sent off to boarding school at Trinity College in Port Hope,

Ontario, for the entire five-year stint. He was finally in one place long enough to make some real friends. During a visit to D.C., his mother took him to witness the historic Senate Watergate Hearings of May 1973, which culminated in the eventual resignation of President Richard Nixon. At age 13, Mark was likely the youngest person in the gallery.

"I got to watch Jeb Magruder plead the Fifth," says McKinney, "and see all these notorious D.C. names like Senator Sam Ervin, Judge John Sirica, and Senator Daniel Inouye, all of whom seemed kind of mythological to me."

Failing to earn enough credits to graduate in his final year at Trinity, he moved back in with his parents, who had returned to Ottawa in the summer of 1977. There, he enrolled at Lisgar Collegiate, where there were suddenly girls and far too many parties to distract him from his studies. After dropping out mid-year, McKinney moved to Toronto for six months, where he tried his hand at stand-up at the Riverboat, with a set of jokes he had cribbed from *The Tonight Show*.

"I bombed very badly," says McKinney, "and I wasn't much better at being a door-to-door salesman, so I moved back to Ottawa. In the fall of 1978, he made up his grade in night school earning just enough credits to allow him to follow his then girlfriend, Nadine, to Memorial University in St. John's, Newfoundland. Once at university, McKinney volunteered to work at CHMR, the fifty-watt campus radio station where he befriended a fellow student named Norm Hiscock. When they discovered they shared an interest in comedy, the two began collaborating on funny radio ads for school dances and other campus activities. CHMR's record library also exposed McKinney to a kind of music he had somehow missed in his travels — the blues.

"Norm and I had a mutual friend named Roger Howse," says McKinney, "and he was the guy who taught me how to play blues harp. Roger introduced me the music of Mississippi John Hurt and Mississippi Fred McDowell. After Nadine dumped me out of the blue — I found out years later that she was gay — I thought I could relate to the pain that these bluesmen had been singing about, but later I realized the incongruity of a white kid from Ottawa thinking he understood the blues, which eventually found its way into my Mississippi Gary character."

As a child, McKinney had always boasted that he was destined for greater things, at one point even speculating about a run for the prime minister's office, but college life bored him, and after some casual experimentation with acid, his goals became more realistic. He decided to drop out of college. "I think you see young guys like me as serious, slightly bookish guys who don't know where to put their energy," says McKinney. "People might ask, 'What do you want to be?' and you say, 'Well, I'm going to be the head of the UN.' 'Really?' they ask. 'With a D average?' I hated living in a dorm in St. John's. For me, it was just too much like boarding school. Then, the summer after college, my girlfriend dumped me. I carried a torch for her for two years until I found out she was a lesbian, although I'm not even sure that information helped much."

Running out of money, and finished with college, McKinney jumped at Roger Howse's invitation to join him on a "little blues road trip" out to Calgary to meet up with a bass player there. After a few weeks on the road, Howse unexpectedly turned back for Newfoundland, but McKinney opted to forge on to Calgary alone. Upon his arrival in November 1979, the former cow town was Canada's newest oil boomtown, and McKinney's dad arranged a job interview with the head of Petro-Canada, despite Mark's utter lack of interest in business.

One of the only things Mark McKinney had enjoyed about his time at university was making the funny radio spots with Hiscock. He was smitten with comedy, but had no idea how or where he could find an outlet to pursue it. What he didn't realize was that Hiscock's family had also recently relocated to Calgary, and when the two reconnected, they bonded over their shared desire to pursue an artistic path. "We were this little fun gang of two," says McKinney, "and we both enrolled in a course at Mount Royal College called 'How To Write A Movie Screenplay.' We dropped acid a couple of times and wrote comedy into this big black book that I still have somewhere."

All through the following year, the two were inseparable as McKinney went through a succession of day jobs, including delivering booze for Dial a Bottle and refurbishing old pianos at a used piano shop, where he persuaded the owner to hire Hiscock. A coworker at the piano shop told them about the Loose Moose Theatre. Hiscock went ahead to scout out a performance and was so blown away that, the next day at work, he insisted McKinney join him at the next show. After attending a show at the Pumphouse Theatre, McKinney agreed with Hiscock, and the fun little gang of two enrolled in one of Johnstone's improv classes.

Soon, they formed their own two-man Theatresports team called Steel Belted Refugees, the Refugees for short.

Like McCulloch, Mark says it took some getting used to before he found a way into improv. "Whatever it is that you get about relaxing and just being in the moment, I just didn't have it at first. Norm had it, but me, I was too desperately eager to please, and I don't think I figured it out until many years later."

The Loose Moose proved to be a safe space for like-minded comedy nerds to talk about Monty Python or other influential sketch comedy of the day, and Hiscock and McKinney instantly fell in with a tight little scene of fellow improvisers, which included Campbell, van Keeken, and Gemmil, and began performing under a name that Hiscock had suggested, The Audience.

When McCulloch arrived on the scene a few months later, McKinney recognized a true ally. "Bruce and Andrew were doing really superweird stuff in Jerry's Kids, so we all just wound up being the guys that hung out and watched comedy, and were obsessed and did weird stuff, basically. We lived to do comedy."

Garry Campbell says that while most of the boys in their clique were united in their love of Monty Python, *Saturday Night Live*, and other comedy history, McCulloch was something of a loner. "We'd hang out in the parking lot before a show, trying to remember every word from last night's *SCTV*, or breaking down Michael Nesmith's *Elephant Parts*, but Bruce, not so much."

McCulloch's independent side was of particular interest to McKinney, who had also grown up in travel-induced isolation. He was among the only people laughing when McCulloch opted to "tunnel" under the onstage rug at the Loose Moose one night. "It was conceptually interesting," McCulloch insists, "but this was a 150-pound carpet, so I could barely make it through. Nobody got it, and I think it confused everyone except Mark, who made it clear to me that he respected my commitment to this ridiculous choice."

While McCulloch and McKinney both respected Johnstone's rules for Theatresports, they also shared an anarchic desire to break them, but McCulloch recalls feeling shocked by the pushback they got from the judges and audiences. "When you're young, you just think your thing is so superior. You can't imagine why they'd be mad at you. We were these young, sexy, weird guys making fun of their culture there, and we were shocked that they had no respect for that. Still, we had fun, and we were on fire nearly every time we performed. This was our lives; it was important to us."

Feeling they had mastered the Theatresports improv games, The Audience decided to try their hand at writing longer sketches. Around that time, Keith Johnstone moved the company into a converted cattle auction mart that he renamed the Loose Moose Simplex. The new space was a game changer; there was suddenly room to produce plays and other theatrical events. The Audience requested a recurring slot on Saturday nights after the regular Theatresports show ended. Their wish was granted and Late Nite Comedy began, featuring The Audience performing a broad selection of their original sketches and contributions from their friends. Soon, Late Nite Comedy was selling out the 270-seat theatre every Saturday, with fans lining up at 11 p.m. in the cold Calgary night.

"It took off almost immediately," says McCulloch, laughing, "like no other time in my life. We were ripping it up each week with a full ninety-minute show of all-new material."

Late Nite Comedy was structured as a revue, which meant that each cast member could do a solo bit, stand-up, or even musical numbers in among the sketch material. Bruce McCulloch used this format to debut risqué ideas that he would return to in the coming years, such as the all-nude scene "Naked for Jesus" or his naive rock 'n' roll song "The Daves I Know."

"I thought 'Daves' was a funny and relatable song," says Norm Hiscock, "but it was also a moment of clarity for me about Bruce. It showed me that he already had his own comedy aesthetic, even while we were all still trying to find ours."

The Audience would play wherever and whenever they could, even risking their lives at one particularly dangerous gig at a penitentiary. In some ways, improvisers thrive on danger, and as The Audience found their collective comedy voice, McKinney and McCulloch began to refine a bohemian style that was as informed by experimental theatre as it was by sketch comedy. Whatever it was, it was working, and in a very short time they had become the de facto kings of Calgary comedy.

"It was wildly exciting," says McKinney. "We were still in our teens and early twenties, but we were already going 'What the fuck do we do now?'"

In the spring of 1983, The Audience staged a best-of show that sold out a 600-seat theatre. Twice. It was a turning point for the troupe, and even their fans suggested that it was time to get out of Calgary and take their act to the big time, wherever that was. McKinney was fond of Vancouver, but McCulloch's early trips to Toronto told him "Go east, young man" just as his friends Diamond and Connelly had before him. To facilitate the move, McCulloch opted to scout out the Toronto scene ahead of the troupe.

"Our last six months in Calgary was just the countdown to us moving to Toronto. Mark wasn't quite ready, but he charged me with the task of finding him an apartment, one that had a fireplace, for $200 a month. 'OK, I'll do that, Mark.' I probably insisted that we had to go, and I just kept repeating, 'We're going. We're going. We're going.' I wasn't so much a bully about it as a bull."

Amazingly, despite their run of sold-out Saturday nights, The Audience had taken no profits from the Late Nite Comedy shows, as they were technically renting out the stage from the Loose Moose Simplex. But shortly before they packed up the truck and headed east, the general manager of the Loose Moose told them he had been tallying up the money they'd been making from the door, and as a gesture of goodwill, he agreed to hand over the whole sum as a going-away present.

"It was over four thousand dollars," says McCulloch, "which was worth a bit of money in 1984. Our Toronto dream became a real possibility. Looking back, it was one of those things, you know, the thing within the thing that makes the thing? I think without that money, it would have been hard. All of a sudden, we had this troupe bank account."

According to McKinney, a portion of their Late Nite Comedy windfall was spent on treating the Loose Moose staff and the entire Late Nite Comedy cast to a concert featuring David Bowie, Peter Gabriel, and The Tubes at Edmonton's Commonwealth Stadium on a warm August night in 1983.

"We rented an entire bus," says McKinney, "it was epic. I got very emotional when Bowie did 'Heroes' as it summarized all my hopes and fears with the move to Toronto looming. Years later when I was at *SNL* I was at the craft table when someone asked to pass the milk. It was Bowie. I contemplated telling him tell him how much that meant, but then just passed the carton."

And so it was that Bruce McCulloch, Mark McKinney, Garry Campbell, and Frank van Keeken pulled up their stakes and made the move to Toronto. Shortly before they left, they competed in one more Theatresports tournament with a team from Toronto that featured an improviser named Briane Nasimok.

"Briane stuck around and saw our Late Nite Comedy show," McKinney remembers. "After our show, we all hung out together. At this bar somewhere, he told us, 'Oh, you know, your sketches, they remind me of these other guys out in Toronto. You should look 'em up when you come out.'"

As they made their way toward Toronto and their destiny, the four members of The Audience back-pocketed Nasimok's recommendation and wondered just what kind of people would give their comedy troupe such a dumb name — the Kids in the Hall.

TWO

Kevin and Dave Flee the Suburbs

Kevin Hamilton McDonald entered the world at Montreal's Queen Elizabeth Hospital on May 16, 1961, and he can confidently tell you that he entered it at precisely 6:44 p.m. "I know this because in my flaky years, I became an astrology nut and I researched the exact time of my birth," says McDonald. "I also know that this makes me a Taurus with a Gemini moon and a Scorpio rising. And you know us Scorpio risings are slow-to-quick to anger, but I'm also stubborn like a Taurus, although I tend to give in like a Gemini because I see both sides. All of this makes me passive-aggressive; I'll make a person go through an hour of hell, and then agree with them at the end. But enough about me."

As a boy, McDonald says he knew he wanted to pursue either drama or comedy, but comedy was not his first choice, as he had been equally impressed with both the slapstick comedy of Jerry Lewis and the dramatic work of

Marlon Brando. This changed soon after a writing assignment for his fifth-grade English class gave him his first taste of laughter. "I had written a funny story about a family vacation we'd taken in the Bahamas, and it had gotten tons of laughs when I read it to the class," says McDonald. "But instead of that making me think I wanted to be a comic, it kind of made me want to be a writer. So, one month later, when we had another assignment, I thought, 'Well, I wrote my comedy story. Now I'm going to write my dark Hitchcock thriller.' As I was walking up in front of the class to read this story I'd written about somebody planning to kill someone, I began to realize that my classmates were expecting another funny story from me. I hate to disappoint people, so I started sweating because I knew I was about to let the audience down. They wanted humour. So, when I got up there, I pretended to read as I improvised a whole other, much funnier story about me playing football. It got even more laughs than the first time. Walking back to my desk, I was half-happy and half-depressed, thinking, 'Oh, I guess I do comedy then.'"

Just as Bruce McCulloch and Mark McKinney had done, young Kevin McDonald began to call upon his latent comic ability to cope with any conflict in his life. Despite showing some athletic ability in football, McDonald was an overweight kid, and self-deprecating body shame became an early part of his comedy. There was real pain behind the joking, and he promised himself that he would one day shed the weight, but in the meantime, his love of Jackie Gleason and John Belushi inspired him to be what he calls "the funny, fat guy."

"I admired a lot of overweight comics," says McDonald,

"but they all had a physical energy I lacked. Plus, they were also geniuses. Later, there was John Candy, and while he couldn't do a cartwheel like Belushi, no one did a double take with as much energy as John Candy."

As he delved more into comedy history, Kevin came across a Don Rickles quote that changed his life: "Some people say funny things; other people say things funny."

"I was deeply affected by that," says McDonald, "and I realized that I had instinctive comedy timing. I would watch sitcoms, and felt that I could recite the dialogue and make it even funnier in my own voice."

Performing in school plays, he explored his physicality on stage and felt an affinity with actor Gene Wilder, who had made a deep impression on him in Mel Brooks's films like *Blazing Saddles* and *Young Frankenstein*. "Gene Wilder had curly hair and I had curly hair. And I was also aware that he cowrote *Young Frankenstein*, so from about fifteen or sixteen on, I thought I was going to be a writer and performer. Comedy just seemed to tie it all together."

His father, Hamilton McDonald, was a dental equipment salesman in the Montreal area, and his mother, Sheila, was a stay-at-home housewife. When Kevin was two years old, a sister, Sandra, joined them. "My dad was the kind of guy who would introduce himself by saying 'Hi, my name is Hamilton. You can call me Hammy; I've been called worse than that.' I must have heard him say that a hundred million times on sales calls."

When Kevin was seven, Hammy moved the family to Burbank, California, for a period of eighteen months, before returning to Montreal just in time for a series of kidnappings and bombings perpetrated by the Quebec separatist organization, Front de libération du Québec (FLQ), known in Canadian history as The October Crisis. Fearing for his family's safety, Hammy relocated the McDonalds to the significantly less politically charged Toronto suburb of Mississauga.

But even though they were far from the FLQ bombs, the McDonalds were still victims of domestic terror in the form of Hammy's rapid descent into alcoholism. Having been expelled from college for partying too hard, Hammy's drinking had only gotten worse after he started a family. While Sheila McDonald did her best to shield their son from his father's mood swings, Hammy had become violent and verbally abusive by the time Kevin was fourteen years old. "He stopped going to work and was just drinking all day," says McDonald. "He got fired and had to file for bankruptcy, so we literally had to move to the other side of the tracks, across the rail yard, over in Mississauga."

McDonald dropped out of Mississauga's Woodlands Secondary School in Grade 13. He had been the class clown for much of his time there, earning a special award for being Funniest Person in School. As with Bruce McCulloch and his dad, Kevin and Hammy found a connection in their shared appreciation for comedy, particularly for the work of Jackie Gleason, whom McDonald still reveres as a master of timing. "I think my dad also liked Richard Pryor, because he swore," says McDonald, "but he hated most of my favourites like Woody Allen, Monty Python, *Saturday Night Live*, and *SCTV*, which he didn't understand."

Despite coming of age during the so-called stand-up

boom of the late 1970s, Kevin insists he had no interest in pursuing stand-up comedy for himself. "I knew what I could and couldn't do. I'd try to write jokes for an hour and I just couldn't."

When Kevin was nineteen, his father was "unemployed, bankrupt, and blind drunk most of the time," so Sheila and the kids removed all of their possessions from the family home, one piece at a time, and quietly left him over a period of two weeks. "We would wait until he collapsed," remembers McDonald, "then move a few more boxes at night, every night, for a couple of weeks until we had moved back to the other side of the tracks again, this time without my father. That's probably why I stopped going to classes for the second half of Grade 13. I had started looking at community colleges where I could study acting, and I was reading plays over at our local library, where I would 'whisper act' the lines out loud."

Financially depressed since his father's bankruptcy, McDonald received full financial assistance from Humber College to attend their three-year drama program, but was expelled after only four months, just before Christmas 1980.

"It was the week after John Lennon died," says McDonald. "My improv teacher, Jim Petty, hated me because I always fell asleep in his class, and the dean of the college, Jerry Smith, called me a 'one-legged actor,' which was ironic as he was himself an actual one-legged actor who'd lost a leg when a lighting grid fell on it during a production of *Pippin*. I found that hilarious."

But there was one drama instructor at Humber, William B. Davis, later known for his portrayal of the

"Cigarette Smoking Man" on *The X-Files*, who offered encouragement and some crucial advice. "He said it was crazy that I was expelled," says McDonald. "He said, 'You're very good at comedy acting. You should pursue improv.' And he wrote down the phone number for the Second City workshops."

While working up the nerve to call Second City, McDonald continued working as a cinema usher, where his interactions with filmgoers allowed him to practise live situational improv in the style of anti-comedy heroes of the day like Andy Kaufman or Steve Martin. He learned to play to strangers while wearing a Cineplex Odeon usher's jacket. He got laughs and gained confidence until he was ready, at last, to call the number that Davis had given him.

"I honestly thought John Candy or Eugene Levy was going to answer the phone or something," says McDonald, laughing. "What I didn't know was that it was a whole organized system of workshops. You could do workshops for sixty dollars for six weeks, and there was a remote possibility that you could be chosen to audition for the Second City Touring Company or their newest company based in London, Ontario. And if you graduated from that, you might get to be on the 'mainstage' in Toronto. Of course, they probably only told me that to sucker me in, but in a way they didn't have to; I was eager to try it anyway."

Second City director and instructor Allan Guttman recalls the time in 1980 when the "heavyish and somewhat rumpled" McDonald first entered his class: "He was wearing glasses," says Guttman, "and had an inordinate amount of hair on his head, which bounced when he moved. He was—and this is a compliment—a bit goofy-looking, in a charming, adolescent way, and he spoke in a style that favoured vowels over consonants. He was respectful, enthusiastic, and imaginative."

Guttman says McDonald already possessed an ability to effortlessly inhabit characters who were self-deprecating losers and loners. "He was funny in both a physical and a verbal way, and I recall one moment when he gently mocked me by turning my own words against me. I complimented him on this. He reminded me of a young Lou Costello, and seemed very comfortable being funny."

Guttman had been the piano player for a Second City cast that had included Dan Aykroyd, Gilda Radner, Dave Thomas, John Candy, and Eugene Levy, and McDonald often peppered him for stories hoping to get some valuable insights into the processes of these giants of sketch comedy. "Allan told us a story about the time he noticed that Dave Thomas was sort of straight-manning John Candy," recalls McDonald. "Later, the whole cast was having a drink, and Allan asked Dave why he had done that. Dave told him, 'Well, it's occurred to me from hanging out with John just how funny he is, so I want to introduce the world to him.' That made an impression on me. I always think that's how a comedy troupe should be."

Among his fellow Second City students were Canadian actress Linda Kash (*A Mighty Wind*), comic monologist Sandra Shamas, and future comedy writer Luciano Casimiri. At first, Casimiri thought McDonald was just a loudmouth football player dabbling in comedy. "I was wearing my old high-school football jacket when we met," says

McDonald, "so he thought I was a 'jock.' In fact, it wasn't until many years later that he confessed that he thought I was one of those guys who tried to be funny at a party by putting Cheezies up their nose. In spite of that, we bonded over comedy, and we'd go see movies together and talk about comedy on the phone all the time."

McDonald says he was intimidated at first by a fellow classmate named Mike Myers, who he says arrived "fully formed" to the class. "I was used to being the fastest gun-fighter in the West—meaning Mississauga—but then I met a guy who could outdraw me. I was a lumpy nineteen-year-old potato of potential, and I had to learn a lot. But at seventeen, Mike had it already. I was like Salieri to his Mozart; he was the guy I wanted to be."

Myers remembers being immediately taken with McDonald's vulnerability, both as a person and as the underdog characters he chose to portray on stage. "I loved Gilda Radner," says Myers, "and Kevin always had a sort of Gilda quality to me—that thing where you just wanted to root for him."

The two began talking about writing some sketches together and forming a troupe, but the chemistry just wasn't there. "I think there was always that feeling of a missed opportunity that we didn't team up," says McDonald. "We had this mutual appreciation society. Still, Mike was on a different path, and although our paths would cross in oddly coincidental ways over the course of our respective careers, our paths were not the same."

In fact, Myers's path was about to veer away from McDonald. The rumour was that he was about to be drafted by the Second City Touring Company. At the time, the buzz around Myers within the workshops was so strong that when a young Dave Foley entered the class, Guttman proclaimed him the next Mike Myers.

"Dave was very smart and articulate," says Guttman, "with a high reference level." Guttman immediately told Myers that he and Foley should meet, and even put them in a class together.

"Dave came up to me," says Myers, "and said, 'I've heard about you, and we're supposed to meet,' or something like that. And so we started to hang out and became good friends."

After Myers was inevitably yanked away for the Touring Company, Guttman paired Foley with McDonald to perform an improv called a "mirror exercise," in which two performers face each other and try to move in exact mirror image to each other. McDonald was thrilled and felt he'd met another collaborator as funny as Mike Myers. Not only was there chemistry with Foley, it was instinctive. This new guy had a similarly subversive sense of humour and equal disdain for the rules of the game; they mocked the mirror exercise and broke up laughing. Guttman was not amused.

"Allan was furious with us," says McDonald, "but right away, Dave and I had established a chemistry between us. I love timing, and I felt that Dave had the expert timing of Woody Allen. And he thought I was funny too."

It would not be the last time their comedy choices would land them in hot water, but more importantly, this was the beginning of a comedy dialogue that has continued to this day.

"I'd see Kevin do some scenes onstage where he was hilarious," says Foley, "and then Kevin would tell me he loved some scenes I was in. So, Kevin and Luc and I all became best comedy friends from that point on."

McDonald and Foley had much in common besides the fact that they were both exiles from suburban Toronto — McDonald from Mississauga and Foley from nearby Etobicoke. Like Kevin McDonald, young Dave Foley had used comedy as a coping mechanism to survive a chaotic family life and his father's alcoholic mood swings, and like Bruce McCulloch, Foley's father was also a tortured artist at heart.

A highly intelligent and well-read man, Michael Foley was also an alcoholic with severe, but undiagnosed at the time, borderline personality disorder (BPD). Michael was a steamfitter by trade, but Dave Foley says a more apt title would be "construction worker with poetic aspirations."

"I think my dad wanted to be Jack Kerouac," says Foley, "or his favourite writer, Thorne Smith, who wrote these really funny novels back in the Prohibition era that were mostly about getting really drunk, meeting a beautiful girl who has sex with you, then falling into some sort of fantasy world, which I guess was my dad's dream. But no matter how drunk he got, he never fell into that fantasy world. He'd often disappear into his room for days, or six months to a year, at a time. He could sometimes be violent with my mother, but never with any of the kids."

Television comedy provided fleeting moments of solace, and the family — Mom, Dad, Dave, and his siblings Michael, Karen, and Glenn — somehow bonded around influential '70s hit sitcoms such as *All in the Family*, *M*A*S*H*, *The Mary Tyler Moore Show*, and *Maude*. Significantly, Dave's parents let their kids stay up to watch a disruptive new comedy from Britain, *Monty Python's Flying Circus*. Foley identified heavily with Python's disdain for authority.

"I was already a pretty neurotic kid," says Foley, "so TV comedy was one of the things that sort of kept me sane. It was also an effective way to stave off depression."

His mother, Mary, had already travelled around the world before giving birth to her third child, and second son, David Scott Foley, on January 4, 1963. Born in England, Mary Foley came from the kind of working-class background where emotions were suppressed, and Dave recalls her struggling to maintain a "stiff upper lip" in the face of her husband's erratic mood swings.

"Oh, sure, she'd sometimes get angry about things," says Foley, "but then if you wanted to get emotional, she'd just say, 'Oh, don't fuss.' She was somewhat downtrodden, but she just took it, because that's what mothers of her generation did."

When he was in his teens, Foley's visiting English auntie revealed the hidden truth about his mother's thwarted ambitions of being a stage actress, and he was shocked to learn that the two sisters had studied theatre together with legends of the British theatre, including Laurence Harvey and Denholm Elliott. "My mother and my aunt even had walk-on roles at Stratford, but somehow this had never come up until then," says Foley. "I also learned that Mum had travelled extensively throughout Europe, alone, and was on her way to other parts of the world when she met my dad in Canada and got pregnant."

For a brief time, the family relocated to Nova Scotia, but soon returned to Etobicoke, Ontario, where Foley went to school. As he grew up, he began to feel stifled by conventional suburban high-school life. He was an intelligent, if introverted, young man, and he had just started to think outside the burbs when he discovered an alternative learning program based in downtown Toronto, the School of Experiential Education (SEE). Dave convinced his parents to let him enroll, and once downtown, he began to feel more comfortable studying among his fellow misfits, bright kids, and outsiders. Between this newfound sense of community and his burgeoning interest in teenage drinking, Dave's shyness fell away. His budding gregariousness came to full flower during a student camping trip when, after a few drinks, he discovered he possessed the ability to make the other kids laugh. He liked the feeling and, upon his return, assumed the role of the proverbial class clown.

"I remember this one day, in particular," says Foley. "I had been making my friend Evelyn Chupaya laugh on the way to school, when she told me I should try stand-up comedy. This had never occurred to me, so I started going over my comedy albums, trying to absorb the syntax of it all."

After studying the masters — George Carlin, Richard Pryor, Lenny Bruce, The Smothers Brothers, and Shelley Berman — Foley felt confident that he had at least eight minutes of stand-up material. Still unsure if he could get a laugh from anyone but his classmates, he resolved to take his eight minutes down to the Monday-night open mic at

Yuk Yuk's to test it out. Just for safety, though, he brought along a few "ringers," including his dad, older brother, and a few kids from school.

"I was nervous as hell," says Foley, "but once I got the first laugh, I kind of rolled through it. My opening joke was something like, 'I think it's good to get a sense of any shared experiences between the audience and performer, so we have something to base the conversation on. So, I'll ask, is anyone here now, or ever has been, a virgin?' Then I talked about my own virginity loss, which was still fairly fresh at the time, and I said, 'It went terribly! I don't know how to put this delicately, but I've never been very good at threading a needle either.' I got solid laughs for eight minutes! It was a fantastic feeling."

Besides getting all the laughs, Foley's life studies teacher, who had also attended the show, gave him a school credit for the performance. For Foley, just shy of his eighteenth birthday, comedy was now all that mattered, which meant his schoolwork fell behind. In fact, he hadn't really thought much about his studies until the day the head of the school called him at home. "He called to ask me if I was still enrolled," Foley recalls, "and I said, 'Sure.' Then he reminded me that I hadn't been there for the last six months, so I just told him, 'Oh, yeah, then okay, I guess I've dropped out.'"

Still buzzing from his debut set at Yuk Yuk's, Foley worked feverishly over the ensuing weeks to come up with eight new minutes for his next time at the club. He tried his best to emulate his stand-up heroes, particularly Lenny Bruce.

"Lenny was the guy I liked the most," says Foley. "I remember the televangelist Jerry Falwell had just made headlines saying that Jesus Christ was not a wimpy pacifist, so I did this whole monologue about it, with Jesus as this very macho guy talking like Robert De Niro, threatening people from the cross and challenging them to a fight."

With trial and error, Foley's stand-up improved, and he began to get advice, solicited or otherwise, from other, more established comedians. "I'd been knocking my brain out to come up with all-new material every night," says Foley, "but I learned that you were meant to hone your eight surefire minutes and then do it every time, adding three or four minutes here and there until you eventually had a set. The other advice I got was from Yuk Yuk's boss Mark Breslin, who told me, 'You're very funny, but get a haircut!' because I used to have long hair that sort of fell down covering my face from under this tweed fedora."

Foley's one-man, multiple-character monologues were already veering into sketch comedy by the time his grandmother sent him a newspaper clipping about improv classes being taught by Rob Salem, later the entertainment editor for the *Toronto Star*, at The Skills Exchange, an adult learning centre in Toronto.

"I thought improv might help with what I was doing," says Foley. "I mean, after all, Lenny had been really into improv. As I started doing improv and sketch work, I thought, 'Oh, I like this so much more.' I loved being on stage with other people and having conversations, as opposed to just talking at people. It was actually Rob who suggested that I go take Second City workshops."

Foley brought another member of Salem's class with him to Second City, Scott Stewart, who quickly became the fourth member of a subset that included Luc Casimiri and Kevin McDonald, who remembers Stewart as "the nicest guy in the world."

"He was a real crowd-pleaser," says McDonald. "I still remember how very funny he was in his scenes for our workshops."

Now the owner of a popular leather goods store in Los Angeles, where he continues to pursue acting, Scott Stewart remembers being immediately impressed with the intelligence of the comedy choices Foley would make in Salem's class. "Dave was different," says Stewart, "and he had such a great ability for obscure references. Kevin, Dave, Luc, and I were just different from the other people, driven to do improv, and constantly thinking of new places to perform. It was just so highly addictive, from the painful hush of bombing to the supreme joy of bringing the house down."

After one six-week cycle of Second City workshops, McDonald, Casimiri, Stewart, and Foley took a trip across town to check out the newly opened Toronto franchise of Keith Johnstone's Theatresports, recently imported from Calgary. After seeing the games in person, McDonald asked Foley to join a Theatresports team he was starting with Casimiri and Stewart. When Foley said yes, McDonald scrambled to assemble the team he had lied about starting. "I panicked," says McDonald, "and had to call Luc to tell him that we had to start a comedy troupe immediately!"

In hindsight, McDonald's bluff merely expedited the inevitable, and the four improvisers scrambled off to Theatresports the following Sunday night at the Toronto Free Theatre, under their Chekhov-inspired team name,

Uncle Vanya and the Three Sisters. Performing at Theatresports felt exciting and liberating, and McDonald recalls feeling certain for the first time in his young life that sketch comedy was his calling. "I remember Luc telling me that the week goes by quickly and nothing happens until the half hour before we go on in Theatresports, when we're truly alive and awake," says McDonald. "It was thrilling, and to this day, I still think about it. About a half hour before I'm about to perform, anywhere, I just feel truly alive, like I'm about to jump out of a plane."

Over the coming months, Theatresports would become even more interesting with the arrival of a group of brash upstarts just in from Calgary. The Audience had landed, and they were about to push these suburban Toronto boys to even greater heights.

THREE

Scott Thompson Throws a Doughnut

"**Every comedy actor** I knew was on a Theatresports team," says friend of the Kids and frequent Theatresports partner, Mike Myers. "We were like pilots trying to log flight hours, by which I mean stage time and scene work." Myers had gravitated to Theatresports along with a few of his Second City colleagues, including future MuchMusic VJ Christopher Ward and monologist Sandra Shamas, who recalls it as a mecca for aspirant writers and performers of all stripes.

"There were mimes, writers, clowns, and a lot of improv people," says Shamas. "Some of us had studied under Del Close at Second City, and others with Keith Johnstone, so we were all up to snuff, and the conversations that we had were like, 'Well, this is different and exciting; how can we parlay it into something more?'"

Having migrated from Second City, Kevin McDonald,

Dave Foley, Luciano Casimiri, and Scott Stewart, collectively known as Uncle Vanya and the Three Sisters, were beginning to sour on what they saw as Theatresports's needlessly competitive approach to comedy. McDonald says they were more interested in the "Theatre" than the "sports" and, rebels that they were, they began to subtly sabotage the games whenever possible, even creating mock games, such as "Best Scene Until Kevin Gets an Asthma Attack," which involved McDonald running around the inside of the entire theatre space until he started wheezing, effectively shutting down the show, to the disapproval of the Theatresports judges and fellow teams alike.

"They didn't like us doing that," says McDonald. "I mean, we thought it was hilarious, but I remember Sandra Shamas complaining that there should be a rule about games that endangered your life. But it was just like the mirror exercise at Second City. We couldn't stop ourselves from being rebels."

While at Theatresports, Foley's comic mind had made an impression on fellow improviser Briane Nasimok, a regular stand-up at Yuk Yuk's who had deep connections within the Toronto comedy scene, including being the "warm-up" comedian and talent scout for the CTV series *Thrill of a Lifetime*, a cousin to the American program *Star Search* and a precursor to contemporary talent contests like *The Voice* or *American Idol*. Nasimok strongly urged Foley to submit his name to the *Thrill of a Lifetime* producers as a stand-up comedian, and even went as far as ghostwriting the letter for him.

"Apparently, the whole thing was a bit rigged," says Foley, "and Briane made the whole thing happen. In my fake letter to the show, Briane told the producers that 'my dream' was to do stand-up at The Improv, so suddenly, I was this nineteen-year-old flying to L.A. to follow in the footsteps of comics like Howie Mandel and Jim Carrey, rubbing shoulders with legends like Tony Curtis and Father Guido Sarducci."

Even before he failed to find success on the talent show, Foley was already being drawn more toward sketch comedy. In the wake of Theatresports and Second City, there was something of a sketch boom in Toronto, and a spate of independent comedy troupes began springing up all over town. Foley, McDonald, Casimiri, and Stewart were fans of one of the more established troupes, The Frantics — with particular attention paid to their favourite Frantic, Dan Redican — and regularly attended the live tapings of their weekly radio program, *Frantic Times*, at the Ontario College of Art, before scurrying over to the Old Fire Hall theatre at 10:30 p.m. to watch Second City's improv sets. While there was never a cover charge, seating was limited and it was first come, first served. It helped that they were pals with doorman Pat McKenna, an aspiring comic and actor friend who would later appear on *The Red Green Show*. "They had a good cast at that time," says Foley, "great people like Kathleen Laskey, Ron James, Debra McGrath, and John Hemphill. We all loved Hemphill because he was the best improviser we'd ever seen, and we thought he was an absolute genius. And they'd often have guests for the improv set like Robin Williams, Michael Keaton, and former cast members like Catherine O'Hara and John Candy, so it was really great."

Still, while Foley says they all enjoyed improvising, he began to hate what he saw as the doctrine of unscripted improv. "I remember telling Kevin that improv was the new mime," says Foley, "and that everyone was going to hate it in a couple of years. That's when we started to focus on writing scenes instead."

After Rob Nickerson, a director and coach at Theatresports, begged them to lose the name Uncle Vanya (for reasons that nobody can seem to remember today), they adopted the equally uninspired moniker Mixed Nuts as a placeholder until they came up with something better. A few months later, Mixed Nuts were asked to appear on a Global TV sketch comedy program. On the set, Casimiri was speaking to a television producer who suggested that the members of Mixed Nuts should write jokes for established comedians as a way to break into the business. "He said we could be just like Jack Benny's kids in the hall," says Casimiri, "which was Benny's name for the guys outside the writers' room, waiting to sell gags and jokes."

According to Kevin McDonald, that producer got the reference wrong; it was actually from comedian Sid Caesar, who often referred to the young writers of *Your Show of Shows* and *Caesar's Hour* — Neil Simon, Danny "Doc" Simon, Carl Reiner, and Mel Brooks — as his "kids in the hall." Such hairsplitting aside, Foley, Casimiri, McDonald, and — for only a little while longer — Stewart all agreed that the phrase had both a genuine comedy pedigree and childish naiveté that they could relate to. And just like that, they agreed henceforth to forever be known as the Kids in the Hall.

According to McDonald, their disruptive tendencies at Theatresports, which had increasingly alienated them from the management, culminated in an actual freeze-out of the Kids in the Hall one cold and snowy night at the very end of 1982. "Theatresports was having this big, invitation-only New Year's Eve party at Harbourfront Centre down on the waterfront," says McDonald, "and they had apparently forgotten to invite us. We thought maybe it was an oversight, so we went down and knocked on the door, but one of the head guys there refused to let us in. We were literally left out in the cold, freezing in a blizzard by the lake. When midnight struck, Luc said to me, 'Don't worry, 1983 will be the year of the Kids in the Hall.' He was wrong about the year, but I always loved that Luc said that at that moment."

Casimiri was right about one thing: 1983 would bring a significant change to the troupe with the arrival that spring of The Audience.

McCulloch remembers that one of his first tasks upon arriving in Toronto was to seek out his Calgary ex-pat friends, Brian Connelly and Reid Diamond. By the time he caught up with them, Toronto had already changed them. "Brian had dyed his hair black and was playing me records by The Birthday Party," says McCulloch, "and I thought, 'Oh, wow, Toronto's so weird.' Bands like New Order were in the air; it was almost Goth. I lived with Brian for a while. Music was all around, although I was trying to focus on comedy."

Toronto musician, photographer, and barber Don Pyle remembers McCulloch's arrival along with a steady flow of transplanted Calgarians, such as actor Callum Keith Rennie. "These had been the wild kids of the Calgary scene," says Pyle, "and now they were dropped into this equally wild Toronto organism. Bruce stayed in my mother's basement in the Junction area for a time, and he and Reid put together a band called Orion's Belt, with Bruce playing bass and Reid playing guitar. Back in Calgary, Reid and Brian had been in this band called Buick McKane, but when they moved out here, they left their singer behind so I stepped in and we changed the name to Crash Kills Five. That lasted a couple of years before Brian quit the band, which fractured Reid and Brian for a few years. When Bruce eventually moved in with Brian at this crappy rooming house, a kind of halfway house for Calgarians, Brian told Reid he'd let Orion's Belt record on his Portastudio. I came over to visit as they were finishing up, and Reid and Brian just started talking about playing together again. They needed someone to play drums so I said, 'I'll do it.' And they were like, 'Oh. OK.' I had never played drums before, but I had always wanted to learn how."

As Crash Kills Five evolved into the instrumental trio Shadowy Men on a Shadowy Planet, Bruce McCulloch concentrated on creating a beachhead for the invasion of The Audience. "We told everyone that we had moved to Toronto to 'make it,'" says McCulloch, laughing. "I even got an interview with someone from some local paper, whose name I've forgotten, and I told them, 'We've come here to make it!' Mark slowly came out, then Gary and Frank followed, but Norm stayed behind."

Norm Hiscock and his fiancée, Cindy Park, had been studying film together at the Southern Alberta Institute of Technology (SAIT) and were eager to finish their studies before taking on any new challenges. "We'd already made one film together," says Park, "and at that point, Norm was still thinking he'd be a cameraman. I don't think he ever thought comedy could be a career for him because he loved film and he's a great photographer."

Hiscock kept his hand in the Calgary comedy scene, but after completing their studies at SAIT, he and Park moved to Swift Current, Saskatchewan, where he became a television cameraman and she took a waitressing job until they could figure out their next move.

Meanwhile in Toronto, Briane Nasimok was closing the circle and playing matchmaker between the two troupes, regaling the Kids with tales of their sold-out Audience shows back at the Loose Moose.

"We'd heard over and over again, and not just from Briane, that The Audience were just like us, only a couple of years older and a little more experienced," says McDonald. "They already knew how to write sketches. Dave had already seen one of Bruce's stand-up sets at Yuk Yuk's and said he was funny, although when I finally met him, I found him guarded. Still, something told me he was a genius, but he just hadn't done anything to prove it yet."

"When I met Bruce, he kept rubbing my back," adds Foley, "and I kept thinking, 'This weird little gay man's hitting on me.' But it turned out he wasn't gay; that's just what Bruce was like. It was a territorial thing, but I was like, 'What the hell does this guy want?'"

Nasimok had regularly let the Kids use his apartment as a writing and rehearsal space, or just to crash out if they missed the last subway train. He now extended this offer to Mark McKinney, who went out into the city to investigate the comedy scene he'd heard so much about. McKinney was queuing up to Second City's nightly no-cover improv set when McDonald and Foley met him in the line. As with McCulloch, McKinney's reputation as a funny guy had preceded him.

"I'd heard Mark was also a genius," says McDonald, "and Dave had heard that he was probably the best actor of his group. So, we introduced ourselves and then, when Dave and I were somewhere Mark couldn't hear us, I said, 'Yeah, well, *he's* not funny either. I can instantly tell that he's not funny; I just know.' Dave pushed back and said we needed to see them perform first, so the following Wednesday we saw The Audience at Theatresports, and to my surprise, they were as great as we'd heard. I thought Garry Campbell was going to become a big star. He was sort of like Steve Martin, but original and different. And Mark was brilliant at characters in a Christopher Guest or Peter Sellers way. He also had that same perfect comedy timing as Dave."

As McKinney surveyed the Toronto comedy landscape, he concluded that the local chapter of Theatresports had less of an "edge" than the one back in Calgary. Whereas he had studied directly under Keith Johnstone, and had a little more reverence for the "theatre" part of Theatresports, he felt that the Toronto branch was just another place for an improviser to springboard into a career at Second City. He wasn't having it.

"At the time, I was a bit of a swinging dick around there," says McKinney, "because I actually had figured out improv. Maybe it was not having Keith around, or something like that, but I was starting to call myself an actor and take it a little bit more seriously. Once I met all the guys who became the Kids, we bonded over the fact that we all knew we would never be considered for Second City."

As months went by, the ever-impatient McCulloch grew anxious that The Audience weren't taking off in Toronto as rapidly as they had in Calgary. "We came in thinking we were a big deal," says McCulloch. "We felt we were already fully formed, so our simple plan was to swoop in and replicate our quick success in Toronto. We had some good shows at Theatresports Toronto, and made some friends there, but we soon realized Theatresports would not be our next arena. We had to break out on our own."

While The Audience acclimated themselves in the city, the Kids in the Hall were reduced to a trio after Scott Stewart left the group to pursue a solo career as an actor and comedian. Foley, McDonald, and Casimiri had begun writing and performing radio sketches for the Ryerson University radio station CKLN, when Nasimok approached them about a new, weekly variety night he was booking.

"Curtains Up was held every Thursday night at the Soho at the Metz dinner theatre," says Nasimok. "It was intended as a venue for working improvisers and writers to experiment and try out their new stuff, although, to be fair, it eventually devolved into people just going up and doing their party pieces."

Still, Nasimok continued to promote the series and eventually moved it to the Second City's Old Fire Hall theatre. It was here that the Kids in the Hall joined in on the fun, along with other performers, including comedy magician Tony Mason and storyteller Simon Rakoff.

New venues and comedy nights began popping up around town, perhaps none more notorious than Vaudeville After Dark, held at The Ritz, formerly the Vaughan Theatre on St. Clair Avenue West, hosted by the comedy team Al & George (Lara Rae and George Westerholm). Despite rumours that the old theatre was haunted, neither The Audience nor the Kids in the Hall were deterred from sharing a bill at the 800-seat venue. According to Mark McKinney, The Audience were especially thrilled to find a large space where they might possibly replicate their Calgary success with a midnight variety show every Saturday night. "We had developed a real entrepreneurial streak," says McKinney, "so we worked really hard to find a similar audience in Toronto, although it just seemed to be taking forever."

Ever hustling, The Audience kept plugging away in search of a venue that they could call their own. They took the door money they had been gifted from their Calgary run and rented out The Poor Alex Theatre for $100 a night. Once again, the Kids and The Audience were sharing the bill, but it was here that thoughts of merging the two troupes first began to take root. For Foley, the Poor Alex shows mark the moment when he truly "got" The Audience, while McCulloch likewise began to see the Kids in the Hall as kindred spirits.

"I felt that our brains were very similar," says McCulloch, "and we liked each other. They hated Theatresports more than we did, because they wanted to do their own thing. So, we united."

The Poor Alex proved a fertile atmosphere for the cultivation of a shared comedy aesthetic, and a new spirit of collaboration emerged between the two troupes, even though, as McCulloch is quick to point out, The Audience dominated the writing. "It was more us writing scenes and putting those guys in them," says McCulloch. "We weren't true collaborators yet. We had already written over 150 scenes; they had only written a handful at that point."

Both factions had heard that another local improv group, The Out of the Way Players, had recently set the Guinness World Record for Longest Continuous Improvisation. And while nobody bothered to confirm the record, the young comedians were unified in their desire to break it. They staged a two-day event called the Improvathon at the studios of a cable access station in suburban Etobicoke. Briane Nasimok joined them as a guest performer and host for the fifty-hour-long event. "Different cast members would sleep at different times," says Nasimok. "By nine o'clock in the morning, there were only three of us up, and we started inviting viewers to phone in and suggest improvs. If I remember correctly, this was the first time Bruce did his character Troumouth, who sang a song to a plant. The whole weekend was utter mayhem."

The combined troupe bested the previous record by two hours, but according to McDonald, they failed to officially break the World Record, since nobody bothered to notify

The Guinness Book of Records. In the absence of Guinness judges, their attempt was disqualified.

"It became another typical Kids in the Hall story," says McDonald. "We broke the record but were dumb so nobody knew about it."

Disqualification aside, the Improvathon was a successful collaboration and everyone had fun working together. According to Garry Campbell, the boundaries between the two troupes began to fall away. "It didn't take long for us to become just one big group," says Campbell, "and it became more about everybody doing sketches together."

At first, says Foley, The Audience's more aggressive Calgary style seemed to clash with the Kids' decidedly more passive approach. They weren't used to fighting as a way of solving creative problems. "We thought they were just horrible assholes to each other," says Foley, laughing slightly, "and they were really horrible assholes to us too! They really seemed to like being mean to each other, and there were definitely times when Kevin, Luc, and I thought, 'Maybe we should stop doing this; these guys are horrible to be around.'"

Still, the members of The Audience were also the funniest people the Kids knew, so they stayed, although Bruce McCulloch remembers being confused about why they were unhappy all the time. "I really didn't know why they seemed so mad at us," says McCulloch. "I came from a bunch of aggressive men, but then these guys were much gentler, so they had to be dealt with in a different way. I didn't understand that at first."

McCulloch was also beginning to seriously question

the scope of his own ambitions. The Audience had never backed away from any promotional stunt, no matter how silly or difficult, but nothing was working, and they were losing money by self-financing shows that barely anyone attended. The old Calgary magic never seemed to materialize. "We kind of had to fail in order to succeed again," says McCulloch, with the benefit of hindsight. "But at the time, we were probably pushing too hard and waiting for fate to intervene."

Fate turned out to be a theatre student with fearless comedic instincts and a natural hunger for the spotlight. His name was Scott Thompson.

Thompson was a theatre student at Toronto's York University who had recently formed an improv troupe called The Love Cats with his playwriting partner Darlene Harrison (now Treen), and fellow performers Karen Ballard and the late Tim Sims. According to Thompson, he and the other Love Cats were sexually charged performers with a reputation for being unhinged. "Tim and I were particularly brazen," says Thompson. "We would do shows where all four of us would dress up — Darlene and Karen as nurses, Tim and I in pantsuits, that sort of thing. Tim was amazing."

One fateful night in the fall of 1983, Harrison brought Thompson to the Poor Alex to check out the improvisations of The Audience and the Kids in the Hall. For Thompson, it was nothing short of a revelation. "I remember turning to Darlene and telling her, 'I'm going to be in that group,'" says Thompson. "She said, 'You don't even know them.' But I said, 'Doesn't matter.' I just knew. I had a flash; in a way, it was almost like God told me."

Before the show that night, the troupe had taped doughnuts to the undersides of every seat in the Poor Alex in anticipation of a gag that they had planned to do later in the program. Thompson discovered them early in the show, and in a desperate bid for attention he began throwing them at the stage.

"I ruined their show," says Thompson, "but it was kind of a calculated risk. I was like a little boy hoping to attract the attention of a pretty girl. Afterwards, I hung around to meet them, and I remember Bruce was like, 'Are you the fuckin' asshole who threw the doughnuts at us?' And I'm like, 'Yeah.' I think they were a little confused. 'Who would be proud of ruining our show?' But I just knew it was the right thing to do. With almost anyone else, it would not have been the right thing to do, but it was right for them."

Soon after the night of the doughnuts, Mark McKinney came down to Theatresports to check out Thompson performing with the Love Cats. He was immediately impressed with Thompson's unpredictable energy and physicality. As improv troupes are wont to do, the Love Cats solicited suggestions from the audience for a location, and one patron suggested—as improv audience members are wont to do— a public bathroom.

"So, we did this scene where someone pretended to take a shit," laughs Thompson, "and I walked in and pretended to hold his turd up like it was the turd of God or something. We got a zero from the judges, but I think Mark liked what a crazy choice it was. Mark himself is not a crazy person, so I think he looks for it in other people."

For McKinney, Thompson offered the potential for a broader comic palette, a wild card to add to an already impressive hand. But for Thompson, meeting the Kids in the Hall and The Audience marked the culmination of a lifelong search to fit in somewhere, and a left turn from what he had always assumed would be a career in serious drama.

John Scott Thompson, the second son of Philip and Barbara Thompson, was born in North Bay, Ontario, on June 12, 1959. He and his older brother Rand were soon joined by three more boys, Dean, Craig, and Derek, almost enough for a hockey team. Thompson still has fond memories of his earliest days in Northern Ontario.

"I remember the beauty: the lakes and forests, and all the animals," says Thompson. "I played sports because I had so many brothers, but I would sometimes go off and explore the woods, floating on a raft or climbing a tree."

When he was nine years old, Thompson's idyllic forest childhood came to an abrupt end when the family moved south to the Toronto satellite city of Brampton. Dropped into a predominantly Portuguese neighbourhood, he got his first real taste of prejudice while attending Agnes Taylor Public School.

"There was a real divide between the Anglo kids and the Portuguese kids," says Thompson. "But I had Portuguese friends and Anglo friends, so I could go in both worlds, which was a big deal. But Brampton was a very, very white place. In fact, I still have this joke where I say, 'The Portuguese were kind of like placeholders until the real people of colour arrived in the '80s.'"

Thompson and his brothers spent a lot of time in the basement engaged in play fighting, real fighting, and near constant yelling, much to the chagrin of his long-suffering mother, Barbara, the only woman in the household. According to Thompson, she always felt outnumbered and had openly longed for a daughter to keep her company. But it was not in the cards. "She just kept trying. Her sister Fran only had boys too, so it was just not in the genes. When we were with her children, we all looked the same, like seven brothers."

Thompson says his father was a strict disciplinarian, prone to a harsh temper, but being around so many strong and aggressive men made him highly aware of posture and the physical language of people. He became particularly fascinated with the way men act and interact. "I've been studying men my whole life," says Thompson, "how they move, that particular way heterosexual men move and hold themselves."

His fascination with all things male was more than likely coupled with the latent and reluctant realization, at the age of nine, that he was gay. "I'd be so thrilled when certain friends of my father came over and I just loved being around them," says Thompson. "I loved men on television and in movies. Like when I watched *Barney Miller*, all I cared about was Wojo. I was obsessed with him. Then, when my dad took me to see *The Guns of Navarone*, all I cared about was the shower scene, or *Cool Hand Luke* because it's so hot and they never wear shirts. I love prison men. I just want a man to love me like George Kennedy loved Paul Newman. That's real love. You watch it now — that's such a strange homoerotic love story."

But like so many LGBTQ kids of his generation, Thompson was closeted for most of his young life, correctly sensing that it was dangerous to let the wrong people know his truth. Thompson still recalls the heartbreak of being dropped by his best school friend after confessing his love for him. "The worst thing a man could be back then was gay," says Thompson. "You were garbage. Every schoolyard taunt was about being gay. The worst word was 'faggot,' and I knew I was one." Early on, Thompson never thought much about being a comedian, and he remembers being drawn to dramatic screen icons such as James Dean and Montgomery Clift, and harbouring dreams of one day becoming a rugged leading man himself. Even then, he says, he knew that being a gay man would present a huge obstacle to those dreams.

"Even if I had the talent, charisma, or whatever the hell you need to become a movie star, I knew I was the type of person who couldn't keep in the closet. I'd probably blurt it out and be in a scandal after my first movie. So that ended my movie-star ambitions."

Thompson believes that his father was rough on him because he was uncomfortable with his son's latent homosexuality, which he sensed subconsciously. His anger, Thompson believes, was an attempt to "scare the gay out of me."

Thompson soon learned that one of the best ways to pacify his father, and earn his affection, was by making him laugh. Suddenly, the ability to find the funny, whenever he needed it, became vitally important. To soothe his teenage anxieties, Thompson would frequently escape into the glitzy and glamorous television variety shows of the day, and while he never missed the *Dean Martin Variety Show* or *The Sonny & Cher Comedy Hour*, his two favourites were *The Carol Burnett Show* and *The Flip Wilson Show*.

"Flip Wilson and Carol Burnett were my two huge influences," Thompson admits. "I wanted to be either one. I was kind of crazy about Flip Wilson, who was monstrously talented and very attractive. He was a great stand-up, but I especially liked that he played both males and females who were never caricatures. I mean, Geraldine Jones was huge for me; 'The Devil made me do it!' Absolutely."

Thompson enrolled at Brampton Centennial Secondary School, where he began his high-school years as a bookish and exuberant student who got good grades most of the time. But as adolescence set in, a new recklessness began to affect his grades. "I had been one of those horrible people we called 'browners,'" says Thompson, "but in the last couple of years of high school, I discovered bad boys and drugs like acid, pot, peyote, and mescaline. I probably went too far because I was gay, and I always felt I had to prove I was a man."

Thompson was already dealing with enough demons when a sixteen-year-old classmate at Brampton Centennial named Michael Peter Slobodian succumbed to even darker forces, unleashing a lethality that would not only traumatize the school's 1,500 students, but the entire nation of Canada. On the morning of May 28, 1975, just before lunchtime, Slobodian entered the school with a flexible guitar bag containing two rifles, with extra shells stuffed into the pockets of his parka. Once inside the building, Slobodian opened the case and began firing. In a matter of minutes, he had killed Thompson's classmate John Slinger, along with one of his most beloved teachers, Margaret Wright, while seriously wounding fourteen others before entering the boys' room and taking his own life. Up until that tragic day, Canada had never had a mass killing in any school, and while Thompson himself was not physically harmed in the attack, the event would leave him emotionally scarred for decades to come.

"Michael Slobodian sat behind me in English class," says Thompson, still clearly upset by the memory. "And one of his victims, Margaret Wright, was the teacher who made me become a writer. I was always getting into trouble, and Mrs. Wright would say, 'I'm so sick of giving you detention, so I'm going to ask you to write me a poem, and if I like what you write, I'll let you out of detention early.' So I started writing poems for Mrs. Wright. Here was the first adult who really saw something special in me, and then he killed her. She was only twenty-four years old. And six months pregnant."

The event was a rude awaking for Thompson, making it dramatically clear to him that nowhere was safe; violence can come out of anywhere at any time. Today, he believes the shooting has affected his entire life. "Remember, in those days there was no trauma counselling like there would be now," says Thompson. "And, in general, Canadians were much more British back then; you know, 'Stiff upper lip, move on, don't grumble.' I think that, as a nation, Canada blocked the event out entirely. But I could never do that."

For the duration of his school days, Thompson searched for both a creative outlet and gay role models who weren't used as a punchline, or a punching bag, in the public conversation, all the while keeping his truth to himself.

"They were almost all in the literary world," says Thompson, "people like Tennessee Williams, Gore Vidal, or Truman Capote, but all of them terrified me. William F. Buckley Jr. called Gore Vidal a faggot on live television. If I saw Truman Capote on television, even I wanted to hit him. Even the funny ones, like Rip Taylor or Paul Lynde, terrified me because even though they weren't out, I *assumed* they were gay. I thought, 'Oh my god, when I come out, I'll just be a screaming queen like that.' I couldn't be caught liking the music of Queen because Freddie Mercury just seemed so faggy to me, even though it wasn't widely known that he actually *was* gay until after he died from AIDS."

Like that of many LGBTQ teens, especially in the 1970s, Thompson's fear of being found out led to self-loathing. He was even afraid to join the drama club because everybody at school assumed that all theatre kids were gay. "People would tell me I was so flamboyant and expressive," says Thompson, "which is code for gay. They would insist that I try out for the school play, but I knew that if I joined the drama club, it would out me. I didn't want to associate with anyone remotely gay so I deliberately kept myself away."

By his last year at Brampton Centennial, Thompson finally agreed to take the role of old man Percival Browne in the school's production of Sandy Wilson's stage musical, *The Boy Friend*. It was his first time being onstage apart from the one time he narrated the Passion play at his church. He got to sing a couple of songs in *The Boy Friend*, and it felt great. He was hooked. But despite getting good notices, he was still afraid to admit to anyone that he wanted to be an actor. His brothers had ridiculed him so badly after he had confessed his desire to be a ballet dancer that he never spoke of the arts to them again. To appease his parents, he had dutifully applied to Ottawa's Carleton University to study journalism, and to his horror, he had been accepted. He couldn't do it. While looking for a good escape plan, Thompson read about a Canadian-based, non-profit foreign exchange program called Canada World Youth. He wanted to go as far away from Carleton University as he could get, so a year in Africa seemed perfect.

"I had a scrapbook filled with stories of people like Nelson Mandela," says Thompson, "and I really wanted to see West Africa. At the time I left, I wasn't yet prepared to accept being an actor, but Canada World Youth gave me the courage to be who I was, and it changed my life."

As it happened, Africa wasn't available, so Thompson was instead dispatched to spend half of his year in north-west Canada, with the other half in the Philippines. While he found the experience life-changing and eye-opening, he also realized that he was now ready to accept his calling as an actor. Before he left, Thompson had secretly enrolled in the drama program at York University. Upon his return to

Toronto in September 1978, Thompson set foot on the York campus for the first time. Among the first people he met in residence at Vanier College was another outsider, Paul Bellini, who had come to York all the way from Timmins, Ontario.

Paul Bellini, who would go on to become Thompson's comedy writing partner for decades before writing for other programs, including *This Hour Has 22 Minutes*, was part of a small collective of York film students. "Our film kids were me, Tom King, Brian Hiltz, and Liza Hokura," says Bellini. "Scott was on a different floor than us, because he was in the dramatic arts program, but we all ate together in the same dining hall."

Making good on Mrs. Wright's early belief in him, Thompson pursued creative writing courses at York, and had his poetry published in campus papers like *The Artichoke* and *Excalibur*, which were edited by Bellini and Hiltz, respectively.

According to Bellini, Thompson craved constant attention, which he earned by walking the halls of York wearing oversized glasses or generally being loud, nerdy, and impossible to ignore. That's not to say he was one-dimensional, and Bellini, who probably knows him the best, has seen him high and low. "Scott was a serious theatre student," says Bellini, "and prone to these horrible, crushing, black-cloud moods, but he could also be extremely funny. Even after all these years, when Scott is on, he can still be the life of the party."

To break up the monotony of life in the residence, Bellini and his fellow cinema studies students amused themselves by making short films, and Thompson was always happy to appear in them. "We were all like nineteen and making these little experimental films," says Thompson. "I remember doing my first drag as Geraldine Page in *Posteriors*, Paul's parody of *Interiors*. My big line was [in effeminate voice], 'I love it. It's sort of a nice pink.' And then I start crying."

Director Bellini recalls his star as a fearless risk taker who even did his own stunts in one of his films, *Sealed with a Kiss*. "Scott had to fall out of a tree and do all sorts of other stunts," says Bellini. "He was very brave, and just didn't care who else was looking, which I appreciate in an actor."

Despite mingling with many flamboyant, if not openly gay, fellow students, Thompson says that he somehow managed to go through four years in the drama program without coming out. "That's pretty amazing since more than half the class of boys were gay," says Thompson. "But the early '80s were a different time, and I was terrified that if I came out, the next day I'd be camping it up like a screaming queen and immediately become effeminate."

He did, however, come out as a comedian, and by his third year, he and Darlene Harrison were writing comedic plays, two of which Thompson recalls being *The Dark at the Top of the Stairs* and *Not Why, Why Not*. That summer, he attended a musical theatre course at the Banff School of Fine Arts, where he made one of his first significant, if admittedly awkward, stabs at stand-up comedy. In his short set, which he remembers as "very dark, very raw," Thompson opened up about being terrorized by his father's anger. "My routine was about me hiding from my father in the cupboards," he recalls, "and my mother saying, 'Everybody, quick, into the cupboards.' That was the punchline. I was terrible at stand-up back then."

His jokes might have bombed, but a precedent had been set, and like many of the future Kids in the Hall, he began to mine the abject suffering of his youth for material. Back at York, however, he continued to suppress the secret of his sexual orientation. Looking back, Thompson feels that his internalization explains why he became increasingly rebellious on campus and insubordinate to his instructors. Whatever the cause, by his fourth year, and despite getting good grades, Thompson was expelled from York University, after finishing only his English studies. Forced into the real world, he spent the next couple of years pursuing what he calls "straight acting jobs." On the stage, Thompson appeared in *As You Like It* at Toronto Free Theatre, and in a revival of Antony Ferry's *Hey Rube!* for Toronto Workshop Productions. He also appeared in fellow York student Bruce La Bruce's film *Super 8½*, for which he wrote one of the earliest "Buddy Cole" monologues, and booked small roles in film and television.

"I had one line as 'Guy on Roller Skates' in the movie *Hot Paint*," says Thompson, "and I did a bunch of Canadian television like *Street Legal*, where I played a young New York director, and *The Campbells*, where I played Red, a Scottish Fenian."

Other film roles included *Millennium*, a science fiction thriller starring Kris Kristofferson, and Ken Finkleman's comedy *Head Office*, in a cast that included Judge Reinhold, Rick Moranis, and Jane Seymour. "I was basically an extra

with no lines," says Thompson, "although I did a lot physically, because Jane Seymour liked me. I think she had kind
of a crush on me."

As promising as the serious stuff might have been,
Thompson had fallen hard for comedy, which was how he
and his fellow Love Cats ended up at Theatresports. Close
friend Paul Bellini noticed a new fearlessness in him when
he caught the Cats' edgy sets, and marks the troupe as a
turning point in Thompson's transition into a comedian.

Which brings us back to the Poor Alex Theatre and the
doughnut heard 'round the world.

"I had been auditioning every year for dramatic roles
at the Shaw and Stratford Festivals," says Thompson, "but
the Kids in the Hall just changed everything. After that, I
was all about comedy."

When the sprinkles had settled, Thompson had met
the love of his professional life just as The Audience were
merging with the Kids in the Hall. Their budding alliance
was about to find the ideal greenhouse in the backroom
performance space of a tiny restaurant on Queen Street
West called the Rivoli.

FOUR

In the Backroom of the Rivoli

As the two tribes became one, Kevin McDonald remembers feeling a sense of camaraderie with his fellow sketch comedy misfits. "We had become like this street gang, albeit a *comedy* street gang."

As 1984 got under way, the core members of the gang were McDonald, Dave Foley, Bruce McCulloch, Mark McKinney, Luciano Casimiri, Garry Campbell, and Frank van Keeken, frequently augmented by a rotating roster of guest improvisers and stand-up comics from the emerging Toronto comedy scene, including their newest discovery, Scott Thompson. Even when they weren't doing one-off shows together, they would still convene to talk about Python, Woody Allen, or *SCTV*, as comedy nerds are wont to do.

But every good gang needs a clubhouse, and in 1984, Briane Nasimok, forever hustling on their behalf, secured them a regular Monday-night variety slot in the backroom of the Rivoli bistro at 334 Queen Street West. The building itself had something of a colourful past, having been a house of burlesque in 1911, a silent movie house, a gathering spot for revolutionary Trotskyites, a radical bookstore, and finally a diner. The property had been purchased in 1981 by Andre Rosenbaum and David Stearn, the owners of the nearby Queen Mother Café, who had opted to keep the restaurant in the front space, while transforming the backroom into a performance venue for local bands, alternative cinema screenings, performance artists, and clowns. Their friend Nasimok was among the earliest performers at the Rivoli, and he convinced them that a cabaret night, early in the week, might help sell some drinks on an erstwhile slow night.

"I knew that Monday was amateur night over at Yuk Yuk's," says Nasimok, "so we weren't going to fight that audience. Nothing else was happening at the Rivoli on that night, so Andre and David said, 'Sure.'"

While the club had previously hosted the local sketch comedy faves The Frantics, McDonald recalls that the idea of a weekly comedy night was still a relatively new concept on Queen Street. "Briane would be the regular host, but there would be a constantly changing roster of guest performers. He asked me, Dave, and Luc, to be a kind of a comedy 'house band,' which I always figured was because the club had been kind of a rock 'n' roll place. We were expected to improvise for fifteen minutes, probably do around three or four scenes, then Briane would introduce all that week's guests as they came on and off." Among the guests were stand-ups Norm Macdonald and Eric Tunney, and the musical comedy trio Corky and the Juice Pigs, fronted by Seán Cullen.

"We all loved Seán," says McDonald, "and another funny guy named Jon Davies who had a troupe called Sledgehammer Pie, who we all liked and hung out with."

While the comedy world at the time was typically a "boys' club," McDonald says that some of their favourite guest performers were people like Sandra Shamas and Deborah Theaker. "Sandra and Deborah were as funny as any of us," says McDonald, "and not just funny 'for a woman.' Sandra was just *one of us*, and she might have become a member of our troupe had she not had her mind set on writing her own hilarious monologues, which was a good thing because they were brilliant and she became very successful at it."

Shamas had previously worked with the guys at Theatresports, and noted a tangible growth in their improvisational skills when she caught up with them at the Rivoli. "They were unpredictable, and they all seemed willing to go in any direction the scene took them at breakneck speed. There was a real spine of realism that went through all of their strengths, which made them, and still makes them, individually interesting and compelling, and collectively delightful."

At the time, Garry Campbell was living with Frank van Keeken and Kevin McDonald in an upstairs apartment in Toronto's Parkdale neighbourhood, which he remembers as a fairly dangerous and challenging part of the city. "We hadn't been there a year and somebody was murdered in our backyard," says Campbell. "I also remember waking up in the middle of the night in a sleeping bag on the floor with cockroaches crawling all over my body. That was my fantastic welcome to Toronto."

Likewise, McDonald recalls finding yellow crime tape across the threshold of the entrance to their building. "I asked this police officer if I could pass, and he just said, 'Yeah, but be careful. There's a severed finger on the floor.' Welcome to Parkdale!"

In spite of the danger, city life afforded them a wealth of inspiration, and all along Queen Street, new and exciting culture was being forged out of chaos as local culture hubs like the Ontario College of Art pushed the envelope in fashion, design, music, and comedy. Queen Street West had become English Canada's newest answer to Greenwich Village, a mecca where music and comedy were becoming intertwined. The Queen West strip was suddenly overflowing with street life, and barriers were breaking down in all directions. According to Dave Foley, the change had been a long time coming.

"Up until the '80s, Toronto had been so boring," says Foley. "Sidewalk life had been outlawed, and it was illegal to sell hot dogs, jewellery, or anything on the street. Sidewalk patios were even illegal and you could get still arrested for busking."

Their brief introductory run at the Rivoli had felt right to the troupe — they loved the room and felt at home on Queen Street. Attendance, while not huge, had been enough that McCulloch and McKinney felt confident asking Nasimok if the troupe could take over Monday nights on a regular basis. The Audience contingent was always on the lookout for a place to replicate their Loose Moose success, and in a relatively short time, the Rivoli had proven to be the perfect laboratory for the two troupes to grow their hybrid comedy. "We wrote some good stuff at the Rivoli," recalls McDonald, "like Bruce's 'If Elvis Were My Landlord.' We kind of pretended that we had a TV show, so each week we felt we had to write an all-new program. Dave came up with the idea of creating a side stage, midway down the room along the side of the Rivoli's brick wall, as a place to 'cut to' like in a real TV show. I remember Garry Campbell saying, 'I swear to God, guys, at the end of this year we'll have a TV show. It might be only on cable access, but we're gonna have a real TV show.'"

But privately, Campbell was beginning to tire of intertroupe politics and wondered if he would even be around to see a show go to air. Inevitably, with a group of their size and inexperience, tensions began to arise and Campbell admits there were times when each one of them felt sick of seeing the others day in and day out. "We were doing shows on as many nights a week as we could," says Campbell, "and then hanging out socially. It was too much. So, the fact that we got on each other's nerves was not surprising at all."

When Campbell and Frank van Keeken were offered staff writing jobs on a television series called *The Comedy Jam*, they saw it as a chance to break away from the gang. Bruce McCulloch heard the news while the team was writing new material for an upcoming show. "We were all at Frank and Garry's house when they got a phone call," recalls McCulloch. "They came back and told us they got the job, and they were going to be making $710 each. I thought, 'Whoa!' But I also remember thinking, 'Wait, *I'm* the best writer. Why are *they* getting the job?' From that point on, there was never any conversation about whether Frank and Garry were in or out of the troupe; they just sort of faded away."

Even with fewer egos, the infighting within the gang didn't cease, and at one point, they had to stop performing live altogether. While on hiatus, Foley, McDonald, and Casimiri resumed their CKLN gig, eventually inviting McKinney to join in the fun. Then, Luc Casimiri had a falling-out with McKinney and left the show.

As Foley, McDonald, McKinney, and McCulloch prepared for their return to the Rivoli, they finally addressed an issue they had been avoiding for months: What should they call the amalgamated troupe? Was it better to get behind one of their two names, or come up with something new? Foley made the prudent point that they had been building a brand as the Kids in the Hall, and had been promoting their radio show under that name. McDonald was on board with the idea, but McKinney remained attached to the name they had come up with in Calgary, "The Audience," and McCulloch stood by him.

"One of our early managers—I can't remember which one—said that name made us sound exciting as well as funny," says McDonald. "He said it sounded like *punk comedy,* which I suppose we are. But I just remember Bruce standing up and saying 'There's no way I'm going to stick with *that stupid name.*'"

To reach a consensus, a scientific method was needed. They flipped a coin. The Kids in the Hall won. Hesitantly, says McKinney, The Audience conceded defeat. "Obviously, I was very possessive about 'The Audience,'" says McKinney, "but Bruce and I went along with 'the Kids in the Hall' with one caveat: if a better name came to us, we could change it anytime. That never happened, of course."

The Kids in the Hall was now considered a four-man troupe, with Casimiri continuing to drop by now and again, and with frequent appearances by Scott Thompson. In fact, Thompson was becoming so much a part of the show they began to seriously consider inviting him to join the troupe officially. Foley, however, recalls that he and McDonald had their reservations about bringing in Thompson, who was, of all things, a serious dramatic actor. "Kevin and I were always highly suspicious of actors attempting comedy," says Foley, "so we had our doubts. I think it took us a while to figure out that Scott was actually really, really funny, and he brought a lot of energy to the show."

While Thompson was one of their favourite guests, the troupe was also considering inviting Tim Sims from Thompson's crew, the Love Cats, to join the Kids in the Hall, but Foley also made a strong push for adding their old friend from the Second City workshops, Mike Myers. "Mike was very close with Dave," says McCulloch, "and we'd always try to lure him out to do stuff on stage with us. We worked well together."

Just as Sandra Shamas had been, Myers recalls being impressed by how much the Kids had grown since he'd last worked with them. "They had this fantastic, almost punk rock energy," says Myers. "They did real characters that were from the street, from your life, and the subjects of their scenes were very different than what I was doing at the time over at Second City. They had a kind of postpunk cool about them."

While a particularly strong onstage chemistry existed between Myers and McCulloch, some in the troupe openly wondered if including him might be a case of too many great cooks in the kitchen. As they debated that question in 1984, Myers rendered such talk moot by announcing his intention to pursue a comedy career in the birthplace of his comedy heroes Peter Sellers and Monty Python — the United Kingdom. In light of that news, McKinney once again suggested adding Thompson to the troupe, arguing that Thompson's wild energy and unpredictable improvisation choices would give the troupe more of an edge.

"Mark has this diplomatic background," says Thompson, "so I think he's drawn to people who are a little unhinged and physical, and maybe a little dangerous, because it brings out the wild gene in himself."

And so it was, after a dismal performance on a cold winter's night early in 1984, that the Kids in the Hall casually invited Scott Thompson into the fold. "We were all in this cab after a shitty, shitty show," says McKinney, "and we saw Scott scuttling down Queen Street toward the subway. We pulled up, and I leaned out and asked, 'Hey, Scott, do you want to be in the Kids in the Hall?' He looked up and just said, 'Yeah.'"

"I remember in those days we were using The Who's 'The Kids Are Alright' as our theme song," says McDonald, "so we sang it to him on the street and he started crying."

With their lineup finally in place, the true work of the Kids in the Hall had only just begun.

FIVE

Running Free

Prior to Scott Thompson's arrival, the Kids had never really gone "all in" with drag, choosing instead to portray female characters by adjusting their posture and/or voice, or by pulling a big red, oversized sweater (borrowed from McDonald's then-girlfriend, Tiffany) over their jeans as a makeshift dress. At various times, each Kid had systematically taken his turn as "the girl," but according to McDonald, their intention wasn't so much to parody or mock women as to tap into their inner femininity and "inhabit them."

According to Foley, the idea was that if one of them had the big red sweater on, the audience would accept him as "the girl" in the scene. "The thing is, we're mostly pretty feminine guys, but the truth is that Scott is actually the most *masculine* man among us, which might seem ironic to some people. Sometimes we'd play street hockey, and Scott would be the guy who would hit hard, play dirty, or challenge you to a hockey fight."

Thompson had waited a long time to come out; he hadn't even confirmed his sexuality to his fellow theatre students at York University, many of whom were out themselves. While the secret had traumatized him all through college, he feared the very real possibility of stigmatization, particularly at the dawn of the 1980s. In the end, however, his decision to go public came down to just being tired — tired of living in fear and tired of hating himself.

"Any artist, whether they are a comedian, actor, painter, or whatever, has to be honest," says Thompson, "and I wanted to be an artist, so that meant I had to open up about my sexuality."

Thompson says the support of his four straight allies in the Kids in the Hall became an essential element in his ability to be out onstage. Being openly gay was still a big deal in comedy during the mid-1980s, but within the Kids in the Hall, he finally felt safe. He brought to the troupe a newfound candour, along with a selection of wigs and dresses, and generally encouraged the troupe to play around with gender roles in ways they had only hinted at before. "The group protected me and gave me a place to hide," says Thompson, "which allowed me to play other characters and do voices and all that."

When told that the Rivoli's Carson Foster has referred to him as "the Rosa Parks of gay sketch comedy," Thompson laughs at the assertion, but doesn't deny his role in breaking down a few barriers.

"Nobody else was really 'out' in comedy," says Thompson, "so that made me want to be the first. I was very excited by the idea that I could become other people and express myself, and say the things that were unsayable at the time. For example, I remember that saying I was a fag onstage was considered shocking at the time; nobody dared do that. I mean, this was during a very scary time — the AIDS epidemic. There was a very good chance I wouldn't live to be an adult, but there's nothing more dangerous than a person who has nothing to lose, so I felt I could go for broke. It was a kind of freedom."

Foster, who was both the Rivoli's bartender and talent booker, says that beyond the comedy world, Thompson was one of the first openly gay men in Toronto public life, period. Homosexuality had only been officially decriminalized in Canada in 1969, and the mostly closeted LGBTQ community was still reeling from the Metropolitan Toronto Police's "Operation Soap," which took place on February 5, 1981, in which blitzkrieg raids on four gay bathhouses had resulted in the arrests of twenty bathhouse owners on charges of "keeping a common bawdyhouse," and 286 clients, all gay men, charged as "found-ins."

"Those bathhouse raids were Toronto's Stonewall riots," says Foster, "the incident that galvanized the gay rights movement in Toronto the way Stonewall did in New York. So, the fact that the other Kids stood by Scott at this point in the city's history really spoke to their conviction about human rights."

The second Rivoli residency gave the whole troupe the room to make mistakes and push boundaries, including the resurrection of Bruce McCulloch's risqué, all-nude "Naked for Jesus" sketch originally staged at the Loose Moose in Calgary.

"I just remember I played a cop, and I was naked but for my holster and gun," says Kevin McDonald. "Let me tell you, your penis really shrivels up when you're naked onstage. The first time I did it I remember thinking, 'Oh my god, I'm gonna pee, right here on the Rivoli stage.' I remember Dave was the only one of us who wouldn't go all the way."

Sometimes, Foster recalls, the Kids would cross a line with certain crowds. "There were some shows where the audience was packed with a few 'frat boys' who just couldn't get with a scene like 'Running Faggot,' but you know, Scott was only doing what Lenny Bruce had done years before him. Scott was extremely brave."

While McCulloch remained impatient about the Kids' gradual rise, Mark McKinney recalls feeling energized as the Queen Street crowds began showing up for the Kids. "It was very rock 'n' roll. Unlike Second City, which just had that piano player between scenes, we'd blast loud rock music on tape. It was slow at first, but we started to get regulars, and they were bringing in new people, eventually filling more seats in the backroom."

A community emerged around the Kids in the Hall, populated by their various artistic friends. McCulloch's pals Brian Connelly, Reid Diamond, and Don Pyle were now trading as the trio Shadowy Men on a Shadowy Planet, and played their debut show at the Rivoli. Additionally, Connelly was often called upon to design show posters for the Kids. "The Shadowy Men seemed to us like the rock band equivalent of what we were doing as a comedy troupe," says McDonald. "Like us, they were modern, but in a weird way also kind of traditional."

Similarly, Thompson's film student friend from college, Paul Bellini, was asked to lug his bulky video equipment down to the Rivoli to record their sets for posterity. Bellini was thrilled by what the Kids had become, having not seen them since Thompson joined the troupe. "It was genius," recalls Bellini, "and I just knew there was nothing else like it anywhere. They were generating so much great new material every week, and they'd only recycle the really great pieces. I recorded an eight-minute early version of 'Salty Ham,' and they watched my tape, then trimmed all the fat to reveal a tight four-minute scene."

Bruce McCulloch was reluctant to repeat sketches, but says he knew, instinctively, that the ability to edit and refine a sketch would be a handy skill to have down the road. "As a young man, I thought that anyone who even repeated a *character* was a hack. But I started to see the value in trying things more than once, and it was getting harder to come up with something new each time."

McCulloch also says he was feeling burnt out after trying too hard to replicate his early success in Calgary, and the Rivoli era was rife with short-lived yet emotionally draining internal conflicts, some of which would scar their relationships for years to come. Dave Foley, however, says that whatever was going on behind the scenes, they never took their social squabbles onto the Rivoli stage. "We could fight horribly, and it could be just a miserable process getting the show ready all week, but at the moment we walked on stage on Monday night, we loved those four other guys more than anyone else in the world."

The Kids in The Hall were now a unified five-man entity, ready to take on the world. But first they needed to at least conquer Toronto. Promise was in the air. Crowds were small but increasing in size. The Kids grew impatient; it was taking too long to reach the next plateau.

"It was, like, every time we won something, it got snatched back a little bit," says McCulloch. "I had written this sketch about a guy who would walk around repairing food for the hicks and the hipsters. We did it on stage and it killed, just fucking murdered. We were so good that night, it gave me hope about our future." But shortly after this triumph, McCulloch turned on his television to find John Candy appearing in a sketch called "Food Repairman" on an episode of *The New Show*, a Lorne Michaels production. McCulloch would later discover that the similarly themed sketch was penned by future *Simpsons* writer George Meyer. At the time, this coincidence felt to McCulloch like a punch in the face, even if there was no way Meyer could have known about their sketch.

According to McKinney, it wasn't just McCulloch who was feeling deflated; the whole troupe was feeling burnt out and perilously close to packing it all in. "Bruce wanted to quit and go do stand-up, and Dave was getting serious interest from Second City. I say this without any hint of drama, but we probably would have broken up if Scott and I hadn't come up with the idea to do *Croptown*."

Croptown was built around one massive thirty-minute title sketch, a southern gothic mini-play set in a tiny mythical farm town of the same name. "Bruce played this young rebel who wanted to get out and go to the big city, but always got lost," says McDonald. "Dave played a man but because of the lack of women in Croptown, he was referred to as the town's 'prettiest woman.' I played the sheriff, who suffered from maggots, as well as the world's largest prisoner in the world's tiniest jail—it was basically just me in this little jail cell with bars only covering my head. Honestly, I don't remember much else."

The *Croptown* show was also notable for presenting the debut of a sketch called "Barbershop," and another long piece, "The Suburbs," which included many characters that would later show up on the television series. "Bruce and I worked up something for that with our two businessmen characters, the Geralds," says McKinney. "We all had characters and ideas, and we just made all these thematic pieces sort of hang together."

Croptown generated a timely burst of positive energy and the troupe was excited about the challenge of doing longer scenes. Having done mainly club shows, the theatre stage represented a new frontier, and it led to their decision to stage *Lurching Seaward*, their very first best-of show, at Toronto's Tarragon Extraspace.

"Our friend at Tarragon, Catherine May, told us that this little ninety-seater theatre was going to be dark for a week," says McKinney. "She said we could rent it for around $200, but we couldn't even afford that. So, we made a deal to hand out flyers for a lunch theatre downtown to pay the rent."

The first half of *Lurching Seaward* was built from a selection of the Kids' best short scenes from the Rivoli. After an intermission, the entire second act consisted of a one-act play called *Troumouth Wears Green,* starring McCulloch as Troumouth, an early version of his Cabbage Head character. "Troumouth was basically Cabbage Head without the cabbage," says McKinney, laughing. "We wrote a whole story around him and brought in Sandra Shamas to play Troumouth's wife."

Filling a week of shows at the Tarragon presented a challenge, but after days of the Kids handing out promotional flyers up and down Queen Street, the audiences came out, and just before the Wednesday show, McKinney recalls peeking through the curtains to see a packed house. "Then Thursday night was sold out too, and the Friday and Saturday shows were just mayhem. At that point, I recognized this moment — the Calgary crowds were finally here."

Since *Lurching Seaward* was a proper stage production mounted at a legitimate theatre, they felt they could ask their old Calgary friend, writer Zsuzsi Gartner, to persuade her boss, Canada's pre-eminent theatre critic, Ray Conlogue, to cover it for the *Globe and Mail.* In his glowing review, Conlogue praised the "talented and inventive" troupe for its "cleverly performed" comedy. And while he was enthusiastic about the whole cast, he singled out Bruce McCulloch's "extended tour de force" as Troumouth, which he promised his readers "must be seen to be believed."

The impact was immediate, and the troupe was besieged with interview requests and ticket orders. "We were hot because of this rave review in the *Globe,*" says Foley, laughing, "although I remember my friend Rob Salem at the *Toronto Star* refusing to write about us because he didn't think we were ready!"

The day after the *Globe* review, the Kids were rehearsing at the Tarragon when McCulloch took a call from Pamela Thomas, a Toronto-based casting agent affiliated with both Second City and *Saturday Night Live*. Thomas had previously received a tip from Second City's Sally Cochrane about a new sketch comedy troupe she simply had to check out. When she went to see the Kids in the Hall the following week, she agreed with Cochrane; they were hilarious. "It's very rare that you see somebody who just knocks you out," says Thomas. "What I saw in the Kids in the Hall was instinct. It's nothing I can point to specifically; they just had guts, and they had great chemistry. They also played great women, obviously, and who doesn't find that hilarious?"

Kevin McDonald says that while everybody knew Thomas as a big comedy agent and talent scout, they were equally impressed that she was married to one of their comedy heroes, *SCTV*'s Dave Thomas. "We were huge *SCTV* fans," says McDonald, "so in my mind that meant she was connected to the next-level people."

Thomas recalls sending word of her new discovery to *SNL* kingpin Lorne Michaels and brainstorming with her business partner, Diane Polley, the late actress and casting director—and mother of Canadian actor/director Sarah Polley—about ways to help get the Kids to the next level.

When Thomas asked McCulloch to put her *SNL* scouting contingent—which included herself, Polley, and Ivan Fecan—on the guest list for the last show in the run—Bruce shocked his cast mates by telling her that the show was sold out. "The other guys were about to eat me alive, so in the end, we managed to get them in."

Toronto-born producer Fecan had recently been hired as NBC's Vice President of Creative Affairs and was living in Los Angeles at the time of the Tarragon run, and tasked with helping Lorne Michaels smooth out his return to *Saturday Night Live* for the 1985–86 season, after five years in exile. For his comeback year, Michaels sought an entirely new cast, and his transition team, which included Fecan and Thomas, had spent a good part of that summer crisscrossing North America looking at performers. Fecan says he "just happened to be back in Toronto" when Thomas asked him to come to the Tarragon. "Of course I was blown away, but at the same time, Lorne hadn't figured out if he wanted to hire them as writers or new cast members. All of that was still very much up in the air."

Immediately after their closing-night performance, Thomas called McCulloch to tell him that Michaels had requested a closer look at the troupe in action and to ask the Kids to arrange a private audition at the Rivoli, to be attended by a select audience of *SNL*'s Al Franken and Tom Davis, plus Dave Thomas, and Fecan.

McDonald remembers this sudden attention leading to a new flare-up of divisive tensions within the group. "The week before the Rivoli audition, we were all fighting — myself included — about what scenes we should do. It wasn't like us at all."

Mark McKinney says he was horrified at how quickly they had reverted to an "every man for himself" attitude. "At first, the *Globe* review had made us really happy, but the minute there was a laser beam of interest from something like *SNL,* it got kind of weird internally. I'm amazed that we hung together."

The audition was by all accounts a fiasco fraught with tension, as cast members pushed each other aside hoping to shine with a solo piece or to be the star in an ensemble scene. Of the material auditioned, some was clearly not ready for prime time. One such sketch, entitled "Brian's Bombshell," had Foley portraying a young gay man coming out to his parents—Thompson as his loving mother and McCulloch as his dad, stunned catatonic by the news and imagining his son romping around in a gay underworld while a prancing leatherman empties confetti from a bucket marked "AIDS" over him. According to Foley, the sketch was an "obvious extrapolation of both AIDS hysteria and late-twentieth-century homophobia" that was possibly too raw for the *SNL* scouts, and probably too soon for many in the room who were currently losing friends with alarming frequency. A similarly chilly reception greeted non–TV friendly fare like "Running Faggot" and "Farmers on Heroin."

The pressure to get discovered didn't help. Teamwork, the unspoken unity against adversity that had gotten the Kids to this moment, was nowhere to be seen at the audition. "Usually, we were the basketball team that passed the ball a lot," says McDonald, unafraid to toss out a sports analogy, "and we would take turns dunking it. But all of a sudden, we were all fighting about what scenes we were in, and it was like the small-town theatre troupe in Christopher Guest's *Waiting for Guffman*—too much infighting and 'pick me, pick me!' The show ran long—too long for a comedy show — just to make sure everybody felt they were covered and got their solo piece in. After the audition, we had an awkward dinner with the *SNL* guys in the café part of the Rivoli. They said they liked us, thank god, but I just remember Franken stroking his chin and adding, 'You five guys are great, but what can *SNL* do with five guys?' That didn't bode well, I thought."

In the immediate aftermath, each of the Kids wondered if they hadn't blown their shot at being discovered. Then they waited, and waited some more. As they rehearsed for their next show, McDonald wondered if his old job as a cinema usher was still available. The waiting, as Tom Petty once sang, was the hardest part, but when they finally heard from New York, the verdict was even harder. Gathering everyone around in the dressing room after a show at the Rivoli, McCulloch informed the troupe that only he and McKinney were going to *Saturday Night Live* — as writers, not performers.

"Of course we were happy for them," says McDonald, "and we all hugged and gave them our congratulations, but part of me was also devastated."

While Bruce McCulloch says that he felt awkward to be singled out from the troupe, he also admits that he had been training for this moment his entire life, so it was a case of preparation meeting opportunity. "It seemed natural to me since they were interested in the writing aspect of it, and I've always been considered the writer in the group so I didn't feel that guilty. Of course, I wasn't considering how hard it was for the other guys, but I think, subconsciously, I knew that the Kids in the Hall would go on."

SIX

Scattered, Not Shattered

As 1985 drew to a close, the promising future of the Kids in the Hall was suddenly cast into doubt after Lorne Michaels invited Bruce McCulloch and Mark McKinney to join the writing staff of *Saturday Night Live*. The Kids had been elated at the prospect of the five of them heading to the big time, only to see two of their number hired away, and even then, off camera. In reality, Michaels says he wasn't considering *any* of the Kids for the cast at the time. From his standpoint, McKinney and McCulloch were the most developed writers in the troupe; he wasn't breaking up the gang, but merely borrowing two of them for his comeback team.

"I also thought it was just somewhere to begin with the troupe," says Michaels. "I thought, 'This is what I'm doing right now. You guys are great, but you're a distinct voice,' which is why I didn't want to break them up for the *SNL* cast."

McDonald admits to having at least one reservation about Michaels's valuation of the other writers in the Kids in the Hall. "I thought if it was about writing quality, Lorne should also take Dave," says McDonald. "I mean, Scott got better as a writer much later on, and I hadn't really started writing yet—I was too intimidated at that point by the geniuses I was working with—but Dave really deserved to go with Bruce and Mark."

In truth, McKinney and McCulloch had to pass one more audition before signing on to the team, an intimate cross-examination at a Broadway rehearsal hall by legendary *SNL* writers Jim Downey, Jack Handey, Carol Leifer, and Robert Smigel, and future *Simpsons* writers John Swartzwelder and George Meyer, who was the guy who wrote the *other* "Food Repairman" sketch.

"It was a really amazing group of writers," says McKinney, "and our job was to make all these Harvard guys laugh. These were the real 'gatekeepers,' the ones who Lorne trusted. I remember Meyer was a particularly tough laugh, but we got him with a couple of things. Finally, after we held our own, Lorne formally asked us if we were doing anything in September, which I only later realized was his way of saying he's interested in hiring you."

Suddenly thrust into the snake pit of daily life at *SNL*'s offices at 30 Rockefeller Plaza, McCulloch and McKinney struggled to fit in with fellow staffers like A. Whitney Brown and Robert Smigel, while seeing perfectly good ideas such as McCulloch's "Thirty Helens Agree" passed over without a second thought. "While we eventually became pretty good friends with Smigel," remembers McCulloch, "we were just not jiving with most of these new people. I remember George getting mad at me because I wasn't working at the office late into the night the way they all do over there."

To cope, McCulloch turned to stress eating, which resulted in a weight gain of close to fifty pounds, while the two Kids pined for the creative freedom and support they had grown accustomed to back home. As a lifeline, they invited Foley, McDonald, and Thompson down from Toronto to watch them make an episode of *SNL*. While the gesture was appreciated by the other Kids, it was also bittersweet to watch their former comrades getting on with their new, big-city careers.

During the 1985–86 season, while McCulloch and McKinney hoped to improve their credibility with their new coworkers at *SNL*, back in Toronto, the other three Kids assessed their career options. Foley flew out to Vancouver to play the lead role in a feature film called *High Stakes*, having beaten out a then-lesser-known Keanu Reeves. "When the producer Peter Simpson hired me, he told me I'd beat out Keanu," says Foley, "but he said, 'We had to make a choice between sexy or funny, so we went with funny.' Still, I made something like $20,000 for that, which was something like four years' income for me in those days."

Kevin McDonald and Scott Thompson were asked to join the Second City Touring Company, alongside Kids in the Hall founding member Luciano Casimiri. The job, which involved driving around Southern Ontario in a panel van and performing archival material from Second City's fabled Chicago and Toronto casts, was a step down in terms of creative freedom, but the brief improvisational set at the end of every show gave them a chance to bring themselves to the gig.

When he returned from Vancouver, Foley also joined the touring company, but while the old gang was back together in some ways, they experienced the same difficulty fitting in as McKinney and McCulloch did in New York. Having grown accustomed to making their own rules, it was hard to adjust to the institutional nature of Second City. According to Scott Thompson, Second City's dress code — men in suits, women in dresses — was the first clue that things were different there. Just as he had done during his college days, Thompson began acting out onstage and rebelling against the Second City establishment.

"I would openly mock the Second City archival material and just do crazy things. Not surprisingly, it wasn't long before they fired me. I'm not angry about it because it was the best thing that ever happened to me. I just didn't fit in there."

Foley and McDonald stuck it out for a little while longer, although Foley agreed with Thompson that the old Second City material didn't suit them at all. "The improv sets were killing it. This was our moment to bring our style of comedy to the show, and audiences on the road were telling us that we were the best Second City Touring Company they'd seen in a long time. Then we'd go back to Toronto and get yelled at by Second City management for being too Kids in the Hall."

One afternoon after a Saturday matinee on the mainstage at the Old Fire Hall theatre, manager Sally Cochrane summoned McDonald and Foley into her office. Foley remembers, "Sally sits us down and says, 'Now, look, guys, you have to understand that this is not the Kids in the Hall; this is Second City, and we have certain standards—'"

But before she could finish, McDonald leapt to his feet. "I said, 'Then Dave and I have no choice but to quit. We quit,'" says McDonald. "Then I turned to Dave and said, 'Come on, Dave.'"

As bold a move as this was, Foley says that McDonald had neglected to consult with him before speaking. Ultimately, though, McDonald was right and the two walked out of the Old Fire Hall theatre for the last time.

"To this day," says Foley, laughing about it now, "it's like a running joke whenever Kevin's mad about something. He'll say, 'I quit for Dave and me.'"

Thompson and Bellini busied themselves recording with their art punk musical offshoot, Mouth Congress, who moved into sporadic live gigs from 1986 to 1990. It was a loose collective with key players from their York days, including Randall Finnerty, Tom King, Rob Rowatt, Steve Keeping, and Gord Disley, with the odd cameo by Kevin McDonald and Mark McKinney.

"I didn't really think of it as a band," Thompson says on the collective's Bandcamp page. "It was just a group of friends that hung around, smoked pot, and made shit up." (In early 2016, Thompson, Bellini, King, Keeping, and Rowatt, staged a Mouth Congress reunion at The Rivoli.)

Whenever *SNL* was on a hiatus that year, McCulloch and McKinney made the trek home to Toronto to do a Kids in the Hall show at the Rivoli. With the decreased frequency, each show now became a special occasion, and long lineups stretched down the street as their following continued to build. During this period, perhaps out of frustration with their day jobs, the troupe's writing became more focused and elevated as McCulloch and McKinney, now seasoned TV writers, inspired everyone else to tighten their scene work.

"I did this monologue called 'I'm a Cat,' where I would get all feline," says McKinney, "and Bruce and I did an early version of 'Go for Guilt,' and Scott and I did 'Duck Blind,' which was a gay piece without being overtly gay. 'Three for the Moon' was something that Bruce and I wrote together with Dave, and it had this sort of Beat poetry thing that Bruce and I both liked — you know, 'Angry dawn, man staggers out, shattered light, kapow.' We loved that Kerouac kind of stuff and we wanted in on that shit. I think I may have debuted one of my first conceptual anti-pieces, 'Mississippi Gary,' which was fun to do because I got to talk like a black bluesman, but then come clean and admit that I'm just a white kid from Ottawa who listened to too much blues."

The Rivoli audiences were now packed with local celebrities, and Foley recalls the thrill of being appreciated by his heroes from the original *SCTV* and Second City casts, including Martin Short, Dave Thomas, Robin Duke, and Catherine O'Hara, who brought along her sister, the acclaimed singer Mary Margaret O'Hara.

"*SCTV* was one of the first Canadian shows that you

actually wanted to watch," says Foley. "So, it was nice to see these people appreciating us. Kevin and I took a lot of inspiration from *SCTV*, but we always tried to avoid doing things like parodies of TV shows or commercials. They'd already done that better than anyone, so why would we even try?"

Many of the *SCTV* people sent further word to Lorne Michaels that he ought to heed Pamela Thomas's advice and take another look at the troupe as a whole. Michaels sent his twenty-five-year-old brother-in-law, Joe Forristal, to Toronto to scout them again. Forristal had been producing Dennis Miller's "Weekend Update" segments on *SNL*, and had become friendly with McCulloch and McKinney. He loved what they were doing and sent enthusiastic word back to Michaels, who arranged to return to his hometown as soon as *SNL*'s 1985–86 season had wrapped. He wanted to see them perform on their home turf, the Rivoli stage, for a roomful of paying customers, rather than in another intimidating closed-door audition.

As word spread through the Toronto comedy community that one of the most powerful men in the comedy business was coming to town, mayhem ensued as struggling comedians desperately flooded the Rivoli hoping to make Michaels's acquaintance. During their performance, Foley recalls one such woman crashing the stage. "She stood on her head while reciting a poem about how Lorne should go to a club across the street and see their show. Scott cleverly improvised 'Get the fuck off our stage.'"

While the show was once again overlong due to each cast member wanting to get his moment in the sun, their Rivoli showcase was a hit and marked a turning point for them as a collective. While a highly impressed Michaels returned to Manhattan to work out a plan, the Kids went about staging their second fully theatrical show, *Graverobbers from Hipsville*, at Toronto's Factory Lab Theatre. Directed by John Hemphill—one of Foley and McDonald's improv heroes and a standout star of the local Second City cast—*Graverobbers* was a kind of template for a hypothetical *Kids in the Hall* series, complete with their own theme song, "Having an Average Weekend," provided for the first time by their new house band, Shadowy Men on a Shadowy Planet.

"The Shadowy Men were, and are, the coolest," says Bruce McCulloch, "and we all loved Brian's artistic aesthetic, so we also had him draw the poster for *Graverobbers*."

In a television interview to promote *Graverobbers* on CBC's *Midday* program, McCulloch and Foley were asked if they harboured any dreams of one day joining the performing cast of *Saturday Night Live*.

MCCULLOCH: Right now, we're most interested in doing our own thing.

FOLEY: We'd really prefer to do our own show, and have a lot of creative control.

MCCULLOCH: Just a lot of weird stuff. Sometimes it's dark, and sometimes it's happy and sweet.

FOLEY: How about "macabre mirth makers"?

MCCULLOCH: I like that.

Graverobbers from Hipsville was sold out every night, but instead of celebrating, the Kids in the Hall became increasingly anxious as they awaited news of their fate from New York. Would Lorne Michaels once again cherry-pick individual players to send them to *SNL*? Were they getting their own show? Or would it be none of the above? Finally, after an interminable wait, Michaels called Pamela Thomas.

"Lorne told Pam that we were 'of a piece,'" says Kevin McDonald, "and he was interested in finding us a TV show of our own. Not understanding the business, I thought that meant that we already *had* a TV series, but he hadn't really figured out the details. He just knew he *wanted* to get us a TV show. It took him a while to find the right place for us."

Having already redefined American television comedy in the mid-1970s with *Saturday Night Live*, Lorne Michaels says he was convinced that the Kids constituted the next wave, and just as importantly, that they were stronger than the sum of their parts. "They were a real troupe, and I don't like breaking up troupes. But I also saw them as the beginning of the movement toward gender in comedy. The big issues in the '70s were politics and race, which had been going on for a long time. I think there was something new to the way the Kids in the Hall were playing the women's parts more authentically, as opposed to the way Milton Berle did, or even John Belushi when he did Elizabeth Taylor. They weren't doing it as *broad comedy*. They could fit seamlessly into female parts, and it certainly wasn't drag. It was a very different aesthetic, and I thought they were the next step after the original cast of *SNL*."

Lorne Michaels was finally ready to take the Kids — all five of them — to the next level. Their only demand was full creative control, but before Michaels could trust them with the keys, he insisted they endure a six-month New York "boot camp" to toughen them up. Michaels believed that by throwing them headlong into the choppy waters of the American comedy market, far from their Queen Street comfort zone, these five wide-eyed boys would be transformed into the macabre mirth-making men they dreamed of becoming.

SEVEN

Live from New York

Before he could launch a Kids in the Hall project, Lorne Michaels knew he would need a broadcast partner. After shopping the Kids to a few contacts, he found a sympathetic ear in Michael Fuchs, head of programming for Home Box Office, the upstart premium cable outlet better known as HBO. Fuchs expressed substantial interest in producing a moderately priced pilot, with an option toward a full series. While the details were being ironed out, Michaels brought the Kids to Manhattan to familiarize them with the American market. They would share one half of a suite at Michaels's Broadway Video offices, housed in the legendary Brill Building at 1619 Broadway. Here they could write a Kids in the Hall television special for HBO that would function as the pilot Fuchs wanted. For Michaels, the boot camp was essentially a comedy finishing school.

"They just had to get out of Toronto," says Michaels. "They had taken it as far as they could take it there; they'd mastered it. And I thought New York would be a different kind of experience for them because they needed to conceive of a television show that would also play well in America. You have to go where the most talented people are to be able to challenge yourself. And you have to get to a point, particularly if you're going to be speaking to an American audience, where you're not speaking exclusively with a Canadian voice. That's not to say you're trying to pass as American, but you need to have some understanding of the U.S.A. Although, to be fair, New York, particularly at that time, was hardly America."

According to Mark McKinney, the troupe flew into Manhattan from Toronto for an HBO showcase. Held at Manhattan's West Bank, the show was an unmitigated disaster. There is perhaps no tougher crowd for comedy than a room full of professional comedy writers — many of them former colleagues from *SNL* — but material such as "Brian's Bombshell," "Running Faggot," and "Farmers on Heroin" left a politically charged, AIDS-ravaged, 1987 Manhattan audience fidgety and tense.

McKinney speculates that they may have gotten away with far worse up in Toronto, if only because it was a smaller market and, frankly, nobody was watching the first time they used the "bucketful of AIDS" gag. He still wonders if the patrons at the West Bank that night were paying more attention to their own moral rectitude than to the comedy in the sketches.

"Our home crowd had been converted to our point of view," says McKinney, "so they knew where we were coming from with the ridiculousness of this being a father's imagination. Of course it was going to bomb in front of a brand-new audience who had no idea what we were up to. I remember Dennis Miller turning to Robert Smigel afterwards and saying 'McCulloch will never make a buck in this business.' It was a tough night."

Dave Foley was also surprised to discover that their brand of comedy had turned out to be even edgier than anything he saw going on in New York at the time. "It was weird to me that we seemed aggressive and dangerous," says Foley. "I mean, there were some great observational stand-up comics in New York, but there was really only one or two other sketch comedy troupes, and we didn't find them terribly compelling or interesting. Or funny."

Decades earlier, the Beatles had left Liverpool to log their 10,000 hours of stage time in Hamburg's Reeperbahn district, and now the Kids in the Hall embarked on their own formative journey to New York. Mark McKinney acknowledges the boot camp was a deft move on Michaels's part, and feels that being displaced taught them something about their own comedy voice. "We used to think we identified with the Queen West scene, or life in Toronto or in Canada as a whole. But, in fact, it wasn't regionally specific; our audience was mainly broke people, or people from broken families, kids who were trying to be artistic or cool. In Manhattan, we started to realize that there was very little Canadian identification in our material, which was a good thing, because everyone in New York was from somewhere else, anyway. They don't care where you're from, but they care if you're funny or not."

Michaels exerted a kind of paternal guidance on the troupe, an arrangement that would at various times in their relationship awaken childhood father issues within some members. Once a week, the Kids would venture over to 30 Rock, ride the elevator up to the *SNL* offices to get paid, and Michaels would dispense paternal wisdom and advice to his boys. "It was like Lorne was giving us our allowance," says Thompson, "and then we'd just do whatever he instructed us to do that week. We all wanted to make daddy happy."

Thompson also had a sense that this New York trial by fire would give them greater confidence in their material, if it didn't kill them first. "It was an amazing time. We were definitely small-town boys, but Lorne turned us into men. He said, 'Here is the bear pit. I'm going to throw you boys in, and if you come out alive, I'll get you your own bear pit.' The carrot at the end of the stick was so big compared to back in Canada—where there were no carrots at all."

For Kevin McDonald, Michaels was only the latest in a series of surrogate dads for the troupe. "It's the thing that makes us great and horrible. Most of our fathers, except for Mark's, were alcoholics or physically rough with us, and I began to notice that, as a troupe, we'd always find these outside daddy figures and put a lot of trust into them—sometimes too much. Lorne was definitely one of the biggest."

Michaels enlisted his brother-in-law, Joe Forristal, to be Broadway Video's one-man New York transition team for the Kids. Forristal remembers being responsible for "anything and everything," including booking shows and drumming up publicity to help them build a following in New York. "It was hard at first," says Forristal, "because nobody knew who they were yet, and sometimes there would be only four people in the audience. But they'd get onstage and do it anyway. It was a challenge and they rose to it."

At first, Forristal could only find four apartments for the five guys, so while McCulloch and McKinney had places of their own, Foley shared a flat with his then-partner, Tabatha Southey, and McDonald agreed to share an apartment with Thompson in New York's Chelsea district, just steps away from the legendary Chelsea Hotel.

"I'd pass all these five-foot mirrors in the apartment, just watching how big I was," says McDonald. "And Scott always had his skinny gay friends over, so I was pretty self-conscious. Dave and I used to meet at a doughnut shop by the subway before we went up to work. Typically, Dave would get a coffee while I ordered my standard breakfast of a chocolate cake doughnut and a carton of chocolate milk. One morning, Dave was in a bad mood or something and he blurted out, 'You're killing yourself, Kevin! You're going to die from being fat!'"

While Foley's outburst would later inspire the sketch "Fat Hitch-Hiker," its effect on McDonald that day was life-changing. Staring down the suddenly very real prospect of a television career, he made the decision to do something about his weight. "At that very moment, I decided to give up the doughnuts and went on a diet. I didn't want to be 'Fat Kevin' on the TV series."

Eventually, Thompson moved into his own place off Avenue C, in a Lower East Side neighbourhood he describes as "post-apocalyptic," replete with trash-can fires, drug dealers, and the nightly echoes of gunshots. If that wasn't depressing enough, the entire city was consumed at the time by the gloom of the so-called "Gay Plague."

"The spectre of AIDS was all over New York," recalls Thompson, "and there were ghosts everywhere. On the other hand, I had just fallen in love and had my first real boyfriend since coming out, so even though I was living in the epicentre of madness, I was having the time of my life."

In the '50s and '60s, the Brill Building had been the home of Tin Pan Alley music publishers and era-defining hit songwriters like Neil Sedaka, Carole King, and Leiber & Stoller. By the 1980s, its eleven storeys housed the offices of photographers, theatre producers, and Lorne Michaels's company Broadway Video. On a typical day, it was not unusual to spot New York celebrities such as Martin Scorsese or Michaels's friend Paul Simon by the elevator banks. Yet inside the Kids' cramped little writing office, the most glamorous people they interacted with were the two accountants who shared the space.

"The accountants were presiding over a routine audit of Broadway Video the whole time we were writing the pilot there," says McDonald. "They were there before we moved in, and they were still there when we left. Whenever we thought of something funny, we'd look over and see the auditors giggling into their calculators."

As was typical, Bruce McCulloch's impatience returned as the process seemed to stretch out, yet he admits that the Kids' struggle to prove themselves in New York — strangers in a strange land — brought them closer together.

"Sometimes we felt very untalented because it took us a while to come up with some strong new material. Eventually, though, that Brill Building office was where we first wrote up sketches like 'Cabbage Head' and 'Head Crusher.'"

Had it not been for McDonald, Mark McKinney says he might never have thought to create his beloved character Mr. Tyzik, whose catchphrase "I'm crushing your head," has since become one of the Kids' most quoted lines. When McKinney was a child with poor eyesight, he would often compensate by peering through the spaces between his fingertips, putting them around cars and objects to focus on them better. Years later, the "finger view" gag became a kind of low-laughs party piece.

McDonald insists that McKinney pulled out the head-crushing gag during a "double date" that had turned awkward and uncomfortable, despite McKinney having no recollection of it.

"To break the tension," says McDonald, "Mark started pinching his thumb and finger together, saying, 'I'm crushing your head! I'm crushing your head!' The girls stormed out, but it made me laugh. Mark doesn't remember it, but the story is absolutely true. I swear to God!"

Up in their Brill Building office, McDonald suddenly remembered McKinney's crushing hand gesture and it gave him an idea. Their work to date had been tailored to the so-called "black box" stage—specifically, the dark, square, and largely unadorned performance space at the Rivoli. Now, Lorne Michaels was urging them to think outside that box, to generate the kinds of kinetic and visual ideas better suited to television. McDonald pictured the camera's point of view looking through McKinney's two fingers, as McKinney's character crushed the heads of all those who offended him. Agreeing that it was a good bit, McKinney felt that he needed a solid character on which to hang the comedy and thought of a curmudgeonly Eastern European man who had once lived across the hall from him at a Toronto rooming house.

"I'd hear this old guy, probably Yugoslavian, yelling at the hockey games all the time," says McKinney. "So, I started doing a version of this guy in what I call my 'Standard Foreign Voice,' and Mr. Tyzik was born. I think what we both loved about Mr. Tyzik was that his crushing heads device was such a fabulously deluded way of fighting back at power, a more passive-aggressive way of giving someone the finger."

Excitedly, McDonald told McKinney that Tyzik was exactly the kind of visual gag that Michaels had asked them to bring to the show. "I swear to God," says McDonald, "I told Mark if he did this on TV, college kids would be doing it all over the country one day. And I was right."

In addition to daily writing sessions at the Brill Building, the Kids spent some of their time in a Hell's Kitchen rehearsal studio polishing their stagecraft with theatre director John Ferraro and scouring Paul Bellini's VHS tapes of their shows at the Rivoli. They also played an average of two shows a week, and accepted any appearance that Forristal could find them. Their most frequent stages were Carolines at the South Street Seaport and a regular headline show at the West Bank Café. Lewis Black, who would later become known for his apoplectic "Back in Black" segments on *The Daily Show with Jon Stewart*, was the West Bank's artistic director and producer.

"Lewis would introduce our show every night," says McDonald. "He was very nice to us, and we all liked him. He'd do this kind of Mort Sahl thing where he'd come out with a newspaper and start riffing on the headlines of the day. We all thought he was really funny."

Some opening slots were harder than others, and their edgy sketch comedy was sometimes a bad match for stand-ups like Rita Rudner or Richard Lewis. "These poor audiences would come down to Carolines from Wall Street to see their favourite stand-ups," recalls Foley, "but they'd accidentally end up seeing us and hating it."

Rolling Stone journalist David Handelman rode along with the Kids to many of these shows, observing and documenting their routines, both onstage and off, for a feature that would eventually run in the magazine's May 19, 1988, "Hot" issue under the headline "Is America Ready for the Kids in the Hall?" While never decisively answering that mostly hypothetical question, Handelman made a strong case for why America *should* be ready for the Kids, and he compared their absurdist humour to another well-received import, Monty Python. "The Kids excel at taking familiar situations and rendering them bizarre," he wrote, commending more outrageous pieces like "Running Faggot" for plumbing "the demilitarized comedy zone of homosexuality," and applauding the Kids' sympathetic approach to their female characters, which lent an air of "perverse androgyny" to their work.

A self-confessed comedy nerd, Handelman, who has since gone on to a successful career writing for television, still remembers the first time he saw the Kids at Carolines. "I loved what I saw onstage that night. It was anarchic yet intelligent, bawdy but heartfelt, outrageous and subtle, true about humanity, and totally absurdist." Handelman had been invited to Carolines by an actor friend from college, Max Cantor, and was so "bowled over" that he began inviting more friends to come down to see the Kids.

The Kids were finally beginning to catch on with the previously lukewarm New York crowds. After packing out the prestigious Bottom Line club, Mark McKinney remembers having a strong feeling that perhaps America was finally ready for them. "We fucking killed at the Bottom Line. We were up with Eric Bogosian doing twenty minutes and just killing it. This was terribly affirming to us as we went away to do the pilot. We were no longer asking, 'Can we make it in America?' We knew we were good."

Lorne Michaels secured $400,000 in development funding from HBO for the pilot. While this initially seemed like a major commitment, the Kids were dismayed to learn that much of that sum was being used to cover their living in New York. After expenses, there wasn't much left in the budget to actually produce an hour-long special. As it turned out, even HBO's commitment to going ahead with the special was conditional, and the Kids found themselves performing showcase after showcase to generate higher enthusiasm from the executives.

"We did around seven showcases to get HBO finally to say yes. It wasn't like we did one and they went, 'Here's the cheque.' It was more like, 'We're still not sure; we want to bring in another guy.' And meanwhile, we're trying to get a crowd each time, and it's getting harder and harder."

As the troupe neared the end of their six-month New York adventure and the money began to run out, the ever-impatient Bruce McCulloch despaired once more. "It was looking like we'd have to shoot the pilot live at Carolines, real low budget, but I said, 'No. We'll die if we do that.'"

Carolyn Strauss was one of the HBO executives tasked with deciding if the Kids' comedy revolution would be televised. Today, Strauss admits that while a few of her colleagues at HBO expressed reservations about the Kids in the Hall, personally she found them hilarious. "The Kids' characters seemed to come from a very pragmatic, work-aday place, and represented a certain point of view that I hadn't seen that much before. It was a very grounded sort of comedy, and even if it went off into absurd places, I found it very relatable."

Still, a cloud of uncertainty hung over the project until McCulloch remembered Ivan Fecan. A fellow Canadian, Fecan had been a fan of the Kids ever since their days at the Rivoli. While working at *Saturday Night Live*, McCulloch and McKinney kept in touch with Fecan, who had recently joined the CBC as head of programming in Toronto. The stars seemed to be aligning. Now was the perfect timing for Fecan to get in on the ground floor with some fresh Canadian content, provided the CBC could afford to partner with HBO on the special, and possibly the series.

"It was an idea that was so obvious we wondered why we hadn't considered it before," recalls McCulloch. "It just made sense. Ivan was our friend and ally, and now he could save the day."

CBC executives were dispatched to join the HBO brass at the weekly New York showcases, but many of them walked away just as confused and unconvinced as their American counterparts. Not so Ivan Fecan, though, who luckily held the overriding vote.

"The Kids in the Hall," says Fecan, "had a very Toronto sensibility that was fresh and new to us. There was nothing else like them. So, we agreed to have the CBC coproduce the show using our Toronto studios and in-house crews, in partnership with HBO and Broadway Video."

Patriotism aside, Lorne Michaels admits that this multi-national partnership was largely born of economic considerations. The taxpayer-subsidized CBC could provide much of the "below-the-line" costs—production facilities and crew—in exchange for Canadian broadcast rights. "I felt it would only work as a coproduction," says Michaels, "and we needed both Ivan Fecan at CBC *and* Michael Fuchs at HBO, because there wasn't enough money in Canada alone to do it. The primary market would be Canada with support from HBO, who would also air it in the U.S."

HBO's programming at the time was mainly movies, boxing, and stand-up comedy specials. According to Carolyn Strauss, no one at the cable channel was certain that sketch comedy was a safe investment, but the CBC's involvement made it easier to take a gamble on the Kids. "The less you spend, the gutsier you are," says Strauss. "So having someone else willing to defray the costs and shoulder some of the burden for you makes those decisions much easier."

At last Canada was ready for the Kids in the Hall, but were the Kids ready for *them*? It was another in a series of rhetorical questions, but after all the laughter and tears, all the yelling and screaming, and writing and rehearsing, the Kids in the Hall were as ready as they were ever going to be. Their New York adventure had tested them, but they were still unified and eager to head home to Toronto, where they would put all their new ideas and experiences, and the best of their old ones, on tape. As they packed up to fly home, Kevin McDonald recalls feeling "a familiar happy dread" that comes with reaching a new plateau, wondering, as each member of the troupe did, was this the start of something bigger, or was this as good as it would ever get?

EIGHT

Easy to Beat Up, Hard to Kill

Upon their return to Toronto, where they were about to write, rehearse, and shoot their HBO pilot (which HBO was still calling a special), the Kids were given a pre-production office in one of the CBC's older properties on Sumach Street in the city's Corktown neighbourhood. Mark McKinney remembers the "creaky old barn" they were offered being filled with cobwebs and dusty costumes from the sixties. The troupe quickly deemed the space "unsuitable" for making comedy.

"There was no light in there," says McKinney, "and it had windows ten feet above the ground that you couldn't even see out of. Also, the CBC accountants' office was right next door, and we'd had enough of that back in the Brill Building."

In what would become a pattern of disruption and upheaval during their time with the CBC, these brash new Kids on this block made it clear that they were not about to put up with dusty cobwebs, literally or figuratively. "We didn't want to be told nothin' by nobody no how," says McKinney, "and we took that to a ridiculous extreme. It was a double-edged sword because we'd sometimes drive away people who were only trying to be our friends. But then again, we probably *needed* to be a little bit self-absorbed at that time."

Kevin McDonald says it usually fell to Bruce McCulloch to rattle the CBC's cage. "Bruce told them that we don't have to fuckin' do anything we don't fuckin' want to,'" says McDonald, laughing. Somehow it worked, and the CBC agreed to allocate the funding for a place of their own, away from the prying eyes of their corporate overlords.

Thompson's old friend Paul Bellini, now formally hired as an assistant to the Kids, was dispatched to accompany McKinney on a hunt for a suitable office. After searching all over downtown Toronto, they found an ideal location off an alleyway behind 25 St. Nicholas Street, in a sixth-floor loft above the popular gay club Colby's. Ostensibly their writing and production office, the space also served as a kind of private clubhouse. After allocating five individual offices, they furnished a common area with a Ping-Pong table, a comfortable couch, and a large television to watch music videos on MuchMusic while waiting for inspiration to strike.

Within the culture of the CBC, the Kids were viewed as Ivan Fecan's pet project—one that had to be put up with whether they liked it or not. McDonald remembers hearing whispers from inside the CBC that the Kids in the Hall were "difficult." To be fair, he says, the reputation was at least partially earned. "Sure, we *could* be kind of curt sometimes.

Like, if we were having a meeting and someone came over to talk to us, Bruce would say, 'Do you want to give us five minutes?' or 'Get the fuck out. We'll talk to you when we're ready.' Stuff like that."

McCulloch admits that it took them time to learn how to work elegantly within the machine. "Going into that pilot, we absolutely had our dukes up. We questioned everything, the same way a newly signed rock band might say, 'We don't want you to fuck with our sound, man.'"

The Kids' sixth-floor walk-up office had no elevator, making it harder for CBC executives to breathe down their necks, physically, but it also put more pressure on Bellini, their de facto receptionist, to pass along phone messages and memos from the Corporation. "I was the worst receptionist in the history of receptionists," says Bellini, "but I think it was important to the Kids, especially at first, that they only hire people they knew they could trust."

Beyond their risqué material, many at the Corporation took exception to what they saw as the Kids' bullying arrogance toward their established order. Fecan was well aware of the discord, and recalls a betting pool going around the building to guess how long it would be before he was fired for inviting these snotty punks in to tarnish the august reputation of the CBC. "Obviously, they were hysterically funny," says Fecan, "but you must understand that some of our crews, who were not shy people to begin with, just couldn't believe that this material—the cross-dressing, etc.—was going on *at the CBC*. But that was sort of the point of me bringing them there; they were a breath of fresh air, and I thought it was fabulous to have them."

While Lorne Michaels was generally an arm's-length producer, directing operations from his New York office, he did make several trips to Toronto to ensure that the production got off on the right foot. "Early on was probably the only time Lorne was super hands-on in terms of the blocking and other choices," says McCulloch. "I remember him on set saying to somebody 'Get some makeup around Bruce's eyes. People don't like people with little eyes.'"

Michaels says he wanted to make sure the Kids played beyond Canada in the same way he had always tried to have SNL play beyond New York. "Broadcast, which is what I work in mostly, is on in all fifty states," says Michaels. "So, it's a different show every place, you know?"

One issue that raised Michaels's eyebrows was Kevin McDonald's dramatic weight loss. Having shed some seventy pounds on what McCulloch jokingly refers to as the "Fuck You, Food" diet, McDonald was no longer "Fat Kevin," and Michaels was concerned about his health. "When someone loses so much weight so fast," says McCulloch, "they don't look so good at first. People wondered if he was OK." McDonald remembers Michaels taking him aside and feeling him out for signs of an eating disorder, having gone through similar issues with early SNL cast member Gilda Radner. At one point, he remembers Michaels suggesting to him that they postpone shooting the show until he got healthier. McDonald wouldn't hear of it.

"I know one rule of show business: never postpone your big break, because it doesn't come back!" says McDonald.

"But I think Lorne takes all the losses of the people he's worked with to heart. He gave me the number of an elite Toronto dietician, and kept trying to get me to eat pasta. 'Will you have some pasta? Don't go out with the guys,' he'd say. 'Stay here and have some pasta.'"

Getting down to work, and now approaching the special as a true pilot, the Kids began sifting out gems from the 140+ new sketches they had developed during their time in Manhattan. The sketches that emerged found humour in seeming contradictions, such as millionaire dumpster divers or enlightened post-feminist construction workers. They cooked up a TV version of "Brian's Bombshell," the AIDS bucket scene that had caused such a stir in Manhattan, and "Rusty," featuring McCulloch as a young buck with a penchant for geriatric ladies. They also filmed a TV-friendly adaptation of "Naked for Jesus," shot on location less than three blocks from the Rivoli, where the Kids had debuted their version of McCulloch's old Calgary piece. And while they found room for character-driven sketches, such as Thompson's Buddy Cole, McKinney's Mr. Tyzik, and McCulloch's Cabbage Head, there was also a standout ensemble piece called "Reg," in which all five Kids sit around a campfire to toast an absent friend. As the scene progresses, their good-natured remembrances of their fallen buddy slowly begin to reveal a more sinister secret about his death.

FOLEY: It seems like only yesterday we were just a bunch of kids, hanging out, getting Slurpees. Next thing you know, we all got jobs.

MCDONALD: Or girlfriends. Next thing you know, they're moving in with you.

MCCULLOCH: Next thing you know, you're out buying piano wire—good, strong piano wire—and sneaking up on old Reg while he reads.

FOLEY: Jobs become careers...

MCDONALD: Girlfriends become wives...

MCCULLOCH: And Reg becomes a lifeless corpse in your arms.

THOMPSON: It kinda makes you think about the fragility of human life.

MCKINNEY: Ah, not really. Remember how he fought back?

THOMPSON: What a death grip! Almost broke my wrist.

FOLEY: Easy to beat up, hard to kill.

CAST [raising beer cans]: To Reg!

Kevin McDonald says that beyond being one of his favourite scenes, "Reg" provides an insight into the Kids' often self-defeating group dynamic. "That's us in a nutshell. We have five guys lamenting how hard life is after the death of their friend, but then it turns out that they all killed Reg, so they're sad about a problem that they created for themselves."

As they developed their stage sketches for the small screen, Bruce McCulloch says he was mindful of a warning given to him by *SCTV*'s Dave Thomas: many of the best Second City stage sketches bombed on television. Likewise, Dave Foley remembers discovering that some of their favourite pieces didn't always translate to the visual medium. "As time went on, we would go through a lot of the old stage stuff and find it was hard or even impossible to make it work for the show."

One way to break out of the confines of the stage, and even the TV studio, was to shoot certain sketches on film. They knew from the start that certain bits, like McKinney's "Head Crusher," needed to be filmed outdoors, but as they designed the show, they began to think of additional scenes. According to McCulloch, the troupe had even briefly considered shooting the entire show on film, before realizing that they would miss the adrenalin that came from performing in front of a live audience. Ultimately, they opted for a combination of live and filmed pieces, just as *Monty Python* had done roughly two decades earlier.

"All of us quickly fell in love with the idea of using film pieces," says McCulloch, "because it allowed us to think about sketches in a different, more surreal way. I always hoped we'd get even more surreal, actually."

Almost as important as the visuals and the writing was the music. Today, it's impossible to imagine *The Kids in the Hall* without the reverb-soaked twang guitar and thundering garage drums of Shadowy Men on a Shadowy Planet. "It was unanimous that if we ever got on TV, we'd want Shadowy Men to do the music," says McCulloch, "which is weird because nothing's ever unanimous with us."

There was never any doubt that the Shadowy Men's "Having an Average Weekend" would be the official theme for the Kids' television show. It was at once postpunk modern and retro, evocative of the golden age of television comedy, and it had been the official walk-on music of their live shows since *Graverobbers from Hipsville*. But according to drummer Don Pyle, a misunderstanding about song titles during the *Graverobbers* run nearly resulted in another song becoming the theme. "We had put out a 45 with two songs on one side," says Pyle. "It was 'Having an Average Weekend,' then another song called 'Bennett Cerf.' They kept asking us to play 'Bennett Cerf' as their intro, so we did that every night during our run at the Factory Lab Theatre. And every night, they'd be confused, until finally, after five days of doing the show, they said, 'Why do you keep playing that song at the beginning?' We only realized they wanted 'Having an Average Weekend' after they hummed the guitar melody to us."

The cavernous twang of "Weekend" had provided such memorable sonic branding for the Kids that it seemed only logical for the Shadowy Men to compose interstitial music to be played between sketches on the show, and to perform live for the studio audience, keeping the crowd pumped and amused between sketches on taping days. In the minds of the Kids, the Shadowy Men made them cool by association, and the troupe benefitted from their visual touches as much as their music. According to Pyle, the two camps were so joined at the hip that a kind of collective consciousness emerged between the three members of his band and the five members of the Kids. "It was equal elements of all eight of us, really. I mean, if you take Kevin out of the Kids in the Hall, it totally throws the whole equation off. There was no master plan to make a thing that melded together; it was really that our sensibilities are all the same, so we'd just naturally feed off each other, a gang of friends working together. We did a lot of other stuff together too, like Kevin opened a show for our band as a parody of Reveen the Impossibilist called 'Keveen the Impossibilist,' a magician who wasn't very good at magic. And Scott would sometimes sing with us as Buddy Cole. Brian's poster for *Graverobbers from Hipsville* was this really beautiful graphic of the guys in berets and sunglasses digging a grave, so Brian's style became the Kids' signature aesthetic too."

Bassist Reid Diamond brought his own visual flair to the bandstand high above the studio floor at CBC Mutual Street. "We'd be rehearsing or camera blocking out on the studio floor," McCulloch remembers, "and I'd look up and there's Reid, spray painting some props for their bandstand in silver. He'd say, 'Oh, we're going to play inside a huge art deco clamshell this week.' And they would hoist this weird eight-foot clamshell up the creaky aluminum ladder to their stage high above the studio floor."

Robert Boyd was selected to direct their inaugural foray into television comedy. Boyd had previously directed a TV special for Broadway Video, *Superman 50th Anniversary*, and a few of the Kids had enjoyed a comedy documentary he had written and directed called *The Canadian Conspiracy*. Bruce McCulloch was keen on the idea, having written with Boyd on the *Superman* special and one of the Gemini Awards broadcasts for CBC, and Kevin McDonald remembers that, just as with Ivan Fecan, the troupe always tended go with people they met through "Bruce's people."

"Bruce always seemed to know more behind-the-scenes people than the rest of us did," says McDonald, "and of course Lorne was happy with him too, so we had our director."

It was Boyd's idea to use a black-and-white Super-8 movie montage beneath the show's hand-drawn opening credits. Initially, McCulloch found the look "square and unnatural," but eventually he got onboard with what became a distinctive look and feel for *The Kids in the Hall*.

As all the production elements came together, Scott Thompson recalls the excited feeling that something wonderful was just beginning. "It was absolutely exhilarating. I had no doubt that we were going to kill. But at the same time, I was a little nervous."

Some of that nervousness was due to the realization that making television required delegating responsibilities to outsiders. McDonald felt that juggling so many details could become overwhelming at times. "I remember reminding myself to try to enjoy the moment, take it step-by-step, and just worry about rehearsing my scenes. It was the only way we could feel like we had any control."

Lorne Michaels brought a very *Saturday Night Live* approach to staffing and production, including the hiring of key veterans from the *SNL* crew, most notably set designer Eugene Lee and lighting director Phil Hymes. Michaels urged the Kids to adopt *SNL*'s process of taping two complete run-throughs of each episode before two different studio audiences. At *SNL*, these doubleheaders were designated as the "Dress" and "Air" shows, and the thinking was that the first run-through was more or less a dress rehearsal, performed for camera blocking and to gauge how the jokes would play before a live audience. The second, tighter run-through was hoped to be the keeper and, in the case of *SNL*, the one that went out live on the air to North American living rooms at 11:30 p.m. ("The show doesn't go on because it's ready," Michaels famously quipped. "It goes on because it's 11:30.") Since the Kids' show was to be strictly on tape, the best performances from either show could be spliced together to form a more perfect episode. Going live to air was never an option for the Kids, given that they were still learning the intricacies of performing for the TV camera.

"It was certainly hard for me at first," says McCulloch. "They'd tell me, 'Find your camera, hit your mark,' and I'd be like, 'I don't know which camera's mine! What?' Dave took to it right away, though. Somehow he just knew how to block himself in a scene. I mean, he was always a funny guy, but it was sort of a surprise, to me at least, that he was such a natural."

Their collective lack of television experience was never so evident as on the night of the pilot taping before a live audience of mostly friends, family, and fans at CBC's Mutual Street studio. By all accounts, the first run-through of the evening was a disaster; their pacing was off and the energy just wasn't there. Scott Thompson remembers a visibly concerned Lorne Michaels entering their dressing room before the second taping to read them the riot act, pacing like a football coach whose team was getting crushed out there. "He tore us all new assholes. He said, 'I can't believe that after all the work we've done, you go out there and you just throw it away. This is not the group that I signed up for; you can do better than that.' What's interesting is that all five of us were off our game and lackadaisical in that taping. Lorne was ashamed of us, and he said that if we wanted a television show, we had better get it together."

"He warned us that if the second show was just like the first, we wouldn't get a series," adds McDonald. "Scott and I were really spooked by that."

While Michaels can't recall giving a pep talk, he does remember feeling concerned that perhaps the Kids were not ready for prime time. "They had to make this decision that all five of them wanted it, but it couldn't be that two did and three didn't, you know? And of course, it was very hard to get them to agree on *anything*; that wasn't the way they worked."

Michaels knew that the Kids were talented enough for the big leagues, but he also knew that talent without discipline wouldn't translate to a career on television. "It takes so much focus and it doesn't do me any good if they're ambivalent. Then of course, besides talent and discipline, you obviously need luck as well. You either want to play in the big leagues, or you want to work on a smaller scale, which can also be great, but at a certain point, I can only be effective with people who have already decided to turn pro. I didn't know if they were ready."

In order to shake off the bad vibes of the first show, the troupe needed to do something drastic. Locking themselves in the dressing room, just the five of them, they proceeded to trash the place. "All five of us just smashed up the chairs and generally broke up the room," says Thompson. "People were knocking on the door, trying to get in before the next taping, but they backed off and just let us go wild."

A good tantrum, as it turned out, was exactly what they needed to clear the air, and according to Dave Foley, the destruction of their Mutual Street studio's dressing room was also a territorial act—a way to cast out the ghosts of CBC's comedy past. "We didn't want to feel like we had to be respectful of this space just because Tommy Hunter or Wayne and Shuster had taped their programs there. After that outburst, we just pushed past everybody and went out onto the floor in front of the audience in our costumes. The Shadowy Men were playing loud rock 'n' roll, and it was like we'd turned Mutual Street into the Rivoli. We could be *us* again."

Thompson felt that by allowing the controlled demolition backstage, Michaels showed he understood that these five young artists had something to get out of their systems. At this juncture, their newest father figure proved to be a worthy artistic mentor. "Art is a fascinating animal," says Thompson, "and there are certain things you have to allow artists to do that would never be allowed in the real world.

Besides, no one was hurt, and who cares about a few chairs? It really was exactly the right call and we went out and just killed it; we were on fire in that second show."

The second taping captured all the magic they had been looking for, and both the in-studio sketches and filmed pieces like "Head Crusher" (screened for the studio audience on the big Sony monitors high above the bleachers) went over like a dream.

Since they had last seen their old friend Mike Myers, he had returned from London before leaving town again to work at the Second City theatre in Chicago. On a short trip to Toronto, he was invited by Dave and Kevin to watch a VHS tape of their edited pilot. He had been hearing good things about the Kids while he was away, but says he wasn't ready for how much he loved the pilot. "It was perfect," says Myers. "It was so good that I literally took ill. I just had a sense that they'd done it. They had picked all the right pieces. They had that cool Super-8 opening, that cool interstitial music from the Shadowy Men. It was a complete thought from five people at their best. It's funny, I'd just auditioned for *Saturday Night Live*, but I had the odd sensation that everything I had ever done comedically was a waste of time. I didn't know you could do comedy like that, and while I was totally inspired, I also thought, 'Who could ever match this?' The five Kids were a great team, and they complemented each other so well. I was a little envious of how they all found each other."

Ahead of the HBO debut of the pilot—billed as an

hour-long "special" — Broadway Video brought the troupe back to New York for a whirlwind promotional tour. Among their planned activities was a dinner with the troupe, Lorne Michaels, producer Joe Forristal, and *Village Voice* writer Michael Musto. "The Kids were incredibly green with the press at the time," says Forristal, "and unlike Lorne, who is a seasoned pro, they didn't realize that everything they said and did at this dinner would be 'on the record.' So, everybody's drinking, being social and friendly, but the whole time Michael's taking notes for the piece he was writing."

Forristal remembers the Kids being almost stereotypically well-mannered Canadian boys at the dinner, making polite conversation over cocktails and having a delightful night out. But, according to Scott Thompson, the evening quickly descended into chaos after several drinks, when they moved the party over to the trendy Manhattan nightclub Limelight. "You had Michael and Kevin bonding in a corner touching each other, and Dave is at the top of the stairs yelling, 'Do you people know who I am?' before proceeding to fall down the stairs. It was a really wild night. In Musto's story, he wrote something like, 'One of them's gay. One's bisexual. They all took ecstasy.' We got in trouble with Lorne over that story, but in hindsight, why? We were young guys and we wanted to tear things down, like young people are supposed to do. We were in New York City and we were in our twenties having the time of our lives."

After David Handelman's article had appeared in *Rolling Stone*'s "Hot" issue, a steady buzz had been building on both sides of the border all through the summer of 1988 in advance of HBO's October 19 airdate of the special. That day, *New York Times* reviewer John J. O'Connor implored his readers to tune in at 12:25 a.m. to enjoy "five delightfully inventive young men" in the Python tradition of absurdist comedy with a tendency to dress in drag. After spotlighting sketches like "Reg" and "Rusty," O'Connor declared that the Kids in the Hall were writing and performing "some of the freshest and most disarming material the comedy scene has been able to claim in a long while."

Handelman's question hung in the air: Was America—or at least premium cable America—ready for the Kids in the Hall?

NINE

Diving into the Pool

Somewhere near Los Angeles, a twenty-one-year-old comedian named Judd Apatow was watching *The Kids in the Hall* when it aired as an hour-long special on HBO in October of 1988. Apatow was in a room packed with several other up-and-coming comedy writers and performers, including the members of *The Higgins Boys and Gruber* (featuring future *SNL* producer/*Tonight Show* costar Steve Higgins; actor David Anthony Higgins, later from *Ellen*; and Dave "Gruber" Allen, later of *Freaks and Geeks*), plus comedian Joel Hodgson, then on the cusp of launching his own wildly successful cult series, *Mystery Science Theater 3000*. According to Apatow, every one of these emerging stars fell instantly in love with *The Kids in the Hall* that day. "I loved the way they mixed both filmed and live sketches," recalls Apatow. "The whole thing was just so hilariously groundbreaking and cinematic; we were all blown away."

The Kids in the Hall had finally made it onto the air,

and while the critics seemed to like the pilot, there was still no commitment from HBO to a full series. As they waited for news from the network, the Kids tried to distract themselves with rehearsals at Toronto's Tarragon theatre space. It was here that Tarragon's Catherine May called Mark McKinney to the phone to take an important call from Lorne Michaels. "For some reason," says McDonald, "whenever Lorne had news, he asked for Mark. Maybe it was because Mark's father was a diplomat, whereas we were all kind of blue-collar compared to him."

Michaels was calling with the great news that HBO had green-lit *The Kids in the Hall* series with a first season buy of twenty episodes, eight more than they had hoped for. After passing around a liquor bottle at rehearsal, the troupe dispersed to go tell their respective parents and partners the good news.

The next day, the reality truly sank in. This was it. There was no time to party; they had work to do. "I remember years later," says McDonald, "Mark would ask, 'How come we never celebrated moments like that?' We just kept working, and then we had to go off to our separate lives and we rarely hung out together."

Still, their dream of making their own television series was now a reality. Hunkering down in their offices on St. Nicholas Street, the Kids had scenes to write, viewers to capture, hearts and minds to win over, and heads to crush. "And that," says McKinney, "was really when the blur began."

Their longtime champion Pamela Thomas was made a coproducer on the series, and remembers being ecstatic about the twenty-episode buy for the first season. Thomas had been there from the beginning, and was a key player at all the crucial meetings between Broadway Video's Jack Sullivan and HBO's Stu Smiley and Chris Albrecht. Now it was time to celebrate, so Thomas threw an extravagant Hollywood launch party for the troupe at her Pacific Palisades home, paid for by HBO and attended by Dave Thomas and Martin Short. Lounging by the pool, the Kids were in high spirits and it was a rare moment for all involved to let off some steam and give themselves a pat on the back. Some Kids partied harder than others, and Thomas watched with some amusement as Scott Thompson skinny-dipped in her pool.

"Scott said, 'I'm at a Hollywood party, so I'm jumping in the pool,'" recalls Thomas. "We had all worked so hard."

With an estimated price tag of USD$300,000 per episode, anticipation was high at both HBO and CBC in the months leading up to their series debut the following October. The CBC opted to schedule *The Kids in the Hall* on Thursday evenings at 9:30, while HBO looked toward a more grown-up time slot: Fridays at midnight, with repeats.

Broadway Video dispatched a hand-picked team to Toronto to launch *The Kids in the Hall*, with Forristal retained as a series producer, along with fellow producers Jeffrey Berman, Gregory Sills, and Jeff Ross. Arriving in Toronto direct from Los Angeles, Ross was unsure of what exactly he was getting himself into. "Within a day or two I figured it out," says Ross, "but I had to learn all about the troupe's complex personalities while they were all still figuring out how to do a sketch show. Lorne had asked me to go up for two weeks, but I wound up getting an apartment in Toronto and living there for a while. I remember getting a little bit of attitude at first from some of the Canadians, who were like, 'Oh, the big shot American's coming up here to tell us how to make television.' But I'm a good diplomat, and soon things were great with the CBC. And I had a good relationship with each of the guys individually."

Having done well with the pilot, Robert Boyd was hired to direct the series, although according to Mark McKinney, they had given serious consideration to stage director John Ferraro, who had been such a crucial asset for them during the New York boot camp, tightening up their performance chops and cutting the fat out of many of their scenes. "We all liked him, and I think he was hoping that he'd be able to direct our series as well," says McKinney, "but Bruce and Lorne favoured Robert, so we went that way."

According to Don Pyle, Lorne Michaels expressed his concerns about having Shadowy Men on a Shadowy Planet score the entire series just as they were about to go forward. "I've forgotten exactly what Lorne's words were," says Pyle, "but essentially, he said we sounded like 'cheap strip music' or 'cheap porno music.' I know that 'cheap' was definitely in there, although I'm not sure he was saying it as a negative thing. I like cheap strip music!"

But the Kids in the Hall went out on a limb for the Shadowy Men, overriding Michaels and insisting that the band's contributions were essential to their overall package.

"They told Lorne that we couldn't be replicated by some generic studio band," says Pyle. "And that support from the Kids also meant we could negotiate the deal we wanted, and keep our publishing, which was a big deal to us and initially a big sticking point with Broadway Video."

Dave Foley adds that the presence of the band at the tapings heated up the atmosphere in what would otherwise be a cold television studio. "To have Brian Connelly, king of the whammy bar, on guitar was electrifying. It made the actual making-the-show part more fun. I remember the Shadowy Men fifteen feet up and all lit up above us, looking down on the audience from atop their stage. It pumped us all up. I seem to recall that Lorne wanted us to go with a big brass section thing, like *Saturday Night Live*, although to his credit, he never forced that on us. It didn't escape us that after we used the Shadowy Men, big guitars became the sound of comedy for a long time."

By now Norm Hiscock and Cindy Park had made the move to Toronto, and while Hiscock had taken a job as a videographer for a local cable TV channel, Park worked as a producer for television commercials. The couple had stayed in touch with the Kids, and had even attended the taping of the pilot at CBC Mutual Street. Park recalls feeling exhausted by the world of advertising at precisely the moment that she and Hiscock heard *Kids* had gone to series. Seizing the moment, Park approached the troupe and within a week had been hired as a production manager on *The Kids in the Hall*, providing an indispensable professional liaison between the troupe and the suits, and helping to keep Robert Boyd organized.

"Robert was a very busy guy," says Park, "with a lot of power and responsibilities like producing the show, choosing the material, directing the films, sitting in on all the editing, and more."

Organizing the on-location shoots alone would become a full-time job, and Park was promoted to the role of line producer for all the filmed segments used in the show. "We shot a million of these location films," says Park, "so I was not only wrangling Robert, but everyone else, except maybe Scott. That was Bellini's job."

Initially, Paul Bellini's official title was receptionist, but his close relationship with Scott Thompson meant that he soon became the production's unofficial "Scott wrangler." According to Bellini, his ability to steer Thompson to the set also gave him a certain amount of job security. "Cindy basically told me they'd never fire me," says Bellini, laughing, "because as long as I was around, they never had to worry about Scott."

Thompson himself does not dispute this characterization. "I think that they all thought of me as this *wild thing*, and of course, Bellini can corral me in every way, so that role fell to him."

More significantly, as a friend who came up with Thompson at York University, Bellini became Thompson's muse and sympathetic ear in the writers' room, helping him to shape his sketches and write for his voice. "Paul's got an amazing eye and perfect pitch with comedy," says Thompson, "where I don't really. We worked well together because he's more introverted, whereas I obviously have a need to perform."

Yet another of Bellini's duties was to work the typewriter as the Kids were jamming out ideas in the room. "I learned to type so fast that I could transcribe the dialogue as they were writing the sketches," says Bellini. "I learned a lot about writing sketches that way."

A production week for the series began on Mondays, and by Friday they would assemble the two dozen new sketches and perform that at a table read. Bellini would gather up all the troupe's loose, hand-scribbled pages and Post-it notes, and collate them into a neatly typed script for these marathon sessions, after which the Kids and their production partners would select only a handful to produce in the coming week.

"There was always lots of bloodletting," says Joe Forristal, "and sometimes I'd have to be the bad guy and say no to a sketch. But as Lorne always said, 'It's much better that they hate you than each other.' Still, everyone had their input, then it was Robert's task to stand the sketches up and put them on their feet."

Early in the first season, Kevin McDonald was in crisis. Since the pilot, he had felt that Robert Boyd had cut his funniest bits, leaving him feeling like a mere straight man. When he finally spoke up about it, he says he was told to be a better team player. "Robert would tell me it was better for the show that my scenes were cut," says McDonald. "He'd say, 'Kevin, do you want to help Kevin McDonald or do you want to help the Kids in the Hall?'"

McDonald sucked it up for a time, but while his early

days on the high-school football field had taught him the
benefits of "taking one for the team," he was having trouble
quelling the hostility toward Boyd that was rising up within
him. After the first ten episodes, McDonald felt he was
becoming invisible in the series. This was a tipping point.
"I would write my stuff, then they'd film it, but for some
reason Robert wouldn't show it. It was chaotic for everyone,
but I really felt I was being edited out."

Deeply troubled, McDonald confided in Foley, his closest ally in the troupe. "I remember Dave telling me that
he had played an episode of the show for Mike Myers, and
I was so *light* in it that Mike had asked him if I was leaving
the show," says McDonald. "Within the troupe's dynamic,
Dave and I were more like an old vaudeville team, and we
had this intuitive sense of how to develop each other's ideas.
So, Dave was my ally against Robert."

While Foley and McDonald cherished more conventional comedy forms, their natural foils and sometimes
rivals in the troupe were Team Calgary, the dynamic
duo of McKinney and McCulloch, who wrote admittedly
artier pieces that tended toward the moody and cerebral.
McCulloch agrees that these checks and balances kept
the Kids from skittering too wildly to either extreme on
the comedy dial. "Kevin and Dave guarded the jokes, and
they'd put the brakes on when Mark and I brought in some
five-minute Pinteresque scene. Scott was kind of on his
own; he just wanted to fuckin' score. I remember his 'let me
at 'em' thing wasn't so cool for us at first, but in hindsight
I can see that this balance was what made us great. At the
time, you were just fighting for your own weird little area."

Thompson may have only held one vote in their five-man democracy, but it was a powerful and decisive tiebreaker. "Scott was the swing voter when things got deadlocked," remembers McDonald, "and he would go to whatever side he thought was best for the show. I really think that was part of what made the troupe successful, creatively."

Foley took McDonald's concerns directly to Boyd. "Dave told Robert that I was the acid test of the Kids in the Hall," says McDonald. "He told him, 'If you don't think he's funny, then you can't direct us.'"

McCulloch and McKinney, satisfied with their visibility in the show, were having none of it. In hindsight, McKinney acknowledges that their director likely hadn't mastered an essential job for anyone working with the Kids in the Hall — the juggling and nurturing of five fragile egos. "There have been very few people who were able to calmly coexist with all five members of the troupe," says McKinney. "Robert was really good at the beginning, but I could see that his tastes were more in line with Bruce and me, and perhaps he shared that fact a bit more than he should have, and could have been more diplomatic. The other guys picked up on it, and they weren't having it."

McDonald's breaking point came after Boyd "cut away the comedy" from a scene entitled, somewhat ironically, "The Editors." After seeing a rough cut of the sketch and feeling that Boyd had defused all the visual gags, McDonald went home and wrote a detailed ten-page letter to the director, airing his complaints and explaining how one edits a comedy sketch. Admitting that this was "a typical Kevin thing to do," McDonald recalls that the letter was not well received. "I'd listed historical examples of how to cut comedy, from Buster Keaton to Woody Allen's *Zelig*. The next day, Boyd's assistant came to me and said, 'Robert hates your fucking guts. He can't believe you wrote such an insulting letter. He went to film school. Did *you* go to film school?'"

Foley reached his own breaking point while on location shooting one of the recurring "Nobody Likes Us" pieces. In the sketch, Foley's and McDonald's sad-sack characters appear to hang themselves in front of a bank manager's house after failing to secure a loan. According to Foley, after having gone over the fake hanging in preproduction weeks in advance, they arrived at the location to find their director giving what appeared to be last-minute instructions to the riggers about the noose. Fearing for his safety, Foley lost his temper and stormed off the set.

"Robert wouldn't let the director of photography see any of the scripts beforehand," he remembers, "so they'd typically arrive at a location not knowing what they were shooting that day." I said, 'Alright, now you're actually endangering my life.' I got really mad at him and wandered off. When I came back from my little walk, Cindy and I blocked out the whole day with the DP and the rigger. Robert was told to just shut up and stay out of the way."

When Thompson, the swing vote, also began to complain that he felt marginalized, talk turned to mutiny, and it was agreed that something had to change. Eventually, McCulloch and McKinney were forced to come around and agree it was time for a new director.

John Blanchard boasted an excellent pedigree, having directed two landmark Canadian comedies, *Codco* and *SCTV*. While *SCTV* is better known, the strategic importance of Blanchard's work on *Codco* deserves a bit of context. Originally a stage-comedy ensemble from Newfoundland, *Codco*'s Cathy Jones, Mary Walsh, Andy Jones, Greg Malone, and Tommy Sexton wrote and performed absurdist and sexually provocative sketches that reflected their regional identity on a CBC series that ran from 1987 to 1992. Whereas the Kids' scenes were born in the suburbs of central and western Canada, *Codco*'s comedy was filtered through a lens of eastern Canadian life, as typified by sketches such as "Newfie Court," "Leonard Cohen Café," and "Anne of Green Gut," which irreverently deflated the work of beloved Canadian author Lucy Maud Montgomery.

But, according to Foley, while all the Kids were fans of *Codco* and *SCTV*, it was Blanchard's great sense of comedy that made him indispensable. "We benefitted immediately from John's experience and finely honed comedic instincts. For example, he had this idea of developing the home-base set for the monologues we delivered out of character, like 'Are Extraterrestrials Dull?' and 'Menstruation.' We'd stand still on one mark, and John would shoot us from a variety of different camera angles, which added a little bit of dynamism to the look of the show."

As Blanchard became integrated into the crew and various internal squabbles fell away, the show gained a reputation at the CBC for being a fun place to work. "At the beginning, someone once told me that if you fucked up at CBC, you were sent to work on *The Kids in the Hall*, and I don't think it was a lie," says McKinney. "Gradually, we got people joining our crew who could roll with us until we finally had a gang of happy misfits."

Two of the most crucial additions to that happy gang were hair and wig designer Judi Cooper-Sealy and the late makeup artist Geralyn "Geri" Wraith. Both came via *SCTV* and quickly made themselves indispensable in the design of the many characters on *The Kids in the Hall*. In an interview in 2016, Wraith, who succumbed to cancer in March of 2018, described their close-knit team as a kind of family. "I don't think I have ever had, or will ever have again, that level of teamwork and creativity on a show," said Wraith. "What Judi and I did was make the words on paper a reality. The scripts would come in, and all of us would discuss what worked and what didn't."

According to McKinney, the troupe placed enormous demands on Wraith and Cooper-Sealy, who, along with costumer Hilary Corbett and wardrobe assistant Wendy Charette (Moore), became a vital part of transforming their scripted words into three-dimensional action. "Oh my god, I recall them getting irritated at us sometimes because we would change our minds or be particular about certain things. I think Geri was used to working with polite producers, answering to one voice, and now she had five of us!"

In a short statement after her passing, Thompson described Wraith as a "brilliant artist" who was "the calm centre of the show whose talent and kindness were unparalleled," and one of his dearest friends.

For her part, Wraith remembered learning quite quickly how to take each of the Kids' complex personalities in her stride. "Bruce made a few people cry. He once came to me and said, 'People say I'm an asshole. Am I?' I said, 'Yes.' He could be pissy and grumpy, and he always left food to rot in the dressing rooms, but he was a softie underneath it all, and an intelligent little bugger. That said, I always felt respected and taken care of. None of them were assholes to Judi or me. I'd ask Dave about his character and he'd say, 'Whatever you decide; I leave it in your creative hands and I will act along with the makeup and hair.' Kevin was so sweet and always apologizing for everything and nothing."

The Kids had come a long way from the Rivoli days when simply wearing an oversized red sweater and a wig meant you were the "lady" in the scene. Foley credits both Wraith and Cooper-Sealy with transforming them as much as was cosmetically possible into realistic women. "Geri was brilliant at making us up authentically," says Foley, "and Judi had all the right wigs and hair. Plus, we had brilliant wardrobe people. We really only gave them one instruction: 'Don't make it look *funny*; make us look as good as you can.' When it all came together, everyone was on the same wavelength."

TEN

I Can't Stop Thinking about Tony

With better costumes and makeup came a wider variety of nuanced female characters in the series. Like many comedians and actors, the Kids in the Hall modelled many of their female characters on their mothers and sisters. Talk show host Nina Bedford, for instance, was loosely based on Mark McKinney's mother. "The best way to describe Nina is that she's a highly nervous, and I should say a highly unfair, caricature of my mom," says McKinney. "My mom was really smart, but she had a way of sometimes overexplaining things, so I just started to riff on that."

Another of McKinney's ladies debuted in the sketch "Crazy Love." "Melanie is my braces girl," says McKinney, "and she gets brought up to me a lot for some reason. In 'Crazy Love,' Scott played her boyfriend, who had a lot of tarantulas and stuff. That was her first appearance. But there's another sketch, a later film piece directed by John

Paizs, where Kevin's trying to sleep with Melanie, but her dog winds up fucking him."

Bruce McCulloch and Scott Thompson became chattering female office temps for their recurring "Cathy and Kathie" sketches. McCulloch, who typically favoured darker roles with a disposition that more closely resembled his own, says he relished the chance to play the relentlessly optimistic secretary Kathie with a K.

"Kathie was the opposite of me," says McCulloch, "and far closer to my sister Heather, who still lives in Fort Saskatchewan, Alberta. Kathie just wants to be of service to her coworkers, make no enemies, and have a nice time on the weekend. There was such a soul to her. She has little problems, but really she just wants peace and harmony in the world."

Thompson's character Cathy provided much-needed grounding to McCulloch's Kathie. "Kathie is a flibberti-gibbet," recalls Thompson, "whereas my Cathy is an alpha female, with a reservoir of anger that I don't think the other Kathie has. Each of us balanced the other."

Nuanced femininity also ran through the recurring "Hotel La Rut" sketches, which centred on two prostitutes, McKinney's "Silvee" and Thompson's "Michelle." Michelle's rejoinder, "I can't stop thinking about Tony," was based on a real moment in Thompson's life after a lover named Tony broke his heart and ran away to Paris. "I truly just couldn't stop thinking and talking about Tony," says Thompson, "so that whole first speech—I just wrote it all out at home on a piece of cardboard, very quickly."

Inversely, Thompson says that his relentlessly optimistic

housewife Fran, so verbally abused by McCulloch's Gordon in the "Salty Ham" sketch, got her sunny resilience directly from both his mother and his aunt. "I think with most character comedians, their first character is a parent. When I do a businessman, for example, I think, 'That's my dad.' Fran was basically my mother, Barbara, who has a twin named Fran. I gave her my aunt's name, and to be fair, my mom is not quite as energetic as my Fran."

To create Fran's grouchy husband, Gordon, Bruce McCulloch drew on a wealth of comedic material by reciting verbatim the ridiculous things his father, Ian, had said at the family dinner table. "The mushroom pork tirade in 'Salty Ham' was the kind of thing Dad would rant about at my poor mother after a bad dinner," says McCulloch. "When we played Gordon against Fran, it was probably one of the most interesting and exciting writing moments Scott and I ever had. We'd look at each other and think, 'I can play my dad and you can play your mom.' We knew that if we mined these half-remembered transcripts from our lives it was going to be really funny. It was all a kind of comic snapshot of the hell I had lived through as a boy, in the same way that my Gavin character was based on a kid who started talking to my dad and I at the cottage as we were building a veranda. I didn't need to change one word of it."

HBO's Carolyn Strauss felt that by presenting a worm's-eye view of humanity and social mores through the fluid gender of their characters, the Kids were TV revolutionaries, but McDonald is quick to wave off such claims. "Monty Python were the revolutionaries," he says. "*They* were the ones who really ripped things up. They'd do unheard-of things like having a character walk out of a scene halfway through because he didn't like being in the sketch. Our scenes were more about relationships and underdogs, which is in a way what made us kind of punk rock."

Similarly, McCulloch was wary of what Lorne Michaels had identified as the troupe's penchant for "gender politics," and recalls a genuine concern that their comedy would suffer if they were pigeonholed as sexual activists. "Scott obviously wore the gay thing a lot," says McCulloch, "but I never wanted to be known as a gay comedy troupe, because I thought that if we accepted that tag, we could be disregarded more easily. Besides, the fact was we *weren't* a gay comedy troupe. It was probably more significant that we were a group of mainly heterosexuals from the suburbs, where homophobia is rampant, who could cross-dress and kiss each other on the lips and have no problem with it. That was our art, and I think it has more power than if we were a quote–unquote 'gay comedy troupe.'

"Scott played heterosexual characters too. If he hadn't played Buddy Cole, you might not even know he was the gay one. It could have been any of us. Look at Kevin, Dave, me, any of us—we're feminine guys. That was also part of our secret sauce in a way."

Thompson had first improvised as Buddy Cole for Paul Bellini's video camera back at York University. "Paul put a blue gel over the camera," says Thompson, "so the first thing I said as Buddy Cole was 'This is my Blue Period,' and then I went off on a riff. I named him after Buddy's, the pioneering Toronto gay bar that George Hislop used to run, which coincidentally was also the bar where I first came out."

Thompson credits the "homoerotic vampire novels" of Anne Rice — "all the rage at the time" — for his decision to cast Buddy as a world-weary raconteur, and says he initially imagined him as a melancholy 500-year-old vampire who lived in a Paris garret. "Homosexuals and vampires were somehow connected," recalls Thompson. "In reality, Buddy was based on an alpha queen who had broken my heart. He was one of the few effeminate men I'd been with, although he wore his femininity like a sword, which intrigued me. Some people always thought of Buddy as toothless, but I wanted to make him dangerous. I think some of the first lines from the very first monologue came out of those sessions with Bellini. 'It's such a lot of fuss over a few extra esses.' I also gave him a little of the sass that Flip Wilson brought to his Geraldine Jones character. Flip was a huge influence on me. He died so young; it's so tragic he's been forgotten."

Thompson and McKinney took the idea of the "homo-erotic vampire" to literal extremes in their sketch "Dracula," wherein Thompson flipped the script by playing a hockey fan getting cruised by McKinney's gay vampire after a hockey game. "That was a very common thing in Toronto at the time," says Thompson. "A lot of boys were seduced at Maple Leaf Gardens. I definitely had that happen to me, although I wasn't a 'hoser' like my character Brad. But even though Brad allows Mark's vampire to blow him, he's not a gay character; he's just young and opportunistic."

While McDonald shoos away any notion that the Kids were intentionally pushing boundaries, he does acknowledge a certain preference toward dark, obsessive, and broken characters. But there was an unspoken understanding among the troupe that these were never mean-spirited attacks on anybody in particular. "Kurt Vonnegut once said he tried to make all of his lead characters likeable people, then put them through the most horrible shit. I think we do that too. Like in Dave's sketch, 'Country Doctor,' even the character of Death is kind of a funny guy, and you almost feel sorry for him in the end, when I sort of beat him and he slumps his shoulders. We never discussed things like empathy in the writing room, though; I think it would have been horrible if we had."

On rare occasions, such as with their controversial "Dr. Seuss Bible" sketch, the Kids knowingly pushed the boundaries of 1980s television. "It was an idea only Bruce would think of," says McDonald. "Bruce wrote it up as a sketch for Dave, then all five of us jammed it out together. None of the Bible characters were played for laughs; all the comedy comes from Dave's Dr. Seuss. Bruce wrote a lot of funny Seussian rhymes for him and the other characters. But Scott played Jesus straight, with a real empathy for the pain of crucifixion. Of course, since this is a Dr. Seuss story, the crucifixion nails are giant rainbow-coloured silly straws. I also loved the contrast of Jesus saying 'Forgive them, Father, they know not what they do, for they walk through this life in two crappity shoes.' HBO had no problem showing the sketch, but some people at CBC found it shocking, because, after all, we were killing Christ on a comedy show. But to me, it's just like someone getting a pie in the face is always funny; killing Jesus Christ in Dr. Seuss verse just felt funny too. It's not blasphemous to me, and I bet that in the early '70s, way more teenagers turned on to Jesus Christ through *Jesus Christ Superstar, Godspell,* or George Harrison's 'My Sweet Lord.' So there."

Veteran comedian David Steinberg remembers recognizing a little of his own comedy in "Dr. Seuss Bible." In the late '60s, Steinberg had upset CBS, as well as a large chunk of the American television audience, with his religion-mocking "sermons" on *The Smothers Brothers Comedy Hour.* He saw *The Kids in the Hall* as the latest example in a long line of intelligent satirists whose comedy worked on many levels. "The thing about people like the Kids in the Hall, which was also true of Monty Python, Beyond the Fringe, and The Establishment, is they're all off-the-charts smart," says Steinberg. "I made my bones at Second City in Chicago during the mid-'60s, and to me the Kids were a continuation of what we did there combined with what Python did later. They were all so spectacularly gifted, and the storytelling was very cool and sophisticated. 'Dr. Seuss Bible' was even bolder than what I did, which had gotten the Smothers Brothers thrown off the air after my sermons inspired the most negative mail in the history of CBS. Still, if you're doing your comedy right, someone's always going to not like it, which is exactly as it should be."

While such third-rail topics as religion and modern sexuality proved meaty targets for the Kids' comedy, some of their most political material was born of anti-establishment anger at big business and taking on "The Man." McCulloch's time studying business at Mount Royal College had left him fascinated with office life. The obsessive, animal nature of the corporate world was reflected in the way his business-man characters would sniff each other out like dogs while handing out business cards in the scene "Can I Keep Him?" where a young boy finds a lost businessman in the wild and brings him home like a stray dog. "Growing up," says McCulloch, "the antidote to being a punk was becoming a successful businessman. I remember taking some public relations courses with all these people in a room talking and saying nothing, and I found it really humorous. There were typically two kinds of takes we had on businessmen. In the A.T. & Love boardroom scenes, we're all a little dull and silly, and we're wasting time, whereas with the Geralds, it was like a David Mamet take on the animal savagery of negotiating how much a client is going to drink and what's going to happen to her. It's a little dirty, which is really fun."

McCulloch's squash-obsessed Eradicator is another example of Darwinian competition in business, this time set within a corporate intramural squash league. Clad in his black ski mask, the Eradicator takes his competitions far too seriously, and is made pathetic in the process. McCulloch admits that beyond the usual corporate targets, "The Eradicator" was a parody of his own competitive drive and a tenacity he had discovered in himself as a teenage marathon runner and competitive weight lifter back in Calgary. "I grew up playing squash, and there is something about the cage-match element in that sketch. As a kid, I was obsessed with my 10K times and how fast I could do laps, but it was all meaningless, because I wasn't an Olympic athlete; I was just a guy running and timing myself. So, there's sort of a useless competitiveness I have that I think was the comic core of both 'The Eradicator,' and the guy in 'Floating,' a sketch about a competition to see who can lie in the bathtub the longest."

"The Eradicator" was of a piece with many of McCulloch's scenes, including "The Pen," "Into the Doors," and "The Bass Player," where the comedy was driven by the ridiculousness of one man's obsessive nature, be it with his car ("Don't you ever laugh at my car") or with the fact that there was no bass player in The Doors. "That car guy was based on a real person I knew back in Calgary who was just obsessed with his car," says McCulloch. "The guy in 'Into the Doors' is a version of my own youthful obsession that everything in the record is important. It's me and Reid and Brian looking at someone's records and judging them by their taste in music."

Obsessive male pride and what is now sometimes referred to as "toxic male fragility" were at the heart of McCulloch's Cabbage Head character, who had gone through several incarnations since his first onstage appearance in *Troumouth Wears Green*. "Bruce had tried a similar character called Toaster Hands, as in 'Look at me, I have toasters for hands,'" says McDonald, "but there were logistical problems with presenting that. To me, though, Cabbage Head was about how people love to manipulate other people by exploiting their pity."

While McCulloch's characters were often vessels for his social commentary, Mark McKinney worked the other way around. For him, characters were the engine driving the scene. McKinney preferred to "jam out" a character for hours before giving that character a context for a scene.

"When you find the character, the scene will click," says McKinney. "For example, we wrote 'Sick of the Swiss' in just ten minutes one morning after Scott and I had been jamming out the characters."

McKinney's Mississippi Gary character had been lingering in his head since his days on the campus radio at Memorial University with Norm Hiscock. During the first season of the show, Gary made his television debut in a scene opposite McCulloch called "Kathie and the Blues Guy."

"When I was a kid, I listened to a ton of blues music," says McKinney. "It always struck me as really odd, and I'd wonder why I, the whitest of white people, could feel such an empathy for Delta Blues? So, I wrote a sketch about an old bluesman talking in a kind of bluesy gibberish, and I reduced the narrative to bite-size chunks for the people who don't really know anything about the blues, and I created some generic bluesy songs like 'Smokin' on a night train, chewin' on a jelly roll.' The payoff for me was when I broke the fourth wall and admitted, 'OK, I'm not really a bluesman. I'm actually from Ottawa.' But then as I talk about the blues, I would gradually drift back into character."

These characters, and many more, were feeding the incessant demands of the laugh factory that was CBC Mutual Street, in what had become an industrial assembly line pumping out television comedy. Week after week, the Kids would create an entirely new set of material for a live audience of two hundred comedy fans. To keep that audience fresh during the taping sessions, which could sometimes stretch into three-hour affairs, the Kids called upon theirs friends to do warm-up. Luckily, their friends happened to be some of the best Toronto stand-up comics of their generation: Eric Tunney, Boyd Banks, P. J. Heslin, Elvira Kurt, Sheila Gostick, Al & George, Brian Hartt, and Brent Butt. According to Butt, the studio audience at CBC Mutual Street was largely comprised of hipsters in all-black clothing who had followed the troupe over from the Rivoli. "They were a really hip crowd," says Butt, "which meant they'd go any place you wanted to go as a performer. It was a sweet gig for a stand-up."

By the end of the first season, having worked thirteen straight months at a breakneck pace, the Kids were exhausted. The burden of creative control had taken a toll on them, but they still found it uncomfortable to delegate any aspect of the creative process to outsiders apart from John Blanchard or Lorne Michaels. According to Jeff Ross, Michaels could still take a hands-on role in the production if he felt it necessary. "I once saw Lorne sit down with a stack of scripts and a pencil," recalls Ross. "He went through the entire fuckin' thing and made it about 35 percent better in one hour."

While Michaels was rolling up his sleeves and lending a hand on set, the Broadway Video boss was also working behind the scenes to keep the lights on. Unbeknownst to the Kids, there was a growing feeling at HBO that despite the critical acclaim for *The Kids in the Hall*, their small but loyal viewership didn't justify the premium cable channel's continued support. After trying for weeks to convince HBO to renew *The Kids in the Hall* on the grounds that it was the kind of critically acclaimed prestige programming that the cable giant thrived on, Michaels's best efforts failed. The Kids' first inkling that the bottom was dropping out came during rehearsals for the last taping block of the season, when Joe Forristal summoned McKinney to take a momentous phone call from Michaels.

"I could tell Joe knew there was bad news coming because he was fidgeting uncomfortably," says McKinney. "Lorne simply said, matter-of-factly, 'HBO says they're going to pass. They're not picking it up.' He said the series itself wasn't cancelled outright, but our fate was now solely in the hands of the CBC, which didn't feel so good. It felt like a real slap in the face."

Kevin McDonald was blindsided by the news. "We were rehearsing a scene where I was playing a little kid," says McDonald, "and I was sitting on a tricycle when Mark broke the horrible news to us. I remember Scott saying 'Cancelled? But it's only our first season!'"

McKinney admits that nobody in the troupe saw HBO's decision coming, "although, to be fair, that first season was pretty shaky, and we hadn't gotten good at the films or how to get the most comedy out of our production budget." Stunned in their rehearsal room, the troupe closed ranks in what McKinney describes as "a moment of survivors' solidarity." And then, the Kids in the Hall did something that they had rarely done in recent memory; they went to a bar together and got drunk.

"We didn't really get *that* drunk," says McDonald by way of clarification, "but I was in a state of shock, and that hour that we all drank together was the funniest time I remember of us being together. We're funny when things go bad; we do gallows humour well."

ELEVEN

Drugs Are Bad

Down, but not quite out, the Kids in the Hall had been dealt a serious blow by HBO just as they were making an impression on early adopters like Judd Apatow, who says he never missed an episode. For Apatow, *The Kids in the Hall* represented the new benchmark in sketch comedy.

"They were bolder than just about anybody else at the time," says Apatow. "They were often quite absurd, yet there was also something personal and truthful in a sketch like 'Daddy Drank.' And I thought that Scott Thompson's Buddy Cole sketches were really courageous and riotously funny."

Comedian Dana Gould, who worked with Apatow on *The Ben Stiller Show*, recalls accompanying Stiller and Janeane Garofalo to New York's Bottom Line to witness one of the Kids' HBO showcases. Gould instantly identified with and took inspiration from the comedic sensibilities of these like-minded peers from the north. "For us, it was like when Brian Wilson heard *Rubber Soul* and went, 'Ahh, they're doing it!' These guys were our age, our peers, so we thought, 'This is our group now.' Only, they already had their own show and, probably because they were Canadian, a voice that seemed unique to our ears."

Future *Better Call Saul* star Bob Odenkirk recalls being bowled over by the Kids' experimentalism, absurdity, and silliness. He also admits to harbouring mild feelings of jealousy at the time, sensing that — *SNL* aside — there only seemed to be room for one alternative sketch show in America at a time. He and David Cross were itching to launch their own equally original series, *Mr. Show with Bob & David*. "It was ten years after *SCTV*, and now it was *Kids in the Hall*'s turn," says Odenkirk. "But of course, while I loved them, all I could think was, 'Will I have to wait another ten years before it's *our* turn?'"

Meanwhile, up in Detroit, Paul Feig did not discover *The Kids in the Hall* through HBO — he couldn't afford premium cable at the time — and instead caught them on the local CBC station beaming over the Detroit River from Windsor, Ontario. "I remember seeing this guy singing 'These are the Daves I know' and thinking this was hilarious," says Feig. "Pretty soon, I became obsessed with the show. They had a different, mildly subversive take on sketch comedy, and they were writing intelligent sketches that related to the zeitgeist, yet didn't feel tied down to any time. It was completely character-driven and obsessed with real, but odd, characters."

Feig, who would go on to create *Freaks and Geeks* and direct the female-driven blockbuster *Bridesmaids*, found the Kids' comedy to be more evolved than most male-based troupes he had previously seen. Refreshingly, these Canadians seemed extremely comfortable exploring their feminine sides. "Whereas Monty Python had typically played women a little camp," says Feig, "the Kids didn't seem to be mocking their lady characters. Even the fact that there was an openly gay member in the cast seemed so forward-thinking to me at the time."

The near unanimous acceptance of the series by critics and their comedy peers served to make HBO's decision to back out even more painful for the Kids. In the days after the announcement, Joe Forristal visited HBO's New York offices, where he found the atmosphere to be funereal. "The Kids felt like they were losing the baby, and all their hard work had just gone to shit. It was a bleak and uncomfortable time for all of us." But then a funny thing happened on the way to the funeral: Mark McKinney was nominated for a CableACE in the category of Best Actor in a Comedy Series.

Less well-known than the Emmy Awards, the CableACE Awards were established by the cable television community in 1979 as a response to the Emmys' early refusal to nominate cable programming. By the time of *The Kids in the Hall*'s first season in 1989, it was common for HBO to sweep the awards. McKinney's nomination in 1990 was a much-needed lifeline that arrived just as the network was preparing to write off the series. "I'm fairly certain I was nominated purely for that whole 'crushing your head' thing," says McKinney, "which was ironic because at the first read-through, Lorne's only note had been 'Really?

You're gonna do that one?' But then a year and a half later, it wound up saving our baby, because after it aired it was one of our very few hit characters."

In the category of Best Actor in a Comedy Series, McKinney was pitted against Garry Shandling, who was favoured to win for his performance in another HBO series, *It's Garry Shandling's Show*. Despite McKinney's poor odds, HBO graciously agreed to fly the entire troupe to Los Angeles for the ceremony, held that year at the Wiltern Theatre. "The trip was meant to be our swan song," says McDonald, "but I remember being thrilled to be there because I got to meet a personal hero of mine, Muhammad Ali. And then Dave and I found ourselves chatting with Edie Adams, the widow of one of our TV comedy heroes, Ernie Kovacs. She recognized us from across the room, came over, and told us that Ernie would have loved our show. I thought, 'Whatever happens now, I can die a happy man.'"

But their night was about to get even better: In an upset that no one saw coming, McKinney beat out Shandling to win best comedic actor, shocking everyone in the room, including McKinney himself, who hadn't even felt the need to prepare an acceptance speech. "I was shocked," says McKinney, "and in my daze I thanked the Washington Redskins, because Kevin and I were both fans."

After McKinney shuffled off the stage, he was reminded that he had forgotten to thank Lorne Michaels, who was not in attendance. When McKinney finally reached Michaels from a phone booth in the lobby a few minutes later, he was told that the Kids' come-from-behind win would likely be the game changer that would convince HBO to reconsider

"Easy to love, tough to kill..." The troupe circa 1989, posing in their *Kids in the Hall* writing loft clubhouse at 25 St. Nicholas Street, downtown Toronto.

The Audience (pre-Bruce McCulloch) at the Loose Moose Simplex, Calgary, circa 1982–83. *Left to right:* Mark McKinney, Bill Gemmil, Norm Hiscock, Frank van Keeken, and Garry Campbell.

Things were looking up for the pre-television Kids, in Toronto, 1985.

A promotional photograph from HBO's *On Location: Kids in the Hall*, which debuted October 19, 1988.

Three old Calgary punks, backstage at 25 Mutual Street, Toronto, during a taping of *The Kids in the Hall*. Bruce McCulloch (centre) flanked by bassist Reid Diamond (left) and guitarist Brian Connelly (right), both of Shadowy Men on a Shadowy Planet.

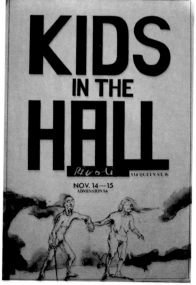

A selection of handmade gig posters and cabaret tickets by various artists.

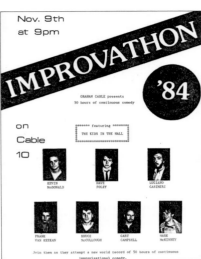

Assorted memorabilia: (*clockwise from top left*) posters for the 1984 Improvathon, the Kids' Rivoli residency (hand-lettered by Brian Connelly), and The Audience's Late Nite Comedy in Calgary (note the cancelled shows); a handbill for the Kids' NYC residency at Carolines; Connelly's poster for *Graverobbers from Hipsville*; and tickets for a *Kids in the Hall* series taping at CBC's Mutual Street Studio 7.

Shadowy Men on a Shadowy Planet
(*left to right*): Don Pyle, Reid Diamond, and Brian Connelly.

Mark McKinney with the author, on location during the filming
of *Brain Candy* in Toronto, circa 1995–96.

Paul Bellini in a rare non-toweled moment,
as a little general with a nice doggie.

Scott Thompson and Bruce McCulloch as Cathy and Kathie.

Bruce McCulloch and Mark McKinney as "The Cops."

"Sex Girl Patrol" (*left to right*): Trudie (Bruce McCulloch), Monique (Mark McKinney), and Ginger (Dave Foley).

Dave Foley and Kevin McDonald as Sir Simon Milligan and Hecubus.

Mark McKinney as Chicken Lady.

Craig Northey, who composed the score for *Brain Candy* and co-composed
(with Jim McGrath) scores for *Death Comes to Town* and *Young Drunk Punk*,
photographed in 2016 at his North Vancouver studio.

In costume for the controversial "Dr. Seuss Bible" sketch (crappity shoes not visible), backstage at The Warfield, San Francisco, 2002.

Author Paul Myers hosting SF Sketchfest's Tribute to the Kids in the Hall at the Palace of Fine Arts, San Francisco, January 26, 2008.

The Shuckton Action News team from *Death Comes to Town*: Heather Weather (Scott Thompson), Levon Blanchard (Dave Foley), Corrinda Gablechuck (Mark McKinney), and Shaye (Kevin McDonald).

Graverobbers from Hipsville redux: Same guys, new graves, and better wine, at Hollywood Forever cemetery, Los Angeles, 2008.

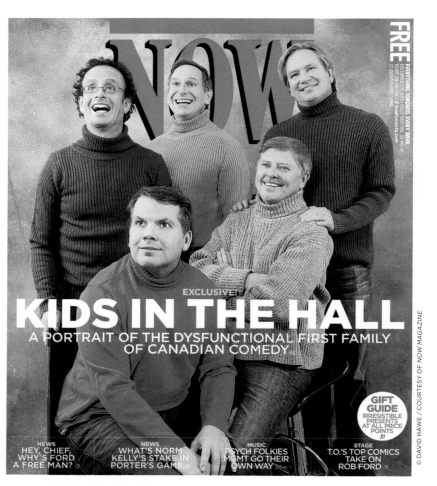

"The Dysfunctional First Family of Canadian Comedy," on the cover of Toronto's *NOW Magazine*, December 2013.

Live table read of *Brain Candy* at the Queen Elizabeth Theatre in Toronto, March 11, 2014 (*left to right*): Gord Downie (The Tragically Hip), Bruce McCulloch, Gregory Macdonald (Sloan), Craig Northey (Odds), Chris Murphy (Sloan), and Thomas D'Arcy.

Mr. Tyzik, the Head Crusher, still crushin' heads — now with video assist. At the Capitol Theatre in Port Chester, New York, May 2, 2015.

Scott Thompson as Buddy Cole, Dynasty Typewriter at the Hayworth Theatre, Los Angeles, March 2018.

"The opening moment of the 2015 tour featured all five Kids decked out in white bridal gowns, a living metaphor for five guys married to a legacy, renewing their vows by merely remembering their lines." At the Capitol Theatre in Port Chester, New York, May 2, 2015.

their decision. "I had been doing all I could to keep the show alive," says Michaels, "and it's never easy. I tried everything I could."

Meanwhile, McKinney was introduced to the man he had beaten, Garry Shandling. "His girlfriend at the time, Linda Doucett, said I should come over and meet him," says McKinney, "but he was kind of mopey and uncomfortable at meeting me, huddled in a corner with his team—Buddy Morra, Larry Brezner, and agent David Steinberg. To her credit, Linda chastised him, 'Garry, be nice.'"

Lorne Michaels's instincts proved to be correct, as HBO's Michael Fuchs informed the troupe that the network would consider doing at least one more season with the Kids in the Hall. "We already knew that we had fans within HBO," says McKinney, "but there's no doubt that winning that CableACE very much spoke their language."

HBO's renewal came with certain reservations, of course, and in a 1990 interview with GQ's Johanna Schneller, Bridget Potter, then–senior VP of original programming at HBO, was only cautiously optimistic about the Kids' prospects: "They did not set the world on fire here their first season so there was a legitimate hesitation to do a second year, but we're committed to them. I think they're evolving into something important."

Regardless of the conditional nature of their support, HBO had given *The Kids in the Hall* a temporary stay of execution, and to celebrate, the troupe hit the road to perform a series of live shows across North America. The shows came partly out of a need to whip up American ratings, but they also provided the troupe with their first glimpse of their growing fan base after just one season on television. A series of live shows also had more practical benefits for the troupe, as the stage had always been the one arena where all five Kids were on the same page. Performing live reminded them all why they loved doing comedy together. "Making the television show could be very isolating," says McKinney. "We were all scattered in various makeup chairs at different times, shooting our one- or two-person scenes. But live, we became a true gang again. In the beginning, it was the Kids versus the twenty-three people who had wandered into the Rivoli on a Monday night, and now it was seven hundred or so people at sold-out theatres in most of the major cities around North America."

Ratings for the TV series may have been low, but as they made their way across the country, the Kids were pleasantly surprised to find audiences knew every word of the sketches featured in season one. Dave Foley likens the experience to being in a touring rock 'n' roll band. And in fact, many actual musicians began turning up at their shows. In Atlanta, for instance, they discovered that Chris Robinson and the Black Crowes were fans. "They wanted to party with us," recalls McKinney, "and we hung out with them in New York when they played on *SNL*."

After a Toronto performance by Nirvana, Scott Thompson was invited backstage to meet Kurt Cobain, a declared fan of the Kids in The Hall. And in Vancouver, the Kids met and bonded with Canadian rockers, Odds. Singer-guitarist Craig Northey was thrilled that the Kids blasted out his band's album *Neopolitan* as their preshow music during their two-night stand at Vancouver's Vogue Theatre. "We'd been watching their taped shows on the road," says Northey, "so when we heard our music at their show, we knew we were going to be friends." The band threw an informal wrap party at their practice space next door to the Vogue, and for Northey, it was the beginning of a long friendship and a fruitful artistic partnership.

Comedian Brent Butt, who opened their shows at the Vogue, compared their reception to Beatlemania. "They came out of the stage door, and there was screaming and flashes going off," says Butt. "I had never seen this kind of fervour for comedy; it felt like the roof was going to blow off the place. It occurred to me that every one of these Vancouver fans must have discovered this Toronto troupe solely through the CBC. I never forgot that: you could actually be famous now without leaving Canada."

Significantly, the tour revealed to the Kids that their audience was largely made up of social outcasts for whom their connection with the troupe was special and strong. "I would hear people saying 'Wow, I love you guys, but I didn't know so many other people liked you too," says McCulloch. "They were outsiders and I suppose so were we."

The Kids in the Hall were certainly outside the mainstream as far as network television executives were concerned. If they were going to keep their television show on the air, a few adjustments would be necessary as they entered their crucial sophomore season. While the Kids had initially vowed that every word of every scene would only be generated from within the troupe, the exhausting demands of the first season had opened them to the idea of bringing in additional writers. "We were always working hard and working fast," says McCulloch. "In fact, it was only later, when I got to see how other American TV was put together, that I realized how quickly we made our show."

McDonald was the first to suggest padding the writers' room. He ran into some initial resistance from McCulloch, but Bruce eventually came around when it was suggested that they only hire from within their circle of trusted comedy friends. One name at the top of their short list was Norm Hiscock, who they all considered to be brilliantly funny, and most importantly he possessed that rare and essential ability to get along with everybody in the troupe. "I knew something had to change," says McCulloch, "so I agreed to bring in Norm. He was a really hard worker and I knew I could work well with him."

While the money wasn't great, Hiscock considered himself fortunate to have an opportunity to write comedy for a living. "Plus, it was kind of an exclusive club," says Hiscock, "since they only hired close friends and people who they thought got the sensibility of the show."

Comic Brian Hartt, who had warmed up their studio audiences during the show's first season, joined Hiscock in this exclusive club. "Brian was Bruce's friend from the stand-up scene, and we liked him too," says Dave Foley. "We knew he could come up with good premises for sketches and be a really good collaborator for Bruce."

Hartt had recently opened several dates on the

Kids' North American tour, where he had bonded with McCulloch over life's deepest questions. "Bruce and I had been partying," remembers Hartt, "and we were just sort of crashed out in a hotel room when out of the blue Bruce says, 'You know who the best rock drummer in the world is? Of all time?' And I said, 'John Fuckin' Bonham.' And he went, 'Fuckin' right.' And I sat there for another ten minutes, totally silent, and then I said, 'Alright, I gotta go.'"

Finally, Thompson encouraged Paul Bellini to put his name in as the third extra writer. As his longtime friend and the only other openly gay man in the room, Bellini had an intrinsic understanding of Thompson's *voice*, and besides, he'd practically been cowriting with Thompson anyway. "I remember Dave wasn't convinced about me because I had no traditional comedy background, either in sketch or stand-up," says Bellini. "He told me I should feel grateful because a lot of comedians would be very jealous of me, and he was right. But I knew what I was doing, and by the end of that year, I had my name on, like, forty things."

With a staff of eight writers, it became necessary to have somebody organize the workflow, so The Frantics' Dan Redican was brought in to supervise the writers' room. "Dan was definitely the funniest and the edgiest member of The Frantics," says Foley. "I think Kevin and I also liked him because he leaned toward the kind of premise-based comedy that we liked to write."

While he was officially billed as a supervising producer, Redican became the de facto head writer, often playing peace broker between various factions within the troupe, and finding the most equitable way to cut somebody's favourite scene. "Otherwise," says Redican, "it would just devolve into a huge fight. To stay neutral, I didn't really bring my own sketches to them, to avoid any conflict of interest."

In the middle of the second season, Redican was replaced by Valri Bromfield, whose resumé included being Dan Aykroyd's early comedy partner at the Second City theatre and appearing in the debut episode of *Saturday Night Live*. "We were very excited," says McDonald. "Valri was a genius. Sometimes when we were writing sketches, she'd pop her head in and come up with great lines."

But even Bromfield didn't last long after the Kids began to feel that she was favouring Thompson. Tensions flared when she dared to suggest replacing the Shadowy Men's theme song with a song about Thompson, sung by his Brazilian boyfriend Satranga de Lima. "It was this world music song," McDonald recalls, "with lyrics like, 'Scott is a free bird, he fly, you can't chain him.' Valri was a brilliant writer and performer, but she maybe wasn't the best producer for us, ultimately."

Unchained as he was, Thompson doesn't deny that he enjoyed the newfound attention that came with being on television, and points to a sketch he wrote for the second season, "A Kid in the Hall Show," that was a tribute to, well, Scott Thompson. "I thought it would be funny to do a character who had nothing to say, beyond 'I'm Scott Thompson.' It was about emptiness and narcissism. I think it was also about wanting to be famous on television. I really did want fame. I love the glamour and the shallowness, all of it. And Americans know how to do show business. I mean, I love Canada, but Canadian show business is extremely lame."

Thompson's love of show business manifested itself in his nerdy and gossip-obsessed character, Weston Esterhazy, who he admits was little more than a heightened version of himself. "I'd get so excited about gossip, and I poured all of that into Weston. I'd put my mouth in that rectangle shape and just jam it all out in the voice of a comic book nerd. Mark's character Virgil was born at the same time, so we'd jam out nerd talk together. Nerds were still outcasts in those days, not like today when they're everywhere."

But as much as Thompson loved show business, he cringes recalling one morning in June 1991 when he and the Kids appeared on *The Joan Rivers Show* alongside fellow Canadian William Shatner, musician Joey DeFrancesco, and humorist Dave Barry. "We were terrible that day," remembers Thompson. "We showed up hungover and dishevelled; I think we were still drunk from the night before. Joan could only get one-word answers from us. The segment was awful, and I felt like we really let show business down. After the show, Joan took us into a room and just tore into us, saying 'What the fuck are you guys doing? I gave you a chance, and you go out like that?' It was just like when Lorne had yelled at us at the taping of our pilot. First we had let down Daddy Lorne, and now we had let down Mummy Joan. We were so ashamed."

Licking their wounds, and sobering up, the Kids set aside their shame and went back to the serious business of making comedy. While writing the second season, they had discovered that the expanded writing staff took some of the pressure off, which in turn allowed some of the less natural writers in the troupe to find and develop their voices. McDonald and Thompson both came into their own that year, becoming prolific sources of sketches and scene ideas. McDonald recalls new scenes and characters being born even while shooting other sketches, which was how he and Foley arrived at their "Sizzler Sisters" characters while working on McCulloch's scene, "Kathie's Pig Nose."

"Dave and I were both playing women in it," says McDonald, "so we were in the makeup chairs in our bathrobes and wigs when we just started improvising in these bad Ronald Colman voices, saying 'We're clearly not two insane people. We're two Sizzler Sisters. Right, Jerry?' 'That's right, Jerry. We're the Sizzler Sisters, and there's no way we've escaped from a lunatic asylum.' By the time we got called to set, we'd written up this scene."

The day after the shoot, McDonald was back in the office typing up the "Sizzler Sisters" when McCulloch entered and began chatting with Foley. "Dave mentioned this bit that we used to do at Theatresports where we'd come out as French-Canadian trappers," says McDonald. "He described how we'd pretend to row a canoe across the stage, singing '*Alouette, gentille alouette*,' and it always got a huge laugh. So, while I'm still typing up the 'Sizzler Sisters' sketch, I can hear Dave and Bruce in the next cubicle, writing up the '*Coureurs des bois*' sketch."

McCulloch plugged the "*Coureurs des bois*" into a favourite theme of his, the drab competitiveness of office culture, and brought it to a gruesome conclusion with Foley and

McDonald's trappers now hunting businessmen for their Armani suit pelts, deep in the wilds of Toronto's Bay Street financial district. It was another strong idea, and after a prolific day, McDonald left the office feeling rather satisfied with both sketches.

But the day wasn't done. Leaving their St. Nicholas Street office, a drug dealer approached McDonald in the side alley, and their interaction inspired yet a third scene. "He asked me if I wanted to buy some hash," says McDonald, "and I said I didn't. Then he said, 'Hey, aren't you that guy on the TV show?' And I said, 'Yes, I am. Thank you.' But as I walked away, feeling flattered, I had this thought that it would be really funny if I called the cops on him. I ran back to the office and I wrote up 'Drugs Are Bad.' So, it was just one of those magic days when the sketches rained down from the Comedy Gods fully formed."

The drug culture of late 1980s Toronto inspired other sketches, such as Thompson's "In Search of Pot," which was based on a "marijuana drought" in the city, while sidestepping its more serious consequences. "Since there was no pot anywhere," says Thompson, "Queen Street was suddenly flooded with cheap heroin, and a number of people in my circle started to experiment with it, which I found shocking."

Thompson says that Bauer, his long-haired stoner character from the decidedly less serious "In Search of Pot" (also seen in McCulloch's "Ham of Truth"), was based on a fellow student he knew back at Brampton Centennial. "Bauer is this guy who had obviously peaked in high school," says Thompson. "Just because you're cool at school it doesn't mean you're going to be cool for the rest of your life. I think Bauer had some troubles when he got older, but he had this kind of stoner wisdom that reminded me of The Dude from *The Big Lebowski.*"

As predicted, Norm Hiscock really did get along with everyone in the troupe, and he began to write with Kids other than Foley. "Norm was at the top of his game," says McDonald, "and we *all* wanted to write with him. In the Kids in the Hall, you couldn't say that about everybody."

McDonald and Hiscock's "Nervous Break(fast)down," which fans often refer to as "Bell Biv DeVoe," came to them one morning when a grumpy Hiscock was absentmindedly flipping through the *Toronto Sun* newspaper, mumbling out the headlines and giving oblique commentary. "Norm opened the paper and said, 'Let's see, what's number one in the charts? Bell. Biv. DeVoe.' And I just started laughing," says McDonald. "It was such a weird thing to blurt out. Then there'd been an earthquake in Ecuador, so Norm just says, 'Whole lotta shakin' goin' on down there.' Now we're both laughing at the idea of this guy having a nervous breakdown. Half an hour later we had a sketch, adding things like 'Your mother's leaving me' and 'Whole lotta milk-ah' while I'm pouring milk on the flowers."

McDonald and Hiscock's morning coffee chats also inspired "The King of Empty Promises," a.k.a. "Slipped My Mind." McDonald recalls: "One morning, I asked Norm what we should write about. He said, 'Why don't we write about that horrible thing you do to people? Remember when you promised you were going to tape that album for our editor Chris Cooper, but you still haven't. That was months ago.' I felt horrible about that, but I knew it was a funny premise, so we finished writing that one in half an hour. When I read out the catchphrases 'will do' and 'slipped my mind' in a kind of Paul Bellini voice, Norm laughed his head off."

While Mark McKinney's characters are indelibly woven into the television series, he claims to have actually written fewer sketches in the show than any of the other Kids in the Hall, but says he found Hiscock and McDonald to be "endlessly positive" influences on what sketches he managed to bring to the table. "I was probably the hardest to write with because I wasn't tremendously disciplined," says McKinney, "and I tended to judge an idea too early unless I could find the character in it."

According to McDonald, Scott Thompson proved himself as a writer when he and Bellini turned in "Girls of Summer," a kind of *A League of Their Own*–inspired sketch, in which Thompson played Buddy Cole as the coach of a lesbian softball team. "I didn't think the sketch would work at all," says McDonald. "All through the shoot, I was just terrible to Scott, telling him how horrible I thought the sketch was. To make matters worse, when the director of the piece, Stephen Surjik, showed us the final cut, none of us laughed."

Everything changed when "Girls of Summer" was screened for the studio audience at the next live taping. It killed, receiving more laughs than any other film they presented that night. As the audience howled in their seats,

McDonald laughed too, and came to the realization that he'd been wrong about Thompson's range and writing abilities. "I had pigeonholed Scott as just a Buddy Cole monologue guy," McDonald admits, "but he was as much a writer as any of us."

But while Buddy Cole may have been his most identifiable character, Thompson expresses a strong affinity for his straitlaced Danny Husk, who'd been introduced in a season one sketch called "Anecdote."

"Dave was convinced that I'd be a really good at playing a straight man," says Thompson, "so I just went into a Danny voice and said, 'Do you mean like this? Well, Dave, I'm just going to stand over there.' I had Danny simply narrate whatever he was doing. Danny may not be the smartest or the bravest, but he's a very decent man. I'm not mocking him; in fact, none of the Kids in the Hall ever really judged *any* of our characters."

Among Thompson's most ambitious Danny Husk sketches was the filmed segment "Kidnapped," which he wrote up with Bellini, Foley, and Hartt. Directed by Michael Kennedy and filmed on location at Toronto's Union Station, the scene focused on a surreal kidnapping plot packed with some absurdist touches — he had to pay his own ransom in two-dollar bills from an ATM — topped off with a fantasy ending sequence where Husk takes flight. "That was such a beautifully shot film," says Thompson. "I wanted Danny flying at the end because it seemed like a really funny way to end the scene; 'Danny's free. He can fly!' I really love it when reality sometimes just goes outside of reality."

TWELVE

Hazy Movies

While Hiscock, Bellini, and Hartt proved an obvious boon to the writing of the show, director John Blanchard and production manager Cindy Park brought dramatic improvements to the overall production values of *The Kids in the Hall*. The five members still had the final say, but they grew increasingly comfortable with delegating control to Blanchard, and allowing Park to enlist a rotating crew of superb film directors, including Stephen Surjik, Michael Kennedy, and Kelly Makin, plus go-to cinematographer David Makin, who was particularly skilled at making 16mm look artsy and moody. "Cindy knew the world of location shoots and was one of the few people who knew how to communicate with all five of us," says McKinney. "She brought in these guys who could really do stuff on film, so they became our rock-steady teddies."

While the quality of the film pieces had drastically improved from the grainy and raw look of the first season's

"Head Crusher" films, Bruce McCulloch was wary that the show might become too slick. In particular, he strongly objected when Park brought in a director from the world of TV commercials to give their filmed opening credit sequence a dramatic makeover for season three. "This guy had done the Black Label beer ads," says McCulloch, preferring not to name names, "and his new intro depicted us at a cool party somewhere, which I thought was something that *Saturday Night Live* would do; not us. We don't go to cool parties in limos. We're not the coolest guys in the room; we're the losers."

McCulloch reluctantly agreed to the new opening of the show, but after that one season, he successfully lobbied for a return to a more vérité look for the remainder of the series.

In hindsight, the choice of a beer commercial director seems especially ironic, given the pain and suffering most of the Kids had experienced as the children of alcoholic parents. Subsequently, drunk dads became a frequent theme in their work, perhaps nowhere more literally than in "Daddy Drank" and "Girl Drink Drunk," both of which were the product of McDonald's reaction to his father's alcohol abuse. The experience had so negatively impacted McDonald that he didn't have his first drink until he was twenty-seven years old. The occasion occurred after a dismal performance in Calgary had left a black cloud over the troupe. McKinney suggested that he and McDonald escape to a nearby bar for a nightcap. "The only place open late was this gay bar with hardly anybody in it," remembers McDonald, "except for this guy mumbling something about suicide. Mark looked around, smiled, and said, 'Tonight, you will have your *first drink.*' Then he said, 'Have a margarita. You'll like it. It tastes just like candy.' Later, when we were looking for ideas for the show, that became the key line in our scene 'Girl Drink Drunk.'"

McDonald admits that "Daddy Drank" was practically a verbatim retelling of his father's drunken provocations, which had triggered gales of uncontrollable laughter from Foley and Hiscock, who encouraged him to write up the scene. "I was a chubby, shy kid, and my dad was well aware that I didn't have any girlfriends. One day, when I came home from school and he was already drunk, he said, 'Hey, Kevin, how many girls called you today? Zero? Right, right. How many girls called you yesterday? Zero? Right. You know what zero times zero equals, dontcha? Fag!' It's kind of a classic joke, even though he was just being mean. I was so hurt that I didn't think it was funny until days later. Then it made me laugh. A lot. In fact, it's safe to say I'm probably a comedian today because of my dad, although I eventually had to go to Al-Anon meetings to really explore the damage it had done to my psyche."

At the Al-Anon meetings, McDonald became aware of his tendency to be a "people pleaser," which is a common trait with the children of alcoholics. Another common trait is overpromising but underdelivering, something McDonald knew all too well as the "King of Empty Promises." Yet, even at Al-Anon, McDonald found ideas for comedy sketches. Feeling increasingly uncomfortable with the tendency of his fellow survivors to blame every problem they'd ever had in their lives on their alcoholic parents, he was inspired to write a scene about self-empowerment called "Freak," framing boundary issues within the world of a circus freak show. "I played a guy whose freak talent was that he could make himself have a nosebleed at will," says McDonald, "only now, after therapy, he was trying to establish boundaries, so he would refuse to make his nose bleed to please others."

McDonald's scene required a variety of circus freaks to populate the scene, so other cast members were encouraged to come up with freak talents of their own. In the process, another hit character was born. "I wanted Mark to play another little silly freak," says McDonald, "so I asked Mark and Bruce for a freaky talent that was still very silly. At one point, fending off some taunting from the freaks, I improvised, 'Go see the Chicken Lady. She's an emotional dependent; she'll lay her eggs at the drop of a hat.'"

In McDonald's first draft, the Chicken Lady is only referred to in passing, but Bruce McCulloch suggested that it might be funnier if they actually *showed* the Chicken Lady. McKinney agreed and volunteered to take on one of his most well-known Kids in the Hall roles. "I was all into being this half-chicken, half-lady," says McKinney, "so Geri and I just played around with her costume until we found it, discussing just how gnarled her feet should be. We knew she had chicken breasts so she had to have big tits, but we didn't want to show them."

Once inside Wraith's costume, McKinney's Chicken Lady came to life. "Mark's a method actor, like Marlon Brando or Robert De Niro," says McDonald, "only with Mark it's in the service of sketch comedy."

After getting comfortable with the physical aspects of

Chicken Lady's oversized, permed wig, which bounced to accentuate her lumpy strut, McKinney struggled to find the perfect voice for his creation. "She had to be shrill and needy, and the costume sort of asked me, 'What would this person sound like?' Then all this shit started coming out about her being blindly horny, and we were off."

Chicken Lady was an instant hit, and McKinney would go on to write many memorable scenes for her. Yet as madcap as she was, there was an air of melancholy frustration to her attempts at intimacy — that same sadness that lurked below the surface in practically every scene the Kids in the Hall ever wrote. Where McDonald and Foley tended to mine it for comic twists, McKinney and McCulloch were more surreal in their comedy, subversively aiming barbs at authority in often poetic or obtuse ways. By way of example, McKinney offers the short "It's a Fact!" films, starring twelve-year-old Jessica Shifman, which he says were his reaction to the tendency of politicians and advertisements to offer up "facts" supported with little or no proof. "What could be more evil," asks McKinney, "than having this smiling red-haired child tell the boldest possible lies she could get away with?"

Similarly, in "The Cops," McKinney and McCulloch found themselves in police costumes for another sketch ("On the Run"), when their uniforms inspired them to start improvising. "We riffed on being these two dunderheaded and nameless cops trying to manoeuvre through life and understand things that they're really too square to get," says McKinney. "I think it's funny that they are two decidedly *Canadian* policemen, always trying to do things by the book."

Comedian Fred Armisen was watching the series from the U.S. and found "The Cops" to be highly instructional. "They exposed me to another side of Canada," says Armisen. "Those running bits with the Cops seemed so foreign to me. It was a real education in terms of revealing the Canadian psyche."

Over the next two seasons, the Cops became a dependable gag they could return to time after time, and a cheap and easy way to inject interstitial continuity and silliness into an eclectic running order. But after a while, the Cops' ubiquity became a sore spot with Thompson, and he and Foley answered with a two-hander street series of their own, "The Hookers." "I wasn't a huge fan of the Cops and they knew it," says Thompson bluntly. "It became a sort of running joke with us. Mark and Bruce were always mocking me, saying 'Look, we got ten more Cops pieces in the show.'"

"The Hookers" centred on Thompson's female sex worker Mordred and her French-Canadian coworker Jocelyn, played by Foley, who Thompson acknowledges was the "pretty one."

"Dave is blessed with these androgynous features that work," says Thompson, "and when he'd walk out as Jocelyn, it caused a lot of homosexual panic in the straight men in the crew, who would be like, 'Damn!' and 'I'd hit that.' And I agree, he's hot! He really is. So, I think that's very transgressive. That must have thrilled his punk heart, even though there's not a gay bone in Dave's body. But just look at him as Jocelyn in the Bauer scene 'In Search of Pot.' He's unreal-looking."

The Cops and the Hookers joined a small roster of recurring Kids characters, like McKinney's Mr. Tyzik and Thompson's Buddy Cole. Another of these was Thompson's Queen, who had first appeared in one of McKinney and Hiscock's "It's a Fact" shorts. "I was always talking about my mum's obsession with Queen Elizabeth and the royal family," says Thompson, "and then Mark said, 'You know, you look kind of like her.' I hadn't seen it until I stepped out of the makeup trailer made up as the Queen and everybody gasped."

Just as the Cops were distinctly Canadian peace officers, Thompson believes that Canada's long-standing ties to the royals informed his characterization of the Queen. "The real Queen was literally on our money, so you would see her every single day of your life. I really do have deep feelings for this woman I've never met, and when she dies, I will absolutely be moved. That said, I think *my* Queen is a little insane. In the "It's a Fact" scene, my Queen throws the little red-haired girl off a pier. I gave her a real barbarism and a violent streak."

Bruce McCulloch also found a recurring character in his uncharacteristically whimsical Flying Pig, which he dreamed up one day while lining up at an ATM in Toronto. "Sometimes, when I was stuck for an idea, I'd ask myself, 'What's the dumbest thing that could happen?' The notion of a flying pig entertaining the bank machine lineup was a really dumb idea for a sketch, so I went ahead and wrote four of them."

Foley and McDonald came up with recurring characters of their own, including Sir Simon Milligan and Hecubus, which McDonald says were inspired by his days with Thompson and Foley in the Second City Touring Company. "We had been walking to rehearsal, and Scott had just told us about how his roommate had come home and walked in on him masturbating. Dave said, 'Oh, you have demons, Scott,' and then it became a conversation about our demons. When they got to me, I told them that I have polite demons, like a demon that would open a door for a lady carrying too many parcels. A lot of this became the verbatim dialogue for 'The Pit of Ultimate Darkness,' which we wrote up the next time Mark and Bruce came back from *Saturday Night Live* to do a Rivoli show."

Scott Thompson's growing identity as the openly gay Kid in the Hall left him at times feeling both typecast as a "gay actor" by the industry at large, and resentful that his own community had not really endorsed him or his troupe as he felt they should have. This dilemma inspired a sketch called "Scott's Not Gay Anymore," in which Thompson stuns his fellow Kids by coming out as a heterosexual man. The sketch poked fun at the attention given to Thompson's sexuality by showing the other four guys not only accepting him as a gay man, but actively exploiting it. "When I tell them I'm straight, the four of them start saying 'Oh my god, you're our cash cow. You can't be straight now!' Having a gay man in the troupe got a lot of press at the time because it was such an odd thing for a person to be openly gay in culture back then."

The sketch also parodied a backlash from certain critics

within the LGBTQ community who complained that Thompson's Buddy character perpetuated an effeminate stereotype of gay men. Paul Bellini disagreed with the backlash, and lamented that Thompson put up with "a lot of bullshit" over it. "He'd agree to appear at fundraisers, only to be treated horribly," says Bellini. "What they didn't see was that Buddy was an alpha male with an effeminate bent, which was an entirely new take on it. Buddy Cole had the whimsy of Bugs Bunny, but there was some real gravitas underneath it. *Xtra!* newspaper wrote a scathing review of Scott, so he sent them a Polaroid of himself reading a parody magazine called *Xcrete!* The feud got really mean, and we rarely got a good mention from the gay press, except in the very first year when *The Advocate* ran a long feature about Scott with photos and everything."

Gay culture influenced the Kids in the Hall in many less obvious ways. If the troupe ever had a mascot, it was surely the image of Paul Bellini wearing nothing but a white terry-cloth towel. According to Bellini, the "Man in the Towel" came to be after McKinney had been peppering him with questions about the Toronto gay bathhouse scene. "Mark's way of writing," says Bellini, "was that you would spend hours talking and eating and doing everything but writing. I happened to tell Mark that I had just been to a bathhouse on Bay Street called the Romans. He asked me what happens in those places, so I told him that you put all your clothes in a locker, and you walk around in a towel past all these other towel-clad men, waiting for magic to happen. Mark started to laugh hysterically, so I said, 'What's so funny?' He said, 'The image of you walking down a hallway wearing a towel, peeking into these rooms, is so funny.'"

When producer Jeffrey Berman suggested that the troupe come up with a prize for a viewers' contest, McKinney joked that they should send out Bellini in a towel. "The room burst out laughing," says Bellini, "then everyone looked at me, asking me if I'd do it. Now, I'm notoriously shy about my body, but I knew it would make me famous, and maybe that would help me get laid. So, that afternoon Norm went to Withrow Park with me and took pictures of me in the towel."

The recurring Bellini contests were a major success, and as a mythology grew around the "Man in the Towel," he began to appear in other sketches, including McCulloch's "Bellini Day" where an entire family celebrates the god Bellini.

"I did a couple of live appearances," says Bellini, "where the place would go ballistic, like a fire had just broken out! This weird little element from the TV show had become real."

When he wasn't disrobing for the troupe, a fully clothed Bellini worked closely with Thompson on "Hazy Movie," the cinematic scene that introduced the world to Thompson's fiercest lady yet, Francesca Fiore, and her partner in crime, Bruno Puntz Jones, played by Foley. According to Thompson, the sketch had been influenced by another big part of Toronto culture at the time, an abundance of cinemas. "I'd probably just seen two films back to back," says Thompson. "In Toronto back then, you could see a goofy American action film then go around the corner to see some high-art, European thing. So I wondered, 'What if one movie invaded the other?' I based Francesca on my Brazilian boyfriend at the time, Satranga. We had thrown a 'genderfuck party,' where everyone came as the opposite sex, so I hired Geri and Judi from the show to make everybody up as their opposite sex. I got Francesca's wig, the polka dots, and the pantsuit and all that, and when I started imitating Satranga's accent, I created this tough-as-nails woman from a *favela* somewhere in South America. I was vague about where exactly in South America because at the time I could never do a specific accent, so sometimes she was from Belize, other times Paraguay or Brazil. But it all makes sense because she's an international woman of mystery and glamour."

The name for Dave Foley's character "Bruno Puntz Jones" was the result of a computer glitch when he and Bellini were playing on the computer and somehow the name appeared. Foley gave Bruno a world-weary European voice, pitched somewhere between the Italian actor Marcello Mastroianni and the British screen idol Ronald Colman. "The two of them were tragic, doomed, almost Goth characters, obsessed with death and murder," says Thompson. "They carried themselves like B-movie stars but there was also this vague idea that Francesca was a whore and Bruno was her boyfriend-slash-partner-slash-pimp."

While they embraced many diverse influences and ideas in their comedy, the core of the Kids in the Hall was always suburban life. The collective memories of kitchen-table arguments and teenage rebellion inspired many of their best sketches, from "Salty Ham" (Gordon and Fran were based on McCulloch's and Thompson's parents) to "Bobby and the Devil" and "Ham of Truth," which channelled their younger selves. In "Bobby and the Devil," the Devil becomes fixated on stealing Bobby's guitar prowess in a scene loosely inspired by the Ralph Macchio film *Crossroads*. Geri Wraith put hours into giving McKinney's Devil a subterranean yet suburban Goth look, modelled ever-so-slightly on Canadian rocker Kim Mitchell. "Back in the '80s, the rock guitar solo was still god, culturally," remembers McKinney. "So in my scene, the Devil was this really, really stupid guy who can't beat a fifteen-year-old in a guitar duel, which is exactly the kind of myth a stoned fifteen-year-old might come up with. I also loved the part where my lovely, double-necked guitar gets transformed into a timid little ukulele, and I get to cry out 'Useless!'"

The struggles of suburban life also inspired McCulloch and Hartt's scenes featuring the relentlessly optimistic and credit-conscious basement band "Rod Torfulson's Armada featuring Herman Menderchuk." According to Kevin McDonald, the band dynamic was an inside joke referring to their troupe's early days at the Rivoli. "On show days, or rehearsals, I'd say, 'OK, we're meeting at one o'clock. Come having eaten.' Most of us would come having eaten, except for Scott and Dave, who'd come an hour late, and say 'We can't start yet. We're hungry. We've got to go eat.'"

"Scott, maybe more than anyone, would live on a half-box of macaroni and cheese or something like that," says McKinney. "So scenes like that, or the one where Bruce and I sing, 'Hodie oten doten day, fattening up our tapeworms,' were just a nod of the hat to the poverty and shittiness of those hungry times."

Bruce McCulloch, who played Rod Torfulson, says the Kids shared the central question on the minds of the Armada, "Do we make it?" "Without question, we're playing weird, rockband versions of ourselves. Kevin is the guy who writes all the songs, but his name is not on the band, even though he works the hardest. Without question, for me the fun of that was being able to do 'band politics,' because the Kids in the Hall were and are a rock band of comedy. I'm obsessed with band politics, how rock bands work, and how they can't rehearse until the other guy comes, and the bass player just wants to play the bass. So I got to do both things."

As season three hummed along, *The Kids in the Hall* was becoming one of the CBC's most prestigious programs and a glittering example of the kind of fresh Canadian content Ivan Fecan had wanted to bring to the taxpayer-funded airwaves. "We felt that as public broadcasters, there should be stuff on our air for younger people too," says Fecan. "And I was very fortunate that I had bosses who would support me in doing what was, for the CBC, very controversial material at the time. It was a good risk, though; it really paid off for everybody involved, from the Kids to the broadcasters. I'm very proud of that period."

But not every Canadian shared Fecan's sensibilities. As the Kids' exposure grew alongside their popularity, bags of hate mail began arriving at the CBC's headquarters, largely from disgruntled taxpayers with buyer's remorse. For Mark McKinney, the outrage over what some critics called "filth" on the people's airwaves was too rich a comic target to resist. His reply was an audacious scene called "Screw You, Taxpayer!"

"I thought we could put a shiny smile on it," says McKinney, "so we wanted to make this crude and vulgar scene, and just get right in your face about the fact that Canadian taxpayers were paying for all of this absurd comedy, whether they liked it or not."

The sketch opens with an over-the-top scene-within-a-scene that is tasteless, racist, and intentionally offensive. Before long, McKinney breaks character, crossing the fourth wall to gloat at how the best part was that you, the Canadian taxpaying viewer, had underwritten the entire distasteful enterprise. "The big payoff for me," recalls McDonald, "was when Mark rallies the whole studio audience to shout 'Screw you, taxpayer!' in unison at the camera. It was brilliant."

As if to prove the Kids could do no wrong at the national broadcaster, the CBC aired the sketch with no strings attached. The only resistance came from south of the border, where HBO refused to air it due to the extremely offensive nature of the material, not to mention that the taxpayer premise was entirely lost on the American audience.

But HBO's refusal to air "Screw You Taxpayer" was the least of the Kids' worries. By the end of their third season, the Kids had run out of second chances. HBO's subscriber base was largely coming to the channel for pay-per-view boxing matches, stand-up specials, and commercial-free movies, and many at the channel remained unconvinced that they should be in the sketch comedy business. The decision to pass on a fourth season was based on simple economics. "We had to think about how much money we could realistically invest in original sketch comedy shows," says Carolyn Strauss. "That said, for me personally, working with the Kids in the Hall was a fantastic experience that showed me the path you could go on to make great television."

While the show would go on thanks to an unwavering commitment from Ivan Fecan and the CBC ("*Thank* you, taxpayer!"), the Kids were back where they started after season one — with no American coproducer to shore up their production budget. The Kids in the Hall were left asking a very Armada question: "Do we make it?"

THIRTEEN

The CBS Years (1993–95)

As a concession to some of the Canadian taxpayer complaints, Ivan Fecan made a significant adjustment to the CBC broadcast schedule in time for the fourth season of *The Kids in the Hall*. He split his prime-time programming into two blocks: "family" prime, from 7 p.m. to 9 p.m., followed by "adult" prime, which ran (after the *CBC News* at 9) from 10 p.m. to midnight. This simple move created a safe zone for potentially controversial and uncensored comedy programs like *The Larry Sanders Show, Codco, This Hour Has 22 Minutes,* and *The Kids in the Hall.* "It allowed a whole generation of Canadians to be exposed to material that may not have been suitable for family viewing," says Fecan.

Not only were his instincts correct, but in the mind of Dave Foley, the decision to air uncensored episodes continues to have a lasting impact on the show in syndication. "Thanks to Ivan, we now have an uncensored version of every episode," says Foley, "which is nice because now, those uncensored versions are the version of record for posterity."

Freedom was one thing, but the Kids would also need money if they were to keep the show's increasingly cinematic production values up to their high standards. CBC could never offer the kind of budget they'd received from HBO. So once more, Lorne Michaels, ever the gentleman hustler, went cap in hand to a succession of American networks in search of a suitable partner. After rejecting a low bid from MTV, he arrived on the doorstep of Rod Perth, Vice President of Late Night at CBS. As it happened, 1993 was a crucial time for CBS, which had once been nicknamed "the Tiffany network" in reference to the perceived high quality of its programs during the tenure of visionary former chairman William S. Paley. In 1990, Paley passed away, and by 1993, CBS was struggling; its late-night lineup was in particular disarray after their much-hyped *Pat Sajak Show* had failed to perform against the syndicated juggernaut that was *The Arsenio Hall Show*. CBS had caught wind of the open secret going around the television industry that the reigning champion of late night, Johnny Carson, was about to step down from NBC's *The Tonight Show*. All three major networks scrambled to step in and fill the void that would be left in Carson's absence, and CBS began to court Lorne Michaels in the hopes he might bring his expertise and his talent roster to create a hit flagship late-night show and put some new polish on the old Tiffany network.

Rod Perth's assistant at the time, Dorian Hannaway, recalls that CBS was eager to try anything to become relevant in late night. "We pictured Lorne bringing in some-body like Bill Murray to host at 11:30 p.m.," says Hannaway, "but in the meantime, we also needed something to go in at 12:30. We tried a lot of different people there, like Bill Maher, Wil Shriner, and even Rush Limbaugh, but nothing was working."

As a goodwill gesture to Michaels, CBS offered to take *The Kids in the Hall* off his hands, slotting them in on Friday nights at 12:30 p.m. Rod Perth enlisted Hannaway to review previous seasons of the show, and assess what it was they had taken on. Hannaway says she was pleasantly surprised by the quality of the work. "The show was wonderful," remembers Hannaway. "So I said, 'I love them. Let me have this.' I knew comedy, so I knew I could work with the Kids."

Hannaway was given full responsibility for the laborious task of culling the best sketches from the previous three seasons and blending them into newer episodes as they were produced. "The Kids had already been on HBO and CBC for three years, so I had to go through three seasons of tapes. I remember we had a CBC cut and an HBO cut, so it was kind of a logistical nightmare because they're so damn polite up there in Canada, they just let the Kids get away with anything. First, I cut together three years of shows, and we ran it as a one-hour special to showcase the Kids in prime time. From then on, we would intermingle half an hour of their HBO shows with half an hour of their new shows for CBS."

For Hannaway, this massive chore became a labour of love and a bona fide career opportunity. "Nobody at CBS wanted to do all that work, so Rod let me supervise the show and, lucky me, it became my first big chance to get involved in a show. I had been a comedy writer and worked on comedy series, so I knew comedy at least, and I was able to work with them, Jeff Ross, and John Blanchard. They were all wonderful to work with because they were so prolific and so unique and so crazy."

While Hannaway was busy with the assembly of the show, Perth went about promoting their new acquisition to CBS affiliates and the press. "My teenagers think they're killer-funny," Perth told the *L.A. Times'* Jane Hall, adding that he was confident his network finally had a hip comedy program with the same broad demographic appeal as NBC's *Saturday Night Live*. Overall, the *Times'* piece presented a unified and optimistic front, but in one of the later paragraphs, a more cautious Scott Thompson expressed his concern over whether or not CBS would ultimately let the Kids be the Kids.

"We're not dirty, but, I think, in a way, we're subversive," Thompson warned, adding that such disruptive comedy might be threatening to the suits back at CBS's New York headquarters. "But the CBS executives seem to want to push the envelope of late-night TV. Hopefully, we'll be writing some stuff that will make them lose some sleep."

The Kids in the Hall arrived at CBS during a time of seismic upheaval in late night. In January of '93, the network announced that that they had also signed David Letterman to host *The Late Show* in the coveted 11:30 p.m. slot, beginning that summer. The troupe was thrilled to have Letterman as their lead-in on Friday nights, but they soon discovered that many of the CBS affiliates were opting out of running them at 12:30, choosing instead to bury their show deep in the middle of their overnight schedule, a place where infomercials and insomniacs typically dwell.

"American network affiliates have real power" says Foley, "which is why you have to do things like 'the upfronts' to charm them. In our case, I assume the affiliates thought our show was too offensive and, who knows, maybe too gay."

Before the start of season four, Jeff Biederman replaced Jeff Ross, who left *The Kids in the Hall* to head up another of Lorne Michaels's properties, *Late Night with Conan O'Brien.* O'Brien's sidekick on the new show was Andy Richter, an improv comedian who had travelled to New York from Chicago, where he had performed at ImprovOlympic Theater and Annoyance Theater. It was there that he first saw *The Kids in the Hall* on television.

"I was a big fan," recalls Richter. "They were funny and very unique, and seemed to be an organic group, like Python. And they wrote wonderfully subversive sketches that made a point. But first and foremost they were funny, which is a very difficult thing to pull off. 'Chicken Lady' was one of my first favourites, and it still is, just because of its wonderful weirdness and subversion of sexual desire."

Since *Late Night* and *The Kids in the Hall* were both Broadway Video productions, it was perhaps inevitable that Richter was introduced to the Kids at an *SNL* after-party at Rockefeller Center in the fall of 1993. "I was very excited to meet them," says Richter, "although I was still a little too shy at first. We eventually became good friends, and over the years Conan would invite members of the troupe to come on to do comedy pieces for our show."

Meanwhile, back in Toronto, the Kids got back to creating what would be their final two seasons. During this time, the writers' room expanded yet again. Norm Hiscock had been named supervising head writer in a room that featured some of their favourite writers from other troupes, including Dan Redican from The Frantics and Andy Jones from *Codco*. "We were in awe of Andy from watching him in the *Codco* days," says McKinney, "and he's just insanely creative."

Significantly, they also hired their first female writer, Diane Flacks, a twenty-seven-year-old solo performer who was a friend of Brian Hartt, and had already appeared as "the girl" in a few sketches, including "Girl Drink Drunk" and "King of Empty Promises."

"They were so respectful and easy to work with," remembers Flacks, "and they were fall-down funny. They made everyone who did a small part on the show feel welcome, like they were happy to have us there. I never had to 'womansplain' anything to them, and I loved the way they played women. I'm an unrelenting feminist; so trust me when I say that, with the Kids, none of us pulled any punches in the pursuit of truth and comedy. Scott and I were instantly sympatico on the outsider political level. Nothing is sacred to him and he has a big, brave heart; I *love* that. Mark is just a fascinating genius, kind and lovely, and I was floored by Bruce's brilliance and still am. His comedy voice *kills* me."

Another new (old) face in the writers' room was Garry Campbell, a founding member of The Audience who had since gone on to his own career writing for television. For Campbell, the reunion was as much social as it was professional, and he was thrilled to be hanging out with his old friends again. "We'd write for a couple of hours, then maybe go to a movie or go for a drink," says Campbell, "but somehow the show still got written."

Norm Hiscock's main task as head writer was to take all the written sketches, including both film and in-studio scenes, and stitch together a cohesive and funny running order to produce an episode that gave equal screen time to all five Kids. Looking back, Hiscock compares his work on the show to the making of a great mixtape. "I experimented with themes to link all the sketches together. Like, one show was all sketches with a 'justice' theme, linked by some interstitial 'Cops' scenes. But there were also themes like family, suburban life, or businessmen that were built into most of the scenes anyway. I'd stare at the cards on the board and try to figure out how to connect them all. I kept a lot of lists."

Hiscock's lists inspired a scene called "Things to Do," in which McDonald plays a man so obsessed with his Things to Do lists, that he is oblivious to being kidnapped during a bank robbery. McDonald admits that director Kelly Makin modelled the bank sequence on Quentin Tarantino's then-recent hit *Reservoir Dogs*. "A few years after our sketch aired, Dave was in a restaurant in Hollywood when Quentin Tarantino came in. He took one look at Dave and said, 'I saw that "Things to Do" sketch. That was a *Dogs* thing, right?' Tarantino saw a sketch of ours, so I can cross that one off my bucket list."

Having famous directors as fans seemed fitting since each of the Kids spent so much time at the movies, and in the later seasons of the show, the sketches were becoming increasingly cinematic. Pieces like "Love and Sausages" from season four and "The Beard" from season five were both based on Hiscock's ideas. He had originally imagined Kevin McDonald for "Sausages" and Bruce McCulloch for "The Beard," but neither scene had set the room on fire when he read them out to the troupe. McCulloch, however, saw potential in "Sausages," and asked Hiscock if he could rewrite it for himself, offering "The Beard" to McDonald.

McCulloch's vision for "Love and Sausages" was far darker than anything Hiscock had imagined, resembling something close to David Lynch's *Eraserhead*. The most expensive and polarizing mini-movie ever shot for the show, the film may have been long on artistic production values, but it was decidedly short on laughs. The Kids were even divided over whether it was wise to devote an entire episode of a comedy program to such bleakness, but when director John Blanchard expressed his desire to axe the piece, the troupe rallied around it. "The more John was against it," says McDonald, "the more Dave and I began to take Bruce and Mark's side. I'm really glad we did. I think it was important for the show."

Scott Thompson drew upon all of his dramatic acting chops to bring a jarring realism to the drooling old grandfather whose cries of "Sausages! Sausages!" became a defining element of the piece. "I only had that one word of dialogue," says Thompson, "so for me it was all about finding that old man voice, yelling '*Sass*-ages,' with just a touch of an East Coast accent. I wanted him to be this drooling, disgusting, and terrifying old man who suffered from dementia, so I asked Geri and Judi to make me as old and decrepit as they could. That makeup and hair was one of their greatest jobs on the whole series. Geri's little boy was so terrified he wouldn't come near me."

On set, both Thompson and McCulloch earned a round of applause from the crew. But while "Love and Sausages" was a beautiful piece of film, the final cut was controversially long, and the entire enterprise had become outrageously expensive. While McCulloch feels unjustly singled out for the indulgences of "Love and Sausages," he believes it was worth the money for Thompson's performance alone. "I loved Eastern European films," says McCulloch, "so yes, I was happy to do all this weirder shit with my clackers and my Communist beard. But it was always a question of how much of the budget resources should go to one person's scene. It wasn't all my fault: Kelly and Norm fell in love with the scene, and even our editor, Chris Cooper, kept saying 'It's seventeen minutes long but I can't think of anything to cut.' I knew the troupe was going to fucking kill me, so I fought hard to get it to a place where it was fun but not as indulgent."

While CBS aired a truncated version of "Love and Sausages," the network generally honoured the Kids' creative vision. Still, Kevin McDonald found it ironic that CBS, who aired the show late at night, "bleeped" them far more than CBC ever did in prime time. "We were on at three in the morning in most places around the U.S.," says McDonald, "but somehow we had more censor problems than we'd ever had before. I remember gently fucking with them in a scene that started with 'Now that the Kids in the Hall are on CBS, these are the kind of scenes you can expect.' And I wrote 'What If Tarzan Got an Office Job?' which was like a really square *Carol Burnett Show* idea. Now, I actually liked *Carol Burnett*, but this was a way of saying *'The Kids in the Hall* will no longer be edgy.' Scott probably has a different point of view on this, but I mostly remember Dorian Hannaway sticking up for us against the network."

Hannaway acknowledges that CBS's Program Practices department was often too quick to shut down borderline edgy material. "CBS was for old people and their parents at the time," she says, laughing. "I remember thinking, 'Why would you buy *The Kids in the Hall* if you didn't want an edgy show?' But I loved them, their comedy was so smart, and I always think that if you can make people laugh, you can do almost anything you want."

Bellini and Thompson tested the patience of the censors on both sides of the border with an episode-long Buddy Cole Christmas special called "Chalet 2000," which was populated by an array of beloved *Kids in the Hall* characters, including Thompson's Queen, who memorably engages in a sexual romp with Canada's national animal, the Beaver, played by a furry McCulloch.

"I loved that the Queen's sexuality was completely awoken by the beaver," says Thompson, with a mischievous grin, "and that Bruce and I exchanged tongue kisses. I was like, 'How fucking subversive are we? I'm a gay man playing the Queen, making out with a straight man dressed as a beaver. A sovereign making out with *the* Canadian animal.' I think the beaver represented, I guess, Canada's primal nature itself. She's England, and Canada's the beast, the untamed wild. Yeah, that's it."

As madcap as the scene was, Kevin McDonald felt that "Chalet 2000" was a noble but ultimately failed attempt that was too much of a solo vehicle for Buddy Cole. "Sure, Scott was gracious enough to write us all into it, and there was some funny stuff, like Norm playing Santa Claus, who had been in a gay relationship with Buddy but they had split up. But we probably should have picked an idea that all five of us could have worked on together."

Similarly, Mark McKinney was the dominant force behind the futuristically glam "Sex Girl Patrol," in which he played multiple roles, including one of the three titular love commandos. McKinney's Monique was joined by McCulloch as Trudie and Foley as Ginger. "Sex Girl Patrol" was a kind of parody of sexy sci-fi romps like Roger Vadim's *Barbarella*. The mini-movie in the sketch was set in the dawn of the third millennium when the forces of "sex negativity" have enslaved planet Earth. McCulloch remembers "Sex Girl Patrol" as an uncommonly developed and high-concept scene for McKinney, who typically preferred the macro focus of detailed character pieces. "But every so often," says McCulloch, "Mark would flex his muscles in a big, almost arrogant way, and he'd pitch a big, stylish piece with lots of costumes."

This time, it was Thompson's turn to take a backseat, and he recalls being outraged over not being cast as one of the three Sex Girls. "Here it was, one of the gayest sketches in our entire series, and they made me play the straight guy. I was one of the thugs working for the angry priest because the guys somehow needed to play these voluptuous women, and they were all 'This is our campy scene.' You can't imagine how upset I was."

"Love and Sausages," "Chalet 2000," and "Sex Girl Patrol" were ambitious sketches that showed how much the Kids had developed since their early cast scenes like "Reg" or "Naked for Jesus." But toward the end of the CBS years, their relentless search for boundary-stretching ideas began to take a toll on the troupe. To put it bluntly, they were exhausted. Dave Foley admits that a few of his later scenes, such as "Quarter-Life Crisis" and "Anal Probing Aliens," were thinly veiled references to job dissatisfaction. "A lawyer quits his job to become a fireman," says Foley, "or an anal probing alien asks 'Why are we doing this? We've been coming here and giving these anal probes and the only thing we've learned is that one out of ten doesn't seem to mind.' The whole scene was a metaphor for the routine of making the show. That was how I felt about it at the time."

As season four came to a close, Kevin McDonald recalls thinking that it was time to return to live studio sketches. "Every one of us considered season four to be a great film year. But that was the worst year for live studio audience sketches. It seemed easier to write films, where you could just cut to reactions and control everything—all of that film stuff. We had almost forgotten how to write live sketches, which are almost like small one-act plays with a beginning, middle, and end. Those are harder to write, especially when you're having such a wonderful time writing and performing the films. So, at the beginning of season five, I remember we talked about it—it was like one of those movies where the coach rallies the sports team, 'Try harder! Do it better!'—and we said, 'Why don't we write better live sketches? Yeah! Why don't we? We'll do just that.' So that's what we did in season five; we had a comeback, returning to the kind of live stuff we'd done on stage."

FOURTEEN

"We're Toast"

As the Kids in the Hall were entering production of their fifth season, their second with CBS, the land-scape of late-night television shifted once again. In 1994, CBS hired Tom Snyder to launch *The Late Late Show*, airing five nights a week at 12:30 a.m. While *The Kids in the Hall* would be allowed to finish its remaining season with the full support of the network, the move effectively meant that CBS was cancelling the series. "Frankly, I think the guys were surprised they had even been picked up for a second year with us," says Hannaway. "I'm sure Tom Snyder would have been thrilled to have Friday nights off, but the network wanted him on five nights a week, so there was no getting around that."

With CBS out of the picture, Lorne Michaels asked the troupe if it was worth having him search for yet another American copartner for a sixth season. In truth, there was interest from MTV, but by now the Kids were exhausted and mostly unified in their desire to quit while they were ahead. The lone dissenting opinion came from Mark McKinney, who admits that he would have been happy if they had stayed on the air indefinitely. "As sketch comedians and as character comedians, it was such a good outlet for us. I didn't quite understand why people wanted to stop at that moment."

Kevin McDonald recalls a lot of thought going into what would be in the series finale, which followed Foley and Thompson's theme of "Endings" as a way to grant some closure to a few of their favourite characters and scenes from the entire series. Thompson chose to have Buddy Cole say good-bye in a sketch called "Buddy's Bar Closes," wherein Buddy's Bar burns to the ground. Eagle-eyed fans noted that a photograph of Kurt Cobain, sent posthumously to Thompson by Nirvana's management after Cobain's death in April 1994, can be seen behind Buddy's bar as it goes up in flames.

Seeing as they were torching the whole series, Dave Foley thought it might be funny to present a series of completely fictitious sketches that were supposedly too hot for TV. "The premise," says Foley, "was that these were the sketches that were censored all these years, and since we're going off the air, we're going to show them to you now. Bruce's Cancer Boy was one of the characters in that. It seemed that cancer had come up in the series a lot, like in 'The Cause of Cancer,' where it turned out that it was Bruce who had caused cancer, so we didn't back away from that stuff."

Foley remembers after writing up "Things We Couldn't Show on TV," they received the funniest and most ironic network note of the series. "We'd written three shocking things like the baseball player getting pressure from a Cancer Boy or the soup that was clearly made out of jizz or shit or something, and then 'Hitler Fucks a Dead Donkey.' When John Blanchard came back from the censors, he said, 'Alright, here's the deal. Hitler can fuck the donkey, but the donkey has to be alive, and we have to see that the donkey is alive.' We laughed for about five minutes, then I said, 'OK, alright. How about this? Hitler fucks a pet donkey, and we'll have a little kid there asking his dad, 'Why is that bad man fucking my donkey?' He said, 'OK, that's fine.' And I said, 'This is way worse than what it was.' It was the best ever."

Bruce McCulloch is grateful that CBS let them finish season five. "I know so many people who've had the rug yanked out before they had a chance to end gracefully. So, while it was a little sad, I felt real closure. We could say good-bye to the series quietly — and by quietly, I mean, going out fucking a fake donkey, screaming and losing my voice as a bad version of Hitler."

Dave Foley suggested the final image in the series, a graveside scene with Paul Bellini's "Man in the Towel" shovelling on the dirt. "This little Italian man in a towel who usually says nothing is dancing on their grave," says Bellini, laughing. "Then I drop a lily and say 'Well, thank god *that's* over.'"

"I remember being out in the field in a deep hole," adds McDonald, "with Paul shovelling mud over us. I'm a little claustrophobic, so there was this combination of horror with the sadness that it really was the end."

Understandably, the last live taping of *The Kids in the*

Hall show before a studio audience was an emotionally charged affair for cast and crew alike. They had fought like dogs, and bonded like brothers, and now they were filming their final Cathy and Kathie scene, as the offices of A.T. & Love—the site of so many of the sketches—were preparing to go out of business forever. Before taping the scene, Kevin McDonald did what he had been doing since the tumultuous night when they had taped the pilot; he went into the men's room and peed in the sink.

"When we first started working at Mutual Street, we didn't have our own backstage washrooms," explains McDonald, "so we had to share the washroom with the audience members. After Lorne chewed us out for our dismal first run-through, we were so shaken that Scott and I wanted to do something symbolic that we'd never done before. So, we went to the washroom and we peed in the sink. After the second taping did well, we decided that, for the rest of the series, whenever we had a bad first show we would go pee in the sink. It became a superstitious ritual."

After presumably washing his hands, McDonald prepared the studio audience for the final A.T. & Love scene. "Before we started, we had made it very clear to the audience that this was our last ever full-cast scene," says McDonald. "I remember at the end, we all took our wigs off and we were all standing there in our dresses, with our wigs in our hands, crying as the audience gave us a standing ovation. Even Mark, the robot, was crying."

Standing arm in arm under the hot lights of CBC's Mutual Street studios, the Kids took a final bow and hugged each other as mascara ran down their cheeks. They scanned the studio floor to take in everyone who had worked on *The Kids in the Hall*, from the office staff to the crews, the producers to the Shadowy Men. In the end, says McDonald, their ragtag crew truly felt like a family. "Although, I think our crew was maybe even sadder than us because at least the troupe planned to work together again, so for us it wasn't good-bye for good."

The official *Kids in the Hall* wrap party was held at Toronto's now-defunct BamBoo Club on Queen Street West, four doors down from the Rivoli, where it had all begun. Each of the invited guests at the party received an engraved commemorative toaster bearing the message "*Kids in the Hall* (1989–94). We're toast."

"The toasters were Mark's idea," says McDonald, "and to this day if I'm ever in Toronto and run into old crew members, they'll inevitably tell me that they still have their toaster."

By all accounts it was one of the wildest soirees Toronto had ever seen, and one of only a handful of moments where all five Kids got together outside of work to take a collective victory lap.

"I remember Bruce saying that if we weren't a troupe, we'd all be his friends," says McDonald, "but since we were working together he didn't want to hang out with any of us. I know it sounds cold to say it, but it's true. With the demands of making a TV show, you'd see all those guys at the studio all the time anyway, so who needs to hang out after work?"

FIFTEEN

Critical Mass

With the television series now behind them, the five Kids in the Hall set their sights on new horizons. A feature-length movie felt like the logical next step. While writing and producing the final season of *Kids*, they had been jotting down possible film ideas in their notebooks. This was no mere pipe dream; Lorne Michaels had forged a production partnership with Paramount Pictures after the success of Mike Myers's *SNL* spin-off *Wayne's World*, and had used some of his newfound Hollywood clout to convince Paramount's John Goldwyn to do a modestly budgeted feature film with the Kids. Such was Myers's symbiotic relationship with the Kids that when he made *Wayne's World 2* in 1993, he hired director Stephen Surjik, who had shot many of the film pieces for *The Kids in the Hall*. Still, as the Kids prepared to enter the world of Hollywood, they afforded themselves a brief moment to take stock of what they had accomplished with the television series, and to bask in the praise of their peers.

In 1988, David Handelman had asked in *Rolling Stone* if American television was ready for *The Kids in the Hall* series. Looking back today, Handelman says he can answer his own question with a resounding *maybe*. "America was hungry for something good, that's for sure," says Handelman. "When the Kids first aired, there wasn't anything else like them, which was both great and slightly hard to overcome."

While the series may have only attained cult status during its original run, Handelman now views *The Kids in the Hall* as the historical bridge between *Monty Python's Flying Circus* and *Kids* contemporaries like *The State, Mr. Show with Bob & David, Exit 57*, and the *Upright Citizens Brigade*. This sturdy bridge has also provided a safe crossing for later series, such as *Broad City, Key & Peele*, and *Inside Amy Schumer*. In rock 'n' roll terms, he compared the Kids to a beloved cult rock band who became legendary even if nobody bought their records at the time. "Kevin once identified the Kids as the comedy equivalent of The Replacements," says Handelman, "another hugely influential band that hardly sold any records but all of the hip people knew and owned them. I agree with that."

Comedian and peer Dana Gould concurs with the cult band analogies, adding that the Kids sharply and perfectly distilled a generation. "If we're talking late-'70s British alternative pop, then the Kids in the Hall were The Jam," says Gould. "If we're talking American bands, they would be R.E.M."

Dave Foley admits that while it's great to hear such glowing praise from critics and peers, he and his fellow

Kids had an almost pathological aversion to basking in it. "It's not for us to say if we were groundbreaking or cutting-edge or not. That kind of thinking is the death of comedy." Modesty notwithstanding, the Kids were well aware that they had made an impression with their peers, particularly a few key players south of the Canadian border. Judd Apatow remained an ardent *Kids in the Hall* fan right up until the end of the series.

"Even in their last season," says Apatow, "when they were probably out of gas, they took it to another level that was even more creative. It got so hysterical because they just had to bust a wall down and find a new vein to mine."

The end of *The Kids in the Hall* opened a door for Bob Odenkirk and David Cross to finally get their shot, as HBO green-lit their series, *Mr. Show with Bob & David*, the following year. "I loved those guys," says Odenkirk. "They're all lively brains with funny characters and interesting voices. And they had a rare inertia and chemistry that was greater than the sum of its parts."

Canadian broadcaster George Stroumboulopoulos says he had never felt a connection with Canadian sketch comedy until *The Kids in the Hall* came along. "Most of what came before them was too colloquial and cute, but the Kids were right in your face. They talked about *my city*, and they were actually saying something very meaningful to my times."

Comedy historian Kliph Nesteroff, author of *The Comedians: Drunks, Thieves, Scoundrels, and the History of American Comedy*, grew up watching *The Kids in the Hall* in a small town in British Columbia where the CBC was the only broadcast signal in town. Nesteroff recalls vivid memories of his fellow high-school students re-enacting the Chicken Lady or crushing heads during their lunch hour. "Somehow, the subversive, gender-bending comedy of *The Kids in the Hall* was what unified the disparate elements of my high school. Nerds, jocks, hippies, cheerleaders, everyone. In Canada, they were brilliant without any contemporary, and they are easily the most influential comedians of my generation. We can argue without much straining that they are one of the greatest sketch troupes of all time."

Meanwhile in New York, Mike Myers recalls swelling with hometown pride whenever anyone told him how much they loved his friends, the Kids in the Hall. "Each season they had gone from strength to strength, and when all the cylinders were firing, they truly reached the level of comedy art."

For members of the NYU-based comedy troupe The State, the impact of the Kids in the Hall was bittersweet. "When *The State* came on MTV in the early '90s," says State member Thomas Lennon, "the first wave of response was that we were 'biting off *The Kids in the Hall.*' This was tough for us to deal with, because at the time, none of us were savvy enough to have actually seen their show. When we did see them, we discovered that they were one of the greatest sketch comedy groups of all time, and their work is as perfect today as it was the day they released it. I am inspired and jealous of their comedy even today, a quarter century later."

Meanwhile, Kevin McDonald remembers thinking that everything was going exactly as he had hoped, and that this critical mass would sustain the Kids into phase two of their master plan. "We always said we wanted to do it the way Monty Python did," says McDonald. "Five years on TV, then we were going to do a movie that was going to be a big hit. The idea was, we could go off and do our individual stuff for a while, then reconvene to do another movie every four years."

Their plan, of course, was entirely contingent upon their first film being a "big hit," and as they reconvened in the summer of 1994 to brainstorm movie ideas, nobody in the Kids in the Hall was quite sure how they were going to pull it off.

SIXTEEN

The Boardroom of Death: Writing Brain Candy

Despite cranking out season after season of television for the last five years — with no breaks — the Kids plunged headlong into writing and preproduction for a feature film just a few weeks after wrapping the series. In reality, the troupe was exhausted, and Mark McKinney, who was about to join the cast of *Saturday Night Live* along with Norm Hiscock as a writer, remembers asking Michaels in confidence if making a feature film was their wisest move at that time. "Lorne," says McKinney, launching into his best Michaels impression, "said something like 'Well, you've got to strike while the iron's hot.'"

Dave Foley had a young family at home, and was also eager to take a short hiatus from the troupe to explore his options in Hollywood. "We had one child," says Foley, "and another on the way, and all of my money from *The Kids in the Hall* was running out." In 1994, he landed a costarring role in Julia Sweeney's SNL spin-off, *It's Pat,* and he signed on to do a CBS pilot called *Mr. Fuller.* Then came a call from former *Larry Sanders Show* writer and producer Paul Simms, who said he had created a new sitcom set inside a radio station that included a role tailor-made for Foley. To Foley, *NewsRadio* seemed like a dream gig. "This show was going to be directed by the legendary Jimmy Burrows, and I'd be working alongside the great Phil Hartman. How could I turn that down?"

Foley recalls feeling excited to tell his fellow Kids about his new job prospects, only to be shocked when the other four instructed him to turn down the pilot on the grounds that it presented a scheduling conflict with one of the dates on the troupe's upcoming live tour. "There was no way I was going to turn down this amazing pilot for one day of a tour," says Foley. "So, I offered to cover their losses on returned tickets and even take out a full-page ad in the *New York Times* to announce any rescheduled dates." The troupe's refusal to accommodate Foley, and his decision to accept the role on *NewsRadio* anyway, marked the beginning of a simmering hostility between Foley and the other Kids that would come to full boil over the dark days and months ahead.

These outside projects notwithstanding, the preproduction and scripting for what became *Kids in the Hall: Brain Candy* began in earnest in late August 1994, when Norm Hiscock accompanied all five troupe members on a two-week writing retreat. While their heroes in Monty Python had opted to write their movies in such tropical locales as Barbados, the Kids settled for the blackfly-infested lakes and forests of Muskoka, two hundred kilometres north of Toronto. The retreat presented Foley and McDonald with a chance to repair their fraying relationship, as the two drove up together from Toronto, blasting out a cassette of Green Day's *Dookie* and stocking up at a liquor store on the way.

"When we got to the Gravenhurst Lodge," recalls McDonald, "we had the whole place to ourselves because it was in the off-season. Mark and I took advantage of it, getting up early to play golf and renting rowboats."

For Bruce McCulloch, the new project represented a light at the end of the tunnel, an excuse to keep a very tired troupe alive by keeping busy. "We just kind of sat there for two weeks at this weird golf resort where we weren't that welcome."

McKinney adds, "We were constantly reminded that we were in the *second*-nicest resort in the area."

Recreation aside, they were there to work, so the Kids began putting in full days, from 10 a.m. to 6 p.m., picking over a wealth of possible film ideas, with the hope of settling on one by the end of the first week and developing it further in week two. Many of their pitches veered toward dark or melancholy themes. McDonald's *Memories* was a wistful homage to Paul Mazursky's *Next Stop, Greenwich Village*, set in 1950s Manhattan, which had originally been performed as a cast scene on their old CKLN radio show. While it contained a lot of inspired comedy, McDonald acknowledges that "it was an awful first draft, and everyone just savaged it."

McDonald was personally fond of McKinney's concept for *The Asshole*, which involved a serial killer going around the city killing assholes. "I would play a cop who goes undercover to infiltrate this whole underground world where assholes live under the subway tracks," says McDonald, "sort of like in the French film *Subway*." *The Asshole* was eventually rejected, as was Foley's proposal, *Planes Are Crashing*, a decidedly pre-9/11 disaster comedy involving a hilarious mix-up with air traffic controllers.

Foley's next idea was a classic anthology movie inspired by one of his favourite Preston Sturges films, *The Great McGinty*. "All five of us would be in this bar in a jungle hotel," says Foley, "and everyone would tell their story of how they wound up there. The big reveal would be that what ties all these people together is that they are all dead. Then, a gong goes off and everyone says, 'Oh boy, here it comes.' And the room starts to fill up with huge army ants attacking everybody and crawling all over them. The last guy in says, 'Oh my god, so we're all in hell?' And the bartender has the punchline at the very end: 'No, no. This is heaven. It's just really overrated.' We talked about it for a while, but we never settled on it."

After discussing and dismissing comedy adaptations of serious works, such as Franz Kafka's *The Trial* and the 1946 Robert Siodmak thriller *The Killers*, the Kids seriously considered an original idea, *Boat Full of Cowards* (also known as *Ship of Fools*), a kind of *McHale's Navy* ensemble comedy in which the Kids would portray a lily-livered battleship crew, steadfastly trying to avoid combat during World War II. "Scott would naturally play a flamboyantly gay, Buddy Cole–like sailor," says McDonald, "and somebody else would be hypochondriac or suicidal, and so on. Mark was going to play this gung-ho, war-loving colonel who ends up aboard our ship after his plane gets shot down, and tries to force us all to go into the battle." Despite early promise, *Cowards* was scrapped after they realized it would be difficult to secure an actual battleship to shoot it on.

Scanning the pile of discarded pitches, it was clear that a kind of darkness had permeated their collective unconscious. It was into this lingering air of depression that McKinney stopped the room cold by uttering one word aloud: "Prozac."

While the pharmaceutical giant Eli Lilly had discovered their antidepressant fluoxetine as early as 1972, healthcare providers had only been prescribing it under its non-generic brand, Prozac, since 1986. By the mid-'90s, much had been written about the drug in the popular culture, pro and con, most notably in Elizabeth Wurtzel's bestselling *Prozac Nation*. Scott Thompson had concerns that psychiatric professionals were overprescribing Prozac as a panacea for loneliness, beyond its specifically intended use in treating the clinically depressed. "I do believe there was a place for it," says Thompson, "but I think society went a little crazy with it. No pun intended. Life isn't about *always* being happy, and it's silly to pretend that it is. Sometimes you just have to ride it out."

After vetoing every one of their other movie ideas, Hiscock felt that McKinney's Prozac idea seemed to offer the best opportunity to develop characters and relevant plotlines. "We imagined all these different people could be medicating themselves," says Hiscock, "but the premise could also work as a parody of big business, which was another theme central to the Kids' comic DNA."

After dismissing McKinney's original title, *The Pill*, on the grounds that it might be mistaken for a film about birth control, they moved to develop a viable screenplay with the working title, *The Drug*. While he had initial reservations about tackling such a dark subject, Bruce McCulloch says he was glad to have a topic that would force them to get out of their comfort zone. "It was a bit steelier in tone and more satirical than some of our other stuff, but God bless us for writing something that didn't just feature all our hit characters from the show."

Satisfied that they had met their goal of an idea by the end of week one, the Kids prepared to break the movie down over the following seven days, at the end of which Hiscock was to gather up their notes and write a first draft before he and McKinney started at *Saturday Night Live*. During the week, each of the Kids imagined their own drafts of *The Drug*, and by the end of the retreat, Hiscock was struggling to collate their diverse elements into a coherent whole. True to form, the Kids had once again become deadlocked by their own democratic ideals, yet Hiscock remained optimistic: "At that point, even Dave was confident that we had something, so I made this weird Frankenstein's monster draft of the best drafts, and I went through it and rewrote the first act of the movie."

While it was unanimous within the group that the film's miracle drug would be called GLeeMONEX—they had even gone so far as to invent its generic name, Duoroflouriximinimum 602 — there was little else they agreed on, and as the summer wound down, Foley recalls beginning to doubt that they would ever settle on a suitable shooting script. "At that point, I really didn't like the script at all. I'd been pushing for a story that was more concise, saying 'Look, we don't have a second or third act.'"

Foley remembers being far more excited about the screenplay he had just written with David Anthony Higgins and *Simpsons* writer/producer Jay Kogen. Compared to *The Drug*, the writing process for *The Wrong Guy*, a proposed Foley-starring vehicle, had been painless. "David, Jay, and I would get together and in a weekend knock out forty pages of *The Wrong Guy*," says Foley, "whereas with the Kids, it seemed to take six months to get even five pages written."

Regardless of Foley's souring mood, he continued to give his best suggestions for *The Drug* to Hiscock, who worked diligently to incorporate them into the whole. "Dave had this funny premise for the film," recalls Hiscock. "It was to be set in this sad little town with a lot of funeral homes, where the local industry had fallen apart, leaving all of the townspeople clinically depressed. Then this huge pharmaceutical company selects their community for a town-wide clinical trial of an experimental drug to fight depression."

In Foley's draft, the hero is a clinical researcher who discovers a drug that makes everyone intensely happy. But, in clinical trials, he discovers that his miracle cure comes with one problematic side effect; one in ten users becomes a mass murderer. Horrified, the researcher tries to halt production of the drug, but by this point, the town is already hooked.

"The townspeople love the drug so much that they're willing to live with the murderous side effects," says Foley. "When they decide that they can't let the scientist out of the town to warn the outside world about the drug, the film becomes about him trying to escape. The thesis was 'What will you endure, what price would you pay, to be happy?' Would the town allow all these dead bodies to pile up because everyone else is so happy now?' Sadly, no one else liked that idea, so we scrapped it."

Early in October 1994, Hiscock and the Kids reconvened in the boardroom of Broadway Video's newly opened offices in downtown Toronto to go page by page, line by line, over what had grown into a meandering and unfocused screenplay. The room was tense, as the historically close friendship between Foley and McDonald was tested by Foley's expressed desire to postpone *The Drug* indefinitely in order to go off and make *The Wrong Guy*. An already gloomy mood was worsened by the tragic news of the suicide of McDonald's brother-in-law. At the time, McDonald remembers feeling Foley wasn't very supportive of his family's devastating loss, although he now admits some jealousy of Foley, who he felt was abandoning him: "I resented that 'Mr. *NewsRadio*' was trying to stop our movie to go work on his own film."

Tensions in what McDonald refers to as the "boardroom of death" were high when Broadway Video's Barnaby Thompson arrived to inform the Kids that *The Drug* had to go into production right away, regardless of whether the script was ready. "We hadn't even resolved the third act yet," says McDonald, "and we only had this 'glee coma' idea for the ending that I had frankly ripped off Terry Gilliam's *Brazil*."

For Foley, the pressure to march into a half-baked production at the expense of his own career goals was the final straw. In no uncertain terms, he informed the others that in his opinion *The Drug* was not ready. "The way I saw it," says Foley, "*NewsRadio* was hot. I was living in L.A. but being pushed into this idea back in Toronto that I wasn't thrilled about. I told them that I thought our audience would be just as interested, even more interested, in a Kids in the Hall movie a year from now."

To the others in the room, postponement was a controversial suggestion, and McCulloch remembers straining to understand why Foley would want a year off at this crucial time. "Up until that point," says McCulloch, "I think we just assumed that we were all going to do stuff together. Suddenly, people were busy and you had to book time with them? It was our messy era."

According to Foley, after saying very little during the meeting, Scott Thompson erupted. "Scott started accusing me of only wanting to do my own movie. He was yelling all these things at me like, 'You've got *NewsRadio* now' and 'You don't care about us!' It was pretty harsh."

Up until this time, most intratroupe disputes had been settled by a kind of parliamentary democracy, with McKinney and McCulloch on one side, Foley and McDonald on the other, and Thompson playing the role of tiebreaker. But now, with Foley taking such a hard-line stance against the entire project, the balance shifted. "Suddenly, I was with Mark and Bruce," says McDonald, "and then Scott was with us too. So, for the first time ever, Dave was all by himself; all four of us against Dave. Then Barnaby just went ballistic. I was just crazed, sad, and angry. I left the boardroom in a huff."

Hurt and confused, McDonald did what he had done back when he was having issues with Robert Boyd in the early days of the series; he went home and composed an angry letter to Foley. His plan was to personally deliver the letter to Foley the next day in the boardroom of death. "I was so mad that I wanted him to read my letter out loud in front of the troupe." When Foley refused to read the letter out loud, McDonald insisted until Foley snapped. "Finally," says McDonald, "Dave said, 'Kevin, if you ask me to read this letter one more time, I'm going to quit the troupe.'"

Calling his bluff, McDonald pressed Foley one more time. "So, I just stood up," says Foley, "and I said 'Well, you know what? It's been a great ten years but I'm going to leave now.' And I got up and walked out of the room and quit the troupe."

The next day, Foley flew back to L.A., uncertain if he'd ever talk to, let alone work with, the Kids in the Hall again.

McDonald sees these outbursts as the logical venting of all the pent-up hostility that had accrued over the past decade of working together. But at the time, he felt that Foley wasn't stating his case for postponement in an "articulate" manner; all he picked up was hostility. "Dave seemed so angry and resentful toward the rest of us. Suddenly, it just seemed like there was all this friction between us. Of course, years later, in therapy, I realized I was probably just jealous of his sitcom success."

Meanwhile, back in the boardroom, Hiscock mourned the loss of a valuable asset in the writers' room. "Dave is a great joke writer," says Hiscock, "and another great mind within the group. And even Scott was gone some of the time, flying back and forth to go do *Larry Sanders*, so that left me, Kevin, Bruce, and Mark to make the final adjustments to the script without them."

Although no formal statement was ever made about Foley's departure, Lorne Michaels was given private notice that the Kids in the Hall would continue as a four-piece. At the time, though, Michaels had bigger issues to contend with. Paramount was growing restless about the project, and had even considered pulling out of *The Drug* before the cameras got rolling. In that event, the Kids in the Hall would be paid out for their screenplay, and the picture would be scrapped. But even in the event of that consolation prize, they could not be paid unless all five Kids signed on the dotted line. They needed Foley's signature, so the Kids convinced him to sign the contracts as a legal formality. After Foley had signed, they received word that Michaels had successfully convinced Paramount to go ahead with the filming of *The Drug*. Now contractually obligated to appear in the film, Foley felt he had been tricked and proceeded to draft a list of conditions for his participation, including a limit on the number of characters he would play in the film to minimize his time on set. But it was his insistence that he not appear as a woman in the film that was received most controversially by the other Kids. "I just didn't feel like sitting through hours of makeup," says Foley, "and frankly I didn't want to be there very much at all."

Thompson remembers being furious about his refusal to do drag, convinced that Foley's "Hollywood people" had advised him that it might hurt his straight career. "Dave and I were probably the furthest apart at the time," recalls Thompson, "and I always thought it was my fighting with him that led to his quitting. But, you know, maybe he was right, and all of the gender bending and homosexuality in the Kids in the Hall did hurt our careers. I'm absolutely convinced that's why we never went to the next level like everybody else did."

As offended as Thompson was by the no-drag memo, it was Kevin McDonald who was most hurt by Foley's final condition. "His people sent me an impersonal memo," says McDonald, "which read, 'While Dave is looking forward to working with Kevin, he is also aware that Kevin is going to want to work it out between the two of them and talk about things.' The memo said that if I tried to do that, he would walk, and I would be sued. It was becoming a bitter divorce, although I have to say I was happy to hear that first part about Dave looking forward to working with me."

Paramount sent word that they needed to change the title of the film, as the marketing department felt that certain theatrical distributors and cinema chains would refuse to take a film called *The Drug*. The Kids in the Hall movie would henceforth be known as *Brain Candy*, and would be filmed in Toronto with Kelly Makin directing and his brother David behind the camera.

One week before they were set to begin principal photography, news of another tragedy reached the boardroom of death when Scott Thompson was informed that his beloved younger brother, Dean, had taken his own life. "It's still very hard to talk about," says Thompson. "Obviously, my brother's suicide is the worst thing I've ever gone through. Dean was schizophrenic, and he'd suffered brain damage in a car accident when he was in his twenties. This was another horrible moment; there was just tragedy after tragedy. I was already furious with Dave, but now I felt that he wasn't showing me any sympathy or concern for what happened. We were all on our own trips back then, and I'm sure Dave feels bad about it now."

Taking stock of all the family tragedies they were suffering both inside and outside the production, McDonald began to wonder if there was some kind of a *Brain Candy* curse. "First and foremost, we had gone and done probably the stupidest thing we could do for our feature-film debut — a comedy about depression. Then, my girlfriend Tiffany left me; my best friend in the troupe, Dave, and I broke up; and then my brother-in-law and Scott's brother both kill themselves. It must have affected my thinking because at one point I wanted to write a scene about the lead character's childhood, and I came up with a funny bit about the father killing himself."

Scott Thompson agrees with McDonald's theory of a *Brain Candy* curse. "We all did terrible things to each other. It became an incredibly difficult film to make."

SEVENTEEN

Some Days It's Dark: Filming Brain Candy

" I remember Dave telling me that making this movie was so hard," says Kevin McDonald, "but it wasn't the kind of 'hard' that you could ever describe to people. No one would ever understand."

Considering that chemistry was at the heart of the Kids in the Hall's debut motion picture *Brain Candy*, a dark satire on both Big Pharma and the age of celebrity, it seems ironic that the troupe's interpersonal chemistry was so frayed at the time of filming. Friends since teenagers, McDonald and Foley, the two original Kids in the Hall, were no longer on speaking terms, and a dark cloud hung over the entire enterprise. In spite of these tensions, they were *supposed* to be making a comedy, and Bruce McCulloch remembers relying on the "sheer muscle memory" of their collective comedy history to make it through.

"Dave would come in and kind of grunt and deliver his

lines, then go over and talk to someone else. But about a week into it, I'd catch Dave and Kevin bonding, as men do, by looking at CDs. I'd hear comments like, 'Yeah, Matthew Sweet's pretty cool.'"

McDonald says he still found it awkward to film his first scenes opposite Foley, seeing him for the first time since he had tried to force him to read his letter in the boardroom. "It felt a little sad," says McDonald, "like we no longer had that old chemistry. Yet oddly enough, when I see *Brain Candy* now, I *do* see some of that old chemistry, so maybe it was more in our minds."

McCulloch says he can still feel the pain of the times reflected in the footage. "Of course, once we started fighting, we didn't know where the troupe was going. But we were contractually committed to finish *Brain Candy*. A couple of times, it felt like we could have stopped in the middle of filming, but I just kept saying 'No, just keep pushing. Just keep pushing.'"

Mark McKinney says he was excited about working on the broader canvas of a full-length movie, despite the personal conflicts and everything beyond the cameras feeling strained. "There was *always* a challenge with us to get all of our comedy voices balanced. As a result, the movie itself feels to me a little bit compromised. On top of that, we picked a premise that was not simple. I think the Pythons were so much smarter to riff on the Middle Ages, the Bible, you know?"

After pre-production was complete, Norm Hiscock left the production to begin his new job as a writer on *Saturday Night Live* while he and Cindy Park welcomed their first child into the world. In his place, Garry Campbell returned to assume the role of script supervisor for the shoot. Upon arriving on the set, Campbell immediately noticed that the convivial atmosphere he'd enjoyed on the television series had vanished. "There was so much shit going on when I got there," says Campbell. "The quagmire of ten years together culminated in this animosity running through everything. I think Bruce felt a little on the outside of it all, so he and I just threw a football around and tried to stay out of it."

Thompson recalls that despite being emotionally unavailable to each other, the Kids rallied as a troupe to do the best work they could under the circumstances. "It was a fascinating shoot that way. To me, one of the best moments in the movie is this minute-long Christmas scene between Dave and my character, the old lady Mrs. Hurdicure. Despite our fighting, Dave and I rewrote that scene completely while riding in a van to the set, just passing a piece of paper back and forth without speaking to each other. We didn't speak about anything except what we were doing, which showed to me that we could overcome our circumstances to do the work."

When they were first writing the screenplay, it was assumed that Dave Foley would portray the closest thing to a hero in the film, Dr. Chris Cooper. But Foley had made it clear that he did not want to be on set for longer than the contractual minimum, and one of his conditions for participating was that he would not accept a leading role in *Brain Candy*. The role of Dr. Cooper instead went to Kevin McDonald, who says he worked hard to carry the film despite feeling like an unlikely leading man. For inspiration, he turned to one of his earliest big screen influences.

"It hit me right away that Gene Wilder could be my prototype for how to approach Dr. Cooper," says McDonald, "so I studied *Young Frankenstein*, and the way he takes a straight part but still ends up getting the most laughs. You can see me do that all through the movie. I roll my eyes a bit like Wilder. Now, I'm very limited as an actor, unlike Dave, but our director, Kelly Makin, somehow pulled the performance out of me. Still, I was mainly relying on my comedy timing, because I'm not an actor the way Mark, or Scott, or Dave are actors."

McDonald had originally been slated to portray the film's villain, pharmaceutical boss Don Roritor, but when he assumed the role of Dr. Cooper, Mark McKinney stepped in as Roritor, imbuing him with a few mannerisms and vocal tics that seemed reminiscent of their own comedy CEO, Lorne Michaels. While McKinney acknowledges that Michaels was the *starting point* for his Don Roritor, he insists that he ended up creating a far darker character. "Roritor shared that grand way that Lorne has of being somewhat aristocratic. And the way Lorne always seems to *know* things. The way he imparts advice, he says these things like, 'You know, you'll find…' with such confidence.

"Famously, Lorne told Bernie Brillstein, 'Mark seems to be doing somebody,' and Brillstein replied, 'Lorne, he's doing *you*!' But Lorne was like, 'Really?' Later, he had me up to his office for a talk that was sort of meander-y, and at some point during the conversation he just blurted out, 'I feel a little self-conscious, because you're doing me.'"

Judd Apatow remembers being blown away by Roritor's surreal exaggeration of Michaels' mannerisms. "Mark made a great screen creation," says Apatow, "that was so funny and bizarre that I feel like everybody who's ever done a Lorne Michaels impression since then is doing some version of Mark's Lorne."

Toronto comedian Jackie Harris Greenberg was cast as Don Roritor's secretary, Natalie, one of the few female roles in the film that was played by a female actor. Greenberg was a longtime friend of the troupe and had performed with them both at the Rivoli and on the TV show. She recalls tensions on the *Brain Candy* set, and says she felt sad witnessing the troupe drifting apart. "I was in some scenes with Dave, and while he was working hard and doing his best, you could see there was just so much other stuff going on in his own life."

With Foley working-to-rule, and McKinney and Hiscock off in New York working at *SNL* much of the time, McDonald took advantage of what he calls the "flipped power dynamics" within the troupe, and credits this shift in the balance of power for some new macro-collaborations between himself and McCulloch. "I remember sitting with Bruce, and thinking up the 'cats on the ceiling' bit. Now, I don't really write jokes, but I knew I could get a laugh out of saying 'Cat on my head! Cat on my head! Cat on my head!' I acted this out for Bruce and Kelly Makin, and they laughed their cute little heads off."

McDonald was also impressed with how Scott Thompson stepped up in new ways during the production, transforming a simple gag McDonald had written for Thompson's closeted Wally Terzinsky character and literally making a spectacle out of it. "Norm and I had originally written this thing," says McDonald, "where Wally would come out by going house to house and literally jumping out of their closets screaming 'I'm out of the closet and I'm gay!' But Scott thought it would be funnier, and probably gayer, to do it as a big musical number. And thank god he did, because that's the part of the movie that people love best."

Thompson and Toronto composer Joe Sealy wrote Wally's song, "I'm Gay," and turned it into a mini-musical on a suburban street. Thompson's Terzinsky wasn't that far from his Danny Husk character, and Thompson says that he found the uber-straight Terzinsky's lack of self-awareness inherently hilarious. "Delusional people are just funnier," says Thompson, "because they're constantly saying the opposite of what they're really thinking, and behaving in ways that are completely counter to what they really want. Wally is living in multiple layers of fantasy, and not just the ones in his military-themed gay porn. When he sings the big song, he's in this other fantasy, the one where, when he comes out, everybody will be on board with it and want to help him."

Despite Bruce McCulloch's humble suggestion that he is the least qualified actor in the troupe, he brought a convincing dramatic range to his main roles in *Brain Candy*. McCulloch says his portrayal of Don Roritor's nefarious and vulgar right-hand man, Cisco, became an outlet for his pent-up frustrations on the set. "The whole shoot was probably the hardest thing we've ever been through as a troupe, so it was a relief to write myself a mean character like Cisco, who didn't care about anybody around him. When I was Cisco, I could snap at people and yell things like, 'You're not a fuckin' plate of croissants!'"

On the other end of the scale, McCulloch played Alice, Dr. Cooper's love interest, as a slightly more upbeat version of his delightful Kathie with a K character. "I thought it would be fun to play a girl who was ridiculously in love with Dr. Cooper, but was overcomplicating things in her head," says McCulloch. "Alice was a snapshot of one or six of my old girlfriends, this girl with a complicated inner life that nobody knew about but her."

Finally, McCulloch's most "emo" character in the film was Grivo, the brooding lead singer from the band Death Lurks, who becomes chemically altered after his GLeeMONEX treatments. Whereas Cisco was an outlet for anger, Grivo was McCulloch's way to channel the pain in the air. Additionally, Grivo's disaffected stage persona was a commentary on rock's cult of personality circa the early 1990s, and the ways in which rock stars, such as the recently deceased Kurt Cobain, lived up or down to the expectations their audiences placed on them. "Grivo does very little on stage," says McCulloch. "The power is all in the music, but his fans just think he's intense and amazing."

McCulloch insists that he had no specific rock star in mind for Grivo, but acknowledges a striking similarity to one rock star in particular. "I guess if he were based on anybody, it'd be Glenn Danzig, whom I've never met, but who I assume is probably a sweet guy. I mean, all those rockers are sweet little guys in the end, and I suppose we're *all* just sweet little guys who are all making it up as we go, right?"

When we first meet Grivo, he and Death Lurks are grinding out the Metallica-like dirge-rocker "Some Days It's Dark." Later, after being chemically lobotomized, Grivo's tune changes, and he and the band stun their audience with the sunny folk-pop tune "Happiness Pie." Both songs, and the film's score, were written and performed by their Vancouver-based friend Craig Northey and his band, Odds.

"Everybody in the Kids got along with Craig," says McCulloch. "He's a great musician who had to take a lot of music from all over the map, but give it all a certain cohesive vibe. Craig's job was to tie all the musical ideas together just as Norm tried to sew together the script. And he really brought it home."

While McKinney, Foley, and McDonald had appeared in the music video for the Odds' 1993 single "Heterosexual Man," *Brain Candy* marked the first time Northey had been asked to compose music for the Kids in the Hall. Northey says he worked closely with McCulloch and Makin to provide multiple music cues within an insanely quick turnaround time. "This movie was wall-to-wall music, with all this stuff coming from a million different places. I had our score, with Doug Elliott and Pat Steward from our band, and we used the Odds' recording of 'Eat My Brain,' plus a lot of cools songs by other artists."

The soundtrack to *Brain Candy* would feature the hippest bands of the day, including Yo La Tengo, Cibo Matto, Matthew Sweet, and The Tragically Hip, who ended up creating the title song from a line of dialogue in the script.

"The Hip had given me all these tracks," says Northey, "and it was great to have Gord Downie, rest his beautiful soul, come sing the line from the film — where Dr. Chris Cooper prematurely announces that the drug is ready for the marketplace — in the song 'Butts Wigglin'.' It was perfect for the film."

Northey says he modelled the sound of Grivo's band, Death Lurks, on a variety of early '90s post-grunge bands, who were "just heavy for heavy's sake." The result was so true to life that one of rock's heaviest bands even covered a Death Lurks tune. "One of the funniest tributes was when Tool started doing 'Some Days It's Dark' as their encore," says Northey. "Turns out, they were big comedy fans, just like us, just like *most* bands, so that was really cool."

Among the other *GLeeMONEX* users featured in the film was Thompson's genteel Mrs. Hurdicure, who might not have suffered the demands of rock 'n' roll adulation, but had her own lifetime of sadness and regret to medicate away. One of Thompson's most empathetic female characters, Mrs. Hurdicure was modelled on his beloved Aunt Mary, with notes of his Queen Elizabeth and Fran, the indomitable housewife from the "Salty Ham" sketch. "My aunt Mary was this really sturdy farmwoman," says Thompson. "She dressed and walked just like Mrs. Hurdicure. I think she was the heart of the film."

Having improved the quality of the Kids' films over five seasons on television, brothers Kelly and David Makin were excited to stretch out on something even longer than

"Love and Sausages." And while Kelly Makin acknowledges that their seven-million-dollar budget was not large for a major studio feature, he remembers being determined to put it all on the screen. "I really wanted to give *Brain Candy* some production value," says Makin, "and to elevate the look from the television show, give it more scope and some scale to reach a larger audience than just fans of the series. Our production design had a lot of recurring shapes and colour schemes. For instance, the world of Roritor Pharmaceuticals featured a lot of pill shapes, circles, and retro '60s and '70s colour palettes. Scott's musical sequence, 'I'm Gay,' was highly colour-coordinated, and we had all these matching cars on this uniform suburban street."

Geri Wraith, so integral to the look of the television series, returned for *Brain Candy*, and recalled that broader canvas of the big screen, and the unforgiving nature of cinematographer David Makin's 35mm camera, which presented her with new challenges in terms of detailed makeup design.

"Since Bruce was playing our lead female, Alice, we had to soften his jawline and lose the beard line, which was not easy," she recalled in 2016.

She said a lot of hard work went into the look of McCulloch's most contentious *Brain Candy* character, Cancer Boy. "Bruce had to wear a bald pate in 110-degree weather, and the adhesive holding it down would start to come undone. We had to position the flag on his wheelchair strategically so David's camera wouldn't see it!"

Essentially a parody of the dark and exploitative side of charities and telethon culture, Cancer Boy had barely raised

an eyebrow when he first appeared in the final season of
The Kids in the Hall, but as far as Paramount was concerned,
McCulloch's hairless child had crossed the line of accept-
able taste. Norm Hiscock, however, insists that Cancer Boy
was merely an extension of the same dark comedy streak
that the Kids had built their brand upon. "Cancer Boy was
probably the outer edge of where we would typically go,"
says Hiscock, "but I have to say, we weren't making fun of
cancer. The Kids, particularly Dave and Bruce, had always
explored the darker parts of life."

While he understands the controversy, McCulloch
insists that their real target with Cancer Boy was the commercial exploitation of sick and innocent children by the
media. "These poor little cancer kids are so hopeful," says
McCulloch, "and they almost always have the sweetest
souls. That's why Cancer Boy sings the song that Craig
wrote for him, 'Whistle While You're Low.' It felt to me
like the most soulful thing I've ever done."

While Garry Campbell says that Cancer Boy was one of
McCulloch's funniest creations, he readily acknowledges
how the black humour of the character may have been lost
on the Paramount executives. "To me, it was never about
getting a few cheap laughs at the expense of the terminally
ill. All of us could be fairly cynical at times, but I don't
believe we were ever mean-spirited, and there's a world
of difference between those two things. Still, I remember
being on set at three in the morning, and some Paramount
executive put his arm around my shoulder and walked me
into a darkened hallway. He whispered, 'You've got to talk
to the guys about Cancer Boy. Get them to pull back.'"

But according to McCulloch, all three of their production partners—Broadway Video, Paramount Pictures, and Canadian company Lakeshore Entertainment—had approved the shooting script without flagging the controversial character. McCulloch says he was frankly surprised that they had been allowed to shoot it in the first place. "Of course, you later discover that nobody reads scripts as closely as you think they would. Even after we filmed it, I was saying 'They're going to make us cut it.' And they didn't, at first." It was only after the film had been cut and screened that the studio notified them that Cancer Boy was a bridge too far. After arguing among themselves about Paramount's notes, the troupe came to a consensus that as far as Cancer Boy was concerned, the kid stayed in the picture.

"I remember calling one of our producers," says McKinney, "and telling them, 'No, this is important; we've got to do it. It's funny. It's what people expect from our troupe.' Later, we heard rumours that the chairman of Paramount had lost someone to cancer recently and that's why they didn't want Cancer Boy in the film."

Shortly before Christmas, McCulloch was on the phone with a Paramount executive—McKinney was also on the call—to once again plead the case for Cancer Boy. "I remember pacing in circles around my small apartment," says McCulloch, "and talking on the phone to this guy who was in control of all the purse strings and marketing budgets. I was telling him about Cancer Boy, and how our troupe made decisions, and how important our name was to us. After literally an hour, I was so exhausted that I just lied to him and said, 'It's important because my mother died of cancer.' And he said, 'OK then, you can leave it in.' Of course, my mother did not die of cancer, so when I hung up, I thought, 'Have I just made a deal with the devil?' But it was one of those things where you make up something at the thirteenth hour."

McCulloch phoned Lorne Michaels to tell him the good news that he'd saved Cancer Boy. "He just said, 'Oh good. I already heard, and you should know that they just cut the advertising budget.' So we'd won the battle but not the war."

While Paramount did make significant cuts to their marketing and promotion budget for *Brain Candy*, there were also unconfirmed reports that they attempted to bury the film by reducing their commitment from an estimated 4,000 screens to just over 400. According to Hiscock, the trouble with *Brain Candy* was that, at its heart, the film was in fact a cynical screed on the illusion of happiness and a contemptuous look at corporate greed. At one point, McKinney's angry taxi driver lays out what could be the film's motto: "Life is short, life is shit, and soon it will be over."

Brain Candy was not the kind of madcap, feel-good popcorn movie that Paramount had in mind. "My thinking at the time was that it's OK to be unhappy sometimes," says Hiscock, "so a drug that doesn't let you feel either extreme isn't necessarily a good thing. At the same time, we were signalling our distrust of big business by having Don Roritor declare 'If we can get people to buy this, we can make more money.'"

Hiscock says they wrote at least three different endings for the movie, but besides a musical number where all the

drugged happy people sing a manic showstopper, the endings were dark, bordering on cynical. "The darkest idea
was where Cooper takes his own drug and becomes stuck
in his happiest moment, which is the moment he invented
the drug. We thought that was pretty clever, but it was kind
of dark because it meant that big business won. We shot a
kind of Terry Gilliam *Brazil* ending, but we tested it in front
of the audience and they didn't like it so much."

Hiscock recalls Lorne Michaels being atypically blunt in
expressing his dissatisfaction with what he calls the film's
"coma queen" ending. "Lorne is very direct, and saves his
comments, but he's generally pretty hands-off about content. But in this moment he went, 'OK, I just have to let
you know what you've decided to do. Just think about it.'
Then the studio gave us a little bit of money to reshoot the
ending, so we came up with that more hopeful ending you
see in the finished film, the one where they fall in love."

Michaels insists that he never personally censored any
aspect of *Brain Candy*. "We gave them the tools to write
their movie and they decided to do a comedy art film,"
says Michaels. "And while it's true that Paramount had
notes about some of the content, I never told them to cut
anything."

Kids in the Hall: Brain Candy, dedicated to Scott
Thompson's late brother, Dean, "and all the Deans in the
world," opened theatrically on April 12, 1996. Paul Feig
attended the Hollywood premiere and says that, apart from
a few audible gasps when Cancer Boy first appeared on the

screen, the film killed overall. "I remember tons of huge laughs in the theatre," says Feig. "And I remember leaving the theatre telling people that *Brain Candy* was awesome, and anticipating it was going to be a big hit and looking forward to their next film."

But while the film had its fans and supporters, *Brain Candy* underperformed at the box office, taking in an underwhelming USD$770,280 over its first weekend, before eventually limping along to an estimated total gross of USD$2,654,308, slightly less than a third of its $7,000,000 budget.

Early believer Pamela Thomas was also there on opening night, and has seen the film numerous times since. While she still finds the film hilarious, she is more convinced than ever that a character like Cancer Boy would never be green-lit by a major studio today. "They had so much creative freedom and support in those days. Lorne backed them up, CBC backed them up, and even HBO backed them up. They were pretty much allowed to do whatever they wanted. That's unheard of, isn't it?"

Film critic Janet Maslin savaged *Brain Candy* in the *New York Times,* pronouncing it a "sloppy showcase for the group's costume-changing tricks," adding that "flashes of complete plot incoherence or atrocious taste spoil the effect."

The late film critics Gene Siskel and Roger Ebert, however, were split down the middle. Siskel raved that the film was an "audacious, clever, very funny satire," and a future art-house cult classic, while Ebert's thumb pointed firmly in the downward position.

"Boy, are we apart on this one," Ebert fired back at Siskel. "I did not laugh once. I thought this movie was awful, dreadful, terrible, stupid, idiotic, unfunny, laboured, forced, painful, and bad."

While once again citing the drawbacks of their collective decision-making process, Bruce McCulloch seems at peace with *Brain Candy*'s place in their history. "It was all so painful to make, but in some ways it was worth it. Of course, a film-writing teacher might have some problems with the screenplay, but I think, from scene to scene, it's still a great, well-put-together film."

According to Paul Feig, whose own series *Freaks and Geeks* went on to legendary cult status despite being cancelled after one season, truly innovative comedy isn't always a commercial success. "The general public are not comedy purists. They just want to be entertained. This doesn't necessarily mean they're dumb; it's just that they're not consuming comedy on an intellectual, academic level the way a comedy aficionado, such as myself, would. We are a limited audience."

For Scott Thompson, the loss of his brother and the emotional scars of the troupe's infighting forever mar the *Brain Candy* era. "I remember it being a very sad time. While the end of the series hadn't meant the end of the troupe, the cracks had been showing for quite a while. Now we were at each other's throats."

Many within the Kids in the Hall camp now acknowledge that a dystopian mental health comedy was probably too tall an order for their first foray into the movies. Kevin McDonald compares the career trajectory of the Beatles. "In the beginning, they put out some breezy, fun singles like 'She Loves You' and 'I Want to Hold Your Hand.' Then, they worked their way up to a serious album like *Rubber Soul*, and ultimately *Sgt. Pepper*. Well, with *Brain Candy* we tried to go straight to our *Revolver*, but it ended up being our *Let It Be*. Dave and I started the Kids in the Hall together, so I always felt we were the heart of the group. But then the heart was broken in two, and the two halves weren't talking to each other, so we split up for a long time after that."

In the wake of the film's release, a kind of cold war began within the troupe, as each of them attempted, with varying degrees of success, to establish careers apart from the troupe. This standoff would persist for the next four years. But in their absence, the *Kids* television series had gone into syndication, and thanks to an upstart cable network called Comedy Central, the Kids in the Hall were about to be exposed to the widest television audience they would ever know.

EIGHTEEN

Cold War Kids (1996–99)

In 1991, fledgling cable outlet Comedy Central started up as a relatively hard-to-find cult channel with a decidedly modest viewership. In the days before *The Daily Show with Jon Stewart*, *South Park*, and *Chappelle's Show* put them on the map, Comedy Central's limited financial resources left them largely reliant upon MTV-style "clip shows," vintage HBO stand-up specials, and reruns of syndicated series to fill their broadcast day. In 1995, just as the series was winding down, *The Kids in the Hall* went into syndication, and Comedy Central introduced head crushing to a younger generation of American fans, many of whom had missed them the first time around.

"I read somewhere that, between 1995 and the early 2000s, the two top-rated shows on Comedy Central were reruns of *Saturday Night Live* and *The Kids in the Hall*," says Kevin McDonald. "They ran us three times a day. Even now, some of our fans are surprised when I tell them we started on HBO."

Among the younger fans discovering the show through Comedy Central was comedian Jonah Ray, host of Joel Hodgson's 2017 reboot of *Mystery Science Theater 3000*. "All I needed to hear was one bar from the opening song," says Ray, "to know that I was about to enjoy myself for the next thirty minutes. The Kids were my eye-opening 'Sex Pistols moment' as a comedian, and when I watched them, I said to myself, 'Wait, I can do this too!'"

While the constant reruns grew their fan base, the Kids were actively pursuing solo careers, uncertain if the Kids in the Hall would ever ride again. For two-fifths of the troupe, however, the bond was too strong to break. Estranged since the making of *Brain Candy*, Dave Foley and Kevin McDonald rekindled their friendship after McDonald moved to Los Angeles in 1996, and the two old friends discovered that they were neighbours. "When Dave and I 'broke up,' it seemed like death for the troupe," recalls McDonald. "But when Dave heard that I was in L.A., he somehow got my phone number and reached out to me. We had our first great talk in a long time and I felt like we were friends again. Of course, what Dave didn't know was that I was in the bath when he called. So when we made up, I was standing there, wet and naked, in my bathroom."

Perhaps it was the California sun warming up the recent chill between them, but that night, Foley and McDonald did something they hadn't done since the days before the Kids in the Hall became their day job: they went to the movies together. "We started going to a lot of movies together," says McDonald, "and I'd go over to Dave's to watch the odd hockey game on TV. It felt just like old times, when

I was a film usher and going to meet Dave at the Second City workshops."

Scott Thompson had joined the cast of *The Larry Sanders Show* in 1995, quickly earning acclaim in the role of Brian, Hank Kingsley's openly gay, and openly Canadian, assistant. When he got the role, Thompson told Shandling that he was wary of perpetuating a gay stereotype, a dilemma he battles with to this day, and consciously set about making Brian the polar opposite of Buddy Cole, drawing more on his skills as a serious actor than on his chops as a comedian.

"When Garry told me that Brian was to be a gay character," says Thompson, "I told him two things. I said I didn't want him to be a flake or a silly queen, and I wanted him to be Canadian. Garry readily agreed to both of those ideas. It was a great place to work. Garry was also very good at making sure that I played the beats and didn't try too hard to be funny."

One of the principal producers and writers for the *Sanders Show* was Judd Apatow, who remembers a thoughtful Shandling working closely with Thompson to fine-tune Brian's character. "There were hardly any gay characters on television at the time, so Garry was always asking 'Does this seem correct to you?' And if Scott wasn't thrilled about something, we'd change it."

Apatow's directorial debut was on a 1998 *Sanders* episode entitled "Putting the 'Gay' Back in Litigation," in which Brian sued Larry and the *Sanders Show* for sexual harassment in the workplace. "We all knew it was important to Scott that the episode was handled well," says Apatow. "He was so smart and funny helping us with the script. A lot of his improvisations in rehearsal made it into the show."

Larry Sanders went off the air in 1998, and Thompson now regrets losing touch with Shandling over the ensuing years. The two had only recently reconnected over Twitter in February 2016, when Thompson heard the tragic news of Shandling's death from pulmonary thrombosis the following month. "My last message to Garry was, 'Let's make sure we see each other before one of us is dead,' and he replied, 'Yeah, that would be a good idea.'"

Contacted by email one week before his death to set up an interview for this book, Shandling praised Thompson's contributions to his celebrated series, and explained how a former *Sanders* producer, Paul Simms, had been a huge fan of *The Kids in the Hall*. "Of course, Paul grabbed Dave for that part on his next show, *NewsRadio*," Shandling wrote via email, "and we focused on Scott for our purposes. He was perfect as Brian."

Simms had indeed made a wise choice to cast Foley in the role of Dave Nelson on *NewsRadio*, and the NBC series continued to be a ratings success until the death of costar Phil Hartman in 1998, which led to the series' cancellation after one final season with Hartman's friend Jon Lovitz filling in. Concurrent with his time on *NewsRadio*, Foley finally managed to get *The Wrong Guy* green-lit and released (Canada only) on August 1, 1997. Cowritten and coproduced by Foley, with David Anthony Higgins and Jay Kogen, *The Wrong Guy* had been sold fairly quickly to the Canadian company Paragon, which had a U.S. distribution deal with Hollywood Pictures. By all accounts, making *The Wrong Guy* was the opposite of *Brain Candy*—a painless film shoot in the Toronto area with a supporting cast of all-star Canadian actors that included Colm Feore, Jennifer Tilly, *SCTV's* Joe Flaherty, and the Barenaked Ladies, who appear in the film as singing cops performing the song "Gangster Girl" a cappella. Foley also gave cameos to two of the Kids in the Hall, and while Mark McKinney's piece ended up on the cutting-room floor, Kevin McDonald's small turn as a motel manager made the final cut.

Before filming, Foley had hoped to have *Brain Candy* director Kelly Makin on board, but when he discovered that Makin was already committed to direct *National Lampoon's Senior Trip*, he approached legendary Canadian comedian and director David Steinberg, who was a comedy hero to all three cowriters on the project. By all accounts, Steinberg's set was a fun place to work and filming progressed on time and on budget. But the project ran into trouble when Disney Studios bought out Hollywood Pictures midway through production. According to David Anthony Higgins, Disney was less than thrilled to have inherited *The Wrong Guy*. "The feedback at all of our screenings was amazing. They say a good comedy needs ten good laughs, and we had a hundred. But Mike Eisner, the president and CEO of Disney at the time, did not find us funny, so we became the orphaned stepchild over there." Despite solid support from the influential *Ain't It Cool News* web site, Disney refused to release *The Wrong Guy* in the U.S., and after a short commercial run in Canada, the film disappeared from the mainstream to become a favourite cult film, mostly with *Kids in the Hall* fans who traded wobbly VHS cassettes, dubbed secondhand from the original limited run.

By 1997, Foley was sufficiently close with McDonald again to invite him to do a guest spot on *NewsRadio*, playing the role of Throwdini in an episode titled "Stupid Holiday Charity Talent Show." McDonald says, "Not only was it great to be reunited with Dave, but to get to work with the hysterically funny Phil Hartman was a huge bonus for me."

That year, McDonald also turned in an impressive guest role on *Seinfeld*, playing Elaine's denim vest guy in an episode called "The Strike." Working with Jerry Seinfeld was both inspiring and intimidating. "First of all, I don't think Jerry knew which Kid in the Hall I was," says McDonald, "because he was always calling me Dave. And I remember getting cold stares from everyone when I volunteered an improv line, which apparently the guests never did. Jerry just looked at me and said, 'No,' which felt a little scary."

McDonald also got to work with the legendary Rodney Dangerfield on a low-budget *Godfather* parody called *The Godson* in 1998. "Rodney's trailer reeked of marijuana," remembers McDonald, "but he was a nice man. When I mentioned I was from Toronto, he told me that Jim Carrey was a funny guy. On that film, I also got to work with Dom DeLuise, a hero of mine whose physicality in Mel Brooks's *The Twelve Chairs* really inspired my own comedy."

Mark McKinney had gone straight from the Kids in the Hall to becoming a cast member on *Saturday Night Live*, where he had been working, along with Norm Hiscock, since 1995. At first, McKinney had been thrilled at the prospect of working alongside old friends like Mike Myers and Janeane Garofalo, not to mention comedians he had long admired, including Chris Elliott, David Koechner, and

Michael McKean. But by the end of his first season on the show, he grew frustrated with *SNL* and began to realize just how spoiled he had become from working in his own troupe for the previous ten years.

"In the Kids," says McKinney, "even if my sketch didn't make the other four laugh, I could throw a tantrum and probably get it in. I was totally unprepared for *SNL*'s big-tent, living-newspaper sort of show. It was front-and-centre America, and you needed to have a good sense of what was on the country's mind so you could riff on that. It was a big moment for me at *SNL* when I realized 'I'm not in Kansas anymore.'"

Unlike with the Kids, McKinney was asked to do celebrity impersonations on *SNL*, and over the course of his run turned in memorable performances as Jim Carrey, Paul Shaffer, Gus Van Sant, Ellen DeGeneres, and Judge Lance Ito, from the then-timely O.J. Simpson trial. He also managed to create a few original characters, including his Victorian fop Lucien Callow and one of the two Scottish hooligans in "Scottish Soccer Hooligan Weekly," a collaboration with Mike Myers.

In the middle of McKinney's tenure on *SNL*, Lorne Michaels cleaned house and brought in a mostly new cast. Suddenly, Myers, Garofalo, and Elliott were gone, and McKinney found himself swimming against a new wave of fresh comedy from strong incoming cast members Will Ferrell, Cheri Oteri, and Molly Shannon. "Working with Mike was definitely a case of worlds finally colliding," says McKinney, "but it was good fun, if only for a season and a half. Then he was gone, and I didn't get it together to do a reset and adapt."

After initially resisting the urge to dust off old characters, McKinney and Hiscock decided to give one Chicken Lady sketch a try. But on the night the sketch was set to air, the show was running late and the two found themselves scrambling to make cuts for time. Already flustered, they were further distracted as Courtney Love, an avowed *Kids in the Hall* fan, encountered McKinney in full Chicken Lady costume, and broke his concentration by lavishing him with praise.

"So now I have Courtney Love in one ear while Norm and I are trying to concentrate on condensing this sketch," says McKinney. "By the time I went out, the sketch made no sense, and it was just a pastiche of the scene we had planned. My confidence was completely shot and it became the only time that Chicken Lady ever bombed."

One Saturday night before McKinney left the show, his writer friend David Handelman visited him on set. Almost out of desperation, and to gain control of their destiny, the two sat at McKinney's desk and hammered out a spec script for *The Larry Sanders Show*. While their episode remains unproduced, the script impressed visionary screenwriter and producer Aaron Sorkin, who hired the pair to collaborate on an episode of his short-lived series *Sports Night*. It was the beginning of a long working relationship with Sorkin for both McKinney and Handelman, which included McKinney working as a writer on Sorkin's *SNL*-inspired drama, *Studio 60 on the Sunset Strip*, doing double duty on-screen as fictional TV writer Andy Mackinaw.

Meanwhile, one of McKinney's earliest collaborators, Bruce McCulloch, had music on his mind. As early as 1993, while *The Kids in the Hall* was still in production, McCulloch had made the short film *Coleslaw Warehouse* ("The weirdest thing I ever did," he says), starring *Codco*'s Andy Jones and acclaimed Canadian actor Don McKellar. The music for the film was scored by Bob Wiseman, an original member of Toronto group Blue Rodeo, who offered to help McCulloch explore some of the more musical ideas he had touched on with Kids songs like "Daves I Know." The result was McCulloch's first full-length album, *Shame-Based Man*, released in 1995.

"I didn't grow up liking comedy," says McCulloch. "I only cared about music, beat poetry, and some theatre stuff. I knew about Shorty Petterstein and all that weird shit because my dad was a jazz cat, so a little of that stuff has influenced me. For instance, one of my pieces, 'Never Trust,' is just a list of jokes with music underneath it. I have found that if you include music, it doesn't feel like just a list of jokes."

Coleslaw Warehouse and *Brain Candy* also fuelled McCulloch's interest in directing. As the separation from the Kids became more certain, McCulloch began to flex his directorial muscles with a music video for the Odds' "Make You Mad," and later, The Tragically Hip's "My Music at Work." During the latter shoot, McCulloch struck up a lasting friendship with The Hip's charismatic singer, the late Gord Downie, who invited him to record his second album at The Hip's residential studio, The Bathhouse. Released in 2002, *Drunk Baby Project* reunited McCulloch with his two strongest musical collaborators, Brian Connelly and Craig Northey.

"Bruce and Brian had written some songs," remembers Northey, "and we'd sit in Brian's kitchen writing some more until we had an album."

Producer Susan Cavan, who had also worked on *Coleslaw Warehouse*, played an important role in McCulloch's transition into an alternative career as a TV and film director, and has produced all of his film projects since, including *Dog Park*, which starred Luke Wilson, Natasha Henstridge, and Janeane Garofalo, and the *SNL* spin-off *Superstar*, a vehicle for Molly Shannon's catholic schoolgirl Mary Katherine Gallagher.

As the new millennium approached, the Kids were on speaking terms again, and the cold war began to thaw. McCulloch included McKinney in both *Superstar* and *Dog Park*, and played opposite Foley in Andrew Fleming's Watergate comedy, *Dick*. By the end of 1999, all five Kids in the Hall were sufficiently comfortable with each other to consider thoughts of reuniting, although nothing was on the table.

As the Kids' fan base expanded, thanks to syndication on Comedy Central and the success of their solo careers, the rise of the Internet allowed these new fans to form a community. In the late 1990s, Kids in the Hall fan sites began to emerge, started by fans like Barb Carr, Ed Johnson-Ott, and Trista Lycosky, whose kithfan.org launched in 1997. Among the Kids' most ardent online fans was fifteen-year-old Octavia Phillips from New York, who discovered the series just as Bellini was dancing upon their grave, and connected with like-minded enthusiasts at the newsgroup alt.tv.kids-in-hall. Phillips created a fan site for Dave Foley, and by 1999, "Tavie" had become a valuable liaison between the troupe and their online fan base, working closely with the Kids' long-serving publicist, Nina Weissman, the troupe's "protective den mother and babysitter."

"Even during the downtime after *Brain Candy*," says Phillips, "they all stayed in contact with Nina. She asked me to do web outreach with the fans, and I began setting up their online presence as a troupe in a more official capacity. I've been doing that ever since."

Many of the fans interacting online with Phillips had been too young to witness the troupe during their live tours, and the chat rooms buzzed with demand for some sort of a reunion tour. At home in Canada, a whole generation of fans had memorized every line from the constant reruns of *The Kids in the Hall* on CBC, and later on the Comedy Network, CTV's Canadian cousin to Comedy Central. Since all five members were still alive and actively working, new fans on both sides of the border wanted to see them work together again. In 1999, the Kids' Toronto-based entertainment lawyer David Himelfarb came to them with an offer to reunite at Montreal's prestigious Just for Laughs Festival. The pitch was for the Kids in the Hall to perform a limited run of three shows to be recorded for a one-hour special that they could then shop to a premium cable outlet like HBO or Showtime. "All five had conditions and various emotional baggage," remembers Himelfarb, "but ultimately, all five Kids agreed."

While some of the troupe had worked together or socialized in fractions of two or three since 1996, this would be the first time all five would be together again, so certain conversations were necessary to smooth out the conditions for their reunion. "In 1999, we had to do an initial conference call to discuss our prospects and we were all really nervous on the call. This was the first time that all five of us had talked together in nearly as many years. Dave's father had just got throat cancer and permanently lost his voice, and on the call one of us said to Dave that we were sorry about his father. Dave just deadpanned, 'Well, at least he can't ask me for money anymore,' and we all just laughed our heads off. It was the first dark joke between us in quite a while, and it broke the ice. After that, it was clear that we could work together."

Unfortunately, the Just for Laughs team was unable to deliver a broadcaster, which effectively killed the idea of a televised reunion in Montreal. Despite this setback, the idea of a reunion show had taken root in each Kid's mind, and they were now curious to see if they still had the old chemistry. After talking it over, they opted to go to Montreal anyway, TV special or not, and take a trial run at the reunion. If they were successful, perhaps they could parlay it into some kind of North American tour that could capitalize on their growing fan base and newfound cult status.

And so, like the *coureurs de bois* before them, the Kids in the Hall pulled up their (stretched) metaphorical canoe along the banks of the St. Lawrence River and disembarked in Montreal, just for laughs.

NINETEEN

Same Guys, New Stresses: On the Road Again (2000–10)

For David Himelfarb, the Kids in the Hall's decision to reunite at the 1999 Just for Laughs Festival had been enormously consequential. "After going to Montreal, the whole thing took on a life of its own. And thank goodness, because in the following year we were back on the road and back in business."

Sponsored by Comedy Central, tickets for the Same Guys, New Dresses tour sold out for all shows in a matter of hours. "Comedy Central even sold tickets through their web site, which I believe was a first," says Himelfarb. "There was a lot of hand-holding and a lot of psychology trying to keep everybody happy. But the boys all agreed to play nicely together."

For Mark McKinney, this was the troupe's first formal victory lap since the series had ended, and a chance to bask in the adulation of a newer fan base that had never seen them work on stage. "It was our insane, rock-star tour. We sold out everywhere in record time. We were massive."

Kevin McDonald says he was grateful that Comedy Central had kept their seats warm during the cold war years. "Suddenly, we were told there would be this big audience for us, and we could play in bigger theatres. Bigger than we'd ever played before."

The Kids in the Hall had always functioned best as a live troupe, and even when their interpersonal relationships were the most fraught, they could still make each other laugh. "I loved that this was a live tour," says McKinney. "When someone asks you if you want to do your familiar characters and best scenes for fans who are dying to see you, you say, 'Yes, please!' I think we all knew we could still be good at that."

It had been years since the Kids had mounted a proper theatre tour, and translating over a decade's worth of television sketches to the stage would require a skilled theatre director. Director Jim Millan had first met Scott Thompson as a fellow student in the drama department at York University, and had gone on to start the alternative Crow's Theatre in Toronto. While Millan had been Mark McKinney's neighbour in Toronto's Little Italy, and had occasionally appeared as a background extra on the TV series, he had never formally worked with them until signing on to direct the Kids in the Hall's Same Guys, New Dresses tour.

"Jim was the perfect man for the job," says Himelfarb. "He was an amazingly sensitive artistic director and a fantastic producer who also had the full respect of all the guys."

Himelfarb recalls an upbeat and positive mood as Millan and the Kids worked out the logistics of the tour at Dave Foley's rented home, high in the Hollywood hills. "Jim had three computer screens lined up in the kitchen, and he'd give us all a sense of what the show was going to look like, and how cool the music was going to be. It was fantastic; the guys were giddy, clapping their little hands."

Millan was familiar enough with the troupe to realize that the late-'90s hiatus had probably saved their career in the long run. "If the Beatles had taken a four- or five-year hiatus in 1968," says Millan, "we might have had some great new Beatles music in the '70s. I always tear up at that line in the Clash movie, *The Future Is Unwritten*: 'You just can't endlessly be together.' It's a disaster, no matter who you are."

While Millan says that there was a "surprising amount of goodwill" within the troupe as they prepared for the tour, an air of caution nevertheless hung over the enterprise. "I remember thinking about the kinds of old patterns people fall into," says Millan. "But it was actually pretty great, and very quickly, they set aside childish things, and just delighted in each other's material. It quickly became about the work first. And while we were all on the lookout for the old behavioural patterns that led to the break, everyone was really excited about putting something together. I remember Bruce cry-laughing like a boy at a birthday party. Keeping everybody together all the time could have been disastrous, but they were sharing in all this adulation, so when we all got on the bus together and talked, we made each other laugh, had drinks, and socialized. It was a new beginning. Everyone suddenly realized that this thing was actually the most vital partnership they could have."

The Same Guys, New Dresses tour opened on January 11, 2000, in San Diego and saw the Kids in the Hall back in action for twenty-eight shows in nineteen major cities across North America, before closing on February 28, after two nights at Detroit's State Theatre. The show opened each night in the temp pool at A.T. & Love for a reunion of Cathy and Kathie with a K.

Kevin McDonald says it was pure coincidence that this had been the last cast scene they had shot for the TV series. "It was really about finding a good opening visual for a reunion show," he says. "I think we just liked the image of all of us dressed as women — the new dresses and stuff — but I will say, after we thought of the idea, someone, probably Scott, said, 'You know what I like about this idea? This is how we ended the series.'"

Since it wasn't cost-effective to tour with painted backdrops and unwieldy constructed "flats," Millan created a "lean visual vocabulary" for the tour, using a system of Barco projectors to illuminate large electronic screens behind the troupe. "We considered it a kind of electronic vaudeville," says Millan. "We could project these surrealist mini-films on the screens, but also use them as traditional vaudeville drops for scenes like 'Country Doctor,' where we used a little evocative, country-style music, projected some images of country life, then settled on a really destitute kitchen with just a few pieces of furniture and a white picket fence so that the country doctor could walk by on his way to the house. Then, there'd be a bump in the light as if he'd stepped into the interior, the lights would come up, and there was dying Scott with the Grim Reaper beside him."

A scene like "Comfortable," which had been written for television, was almost impossible to stage in its original format, so Millan suggested stripping it down to a relatively simple set, featuring a couple of key pieces of furniture. "This put all the emphasis on the comedy beats and the gruesomeness of having sex in front of the other couple," says Millan. "Through this translation and innovation, 'Comfortable' ended up becoming a monstrously good live scene for us."

In addition to some new material, such as "Sandwich People" and the evangelical parody "Jesus 2000," Same Guys, New Dresses trotted out some of the troupe's most beloved characters, including the Cops, Mr. Tyzik the Head Crusher, Sir Simon Milligan and Hecubus, Gavin, and Chicken Lady, as well as classic scenes "The Suburbs," "Salty Ham," "Brian's Bombshell," and "To Reg." But there was perhaps no greater example of what rock stars the Kids had become than the hero's welcome afforded Scott Thompson's gay raconteur, Buddy Cole.

"I thought hard about how to introduce Buddy," says Millan, "because we really wanted the audience to enjoy his reveal. We'd have a stagehand come out on a dark stage and put a single bar stool down bathed in a silhouette light. Then, very slowly, another stagehand would bring out a single martini, with this blue light hitting the glass. And then the screaming would begin. It was like a rock show, and it allowed all these Kids in the Hall fans, with all their pent-up love for these guys and their characters, to cheer loudly. In Buddy's scene, Scott was really good at taking his time to have Buddy sashay in slowly to some fabulous club song, and then, as the front light hit him, he'd sit down and say 'Hello, Toronto,' or wherever we were. By this time, the audience was already out of their minds."

According to Himelfarb, it was Dave Foley's idea to film the tour for a documentary, later released on DVD as *Same Guys, New Dresses.* "Dave thought that everything should be recorded," says Himelfarb, "and he didn't want to waste this opportunity. Bruce, on the other hand, was less inclined, and Mark, I think, wanted to discuss it more before committing to the idea. The documentary aspect to the tour became this miserable thing, but at least Kevin and Scott were on board, so Dave, feeling flush in those days from *NewsRadio* and *A Bug's Life*, hired a cameraperson, Darren Ankenman, and a skeleton crew, and they just started filming everything."

Foley remembers McCulloch initially refused to talk in front of the camera. "He'd be OK to do sketches, but he wouldn't be himself behind the scenes. Whenever Darren was shooting, he'd always wave him off."

After agreeing to let McCulloch bring in his producer Susan Cavan, Foley was given more freedom to shoot hours of footage, including a tense moment backstage at Phoenix's Celebrity Theatre, where Foley revealed his intention to have LASIK eye surgery, right in the middle of the tour, amid vocal objections from the rest of the troupe. "The guys freaked out," says Himelfarb. "Not so much because he would hurt himself, but because it would ruin the tour. Why would he do that? It wasn't necessary; he could have done it at any time. You can see it in the movie, I'm trying to get Dave to change his mind while also trying to placate the other four."

"After the tour," says Himelfarb, "Dave spent forever cutting it all together with a lot of help from his wife, Crissy Guerrero. It was a big deal."

What isn't apparent in the final cut of *Same Guys, New Dresses* is that Kevin McDonald was going through a rough time, exacerbated by the death of his mother and a problematic relationship. Today, he acknowledges it must have been hard for the others to be around him for most of the tour. "In the Kids in the Hall, we all take turns being jerks for a period, and during the comeback tour, it was my turn. I didn't sign autographs after the shows; I was a mess. At the time, I had an overpowering girlfriend who came on the tour and wanted me to spend all my time with her and no one else, so I never hung out with the guys. To cope with the grief of losing my mother, I had bought a meditation candle and would just go back to my room after each show and try to meditate, but then I fell asleep one time and nearly burned down the whole hotel."

Same Guys, New Dresses was sold to the CBC as a ninety-minute special, and subsequently released on DVD with additional commentary from Andy Richter, Mike Myers, and Jason Priestley, plus a hilarious contribution from Matt Stone and Trey Parker of *South Park*. While it was a delightful souvenir for fans of the troupe, critical reaction was less than enthusiastic for the film itself. Nathan Rabin, an avowed fan of the Kids in the Hall, criticized the documentary for hovering between low-end cinéma vérité and high-end home movie, writing on the *A.V. Club* that its dependence on "almost perversely mundane backstage footage" detracted from, rather than enhanced, the onstage energy.

Criticisms aside, the 2000 tour re-energized the Kids in the Hall and invited the prospect of future tours, if not future films and television shows. "Being onstage together dissolved all of our feuds," says McKinney, "because on the stage, we have a pure appreciation of each other and of who we are as a troupe. If the motivation to reunite the troupe had been to merely bury the bruising from *Brain Candy* by trying to mount a new TV show or a special, I don't think that would have flown. But the tour was a great way to bring us back."

Apart from the Kids' reactivated career, 2000 was an unpleasant year for Scott Thompson. He had been enlisted by French filmmaker Joel Soler, with whom he was in a relationship at the time, to work on a controversial documentary about the Iraqi leader Saddam Hussein entitled *Uncle Saddam*. Soler had secretly filmed Hussein's barbarous regime, then risked his life to smuggle the footage out of Iraq. Upon his return to the U.S., he had Thompson write and perform the film's narration. When *Uncle Saddam* toured the festival circuit in 2000, it earned both acclaim from critics and death threats from Saddam loyalists. When terrorists firebombed the Los Angeles home Thompson shared with Soler, nobody in authority took it seriously. "This was just before 9/11," says Thompson, "and

I remember the police laughed at us when we told them it was Islamic fundamentalists. That was a phrase that had not really entered the consciousness yet."

According to Thompson, Soler's biggest crime, in Hussein's eyes, was that *Uncle Saddam* made fun of him. "There's nothing that fundamentalist people, regardless of their stripe, hate more than comedy. The powerful start to believe their own shit, and comedy is the enemy of fundamentalists, because it is the enemy of ideology. That's why in fascist societies, comedians are the enemy, because they poke fun at the powerful and mock their ideologies; dictators and fascists hate that."

Thompson and Paul Bellini chronicled the horrific events of this time in Thompson's one-man show, *The Lowest Show on Earth*, which had been scheduled to run in New York City from September 19 to November 4, 2001. But in the aftermath of the 9/11 attacks, the run was abruptly cancelled and Thompson returned to Toronto shaken but still standing.

Working on the Kids in the Hall comeback tour had given Thompson both a safe place to work and a place to renew his energy. And after the success of Same Guys, New Dresses, a second go-around, Tour of Duty, was planned for 2002. The tour would commence in Buffalo, New York, on March 28, and conclude at the Hard Rock Hotel in Las Vegas on May 25. This was the Kids' first foray into a post-9/11 America still reeling from Al Qaeda's sucker punch the previous autumn and wallowing in weaponized jingoism. The Tour of Duty poster depicted the boys in suits and combat helmets instead of new dresses, reflective of the new

Global War on Terror. Even Buddy Cole was transformed, reminiscing on stage about a burqa-clad romp in the Middle East, performing unspeakable sex acts on Saddam's sons. Elsewhere, McCulloch and McKinney, wearing matching grey suits accessorized with American flag ties, performed a kind of Tony Robbins infomercial for a machine that waves the American flag and for an exercise product called "The Amer-Abciser," which sent up the topical notion that jingoism would "keep us safe" from another terrorist attack. Old material like "Dr. Seuss Bible" became newly relevant in an America where some were bruising for a war to pit Christianity against Islam.

Millan returned as director for the Tour of Duty, and their old musical accomplice Craig Northey was enlisted as musical supervisor and a one-man pit band providing musical cues. In addition to appearing onstage as Oliver, Mississippi Gary's guitar player, Northey, also got to perform a short solo set to open the show. "For me, it was the reverse of how comedians like Steve Martin used to open for bands in the '70s," says Northey. "Only I was also the orchestra, alone with my laptop at the side of the stage, providing synthesized pianos and trumpets."

For Himelfarb, managing the regrouped Kids meant accommodating their various solo schedules and working around their family lives. "Dave was always being pulled away by other work," says Himelfarb, "or Bruce was directing Stealing Harvard, or Mark was off doing Guy Maddin's The Saddest Music in the World with Isabella Rossellini, or something. But when they'd get onstage together as the Kids in the Hall, it really was a terrific thing to behold."

After Tour of Duty, the five Kids returned to their solo projects, confident that they could still make live comedy together whenever the desire arose.

In July 2007, the Kids prepared to return to Montreal, selling out the Place des Arts on the closing night of the 25th Annual Just for Laughs Comedy Festival. Having learned how to live together and be confident in their lives apart, these were not the same guys who had tentatively thrown on their old dresses for JFL in 1999. Everyone checked their egos at the door as they convened to write new material together as a group. After rehearsing extensively for a few weeks, they performed a low-key tryout show in L.A. "Whatever got laughs in rehearsals," says McKinney, "made it to the L.A. show, and whatever got laughs in L.A., went to Montreal."

The rehearsals generated over ninety minutes of new material, and even managed to bring back a few crowd-pleasing characters such as Gavin, Buddy Cole, Chicken Lady, Cathy and Kathie, and Mr. Tyzik the Head Crusher. Among the new material was "Let's Rape Kevin," which was funnier than it sounds; "Carfuckers," a film piece that took a cue from David Cronenberg's *Crash*; and "Superdrunk," which featured McCulloch as a crime-fighting superhero ably abetted by his trusty sidekick, Bartender, played by Foley.

Concurrent with the troupe's Just for Laughs return, Kevin McDonald brought a one-man show to Montreal, *Hammy and the Kids*, a biographical recollection of growing up in two dysfunctional families: his childhood with father "Hammy" McDonald and his young adulthood with the Kids in the Hall. The show was born after McDonald's appearance on Carl Arnheiter's talk show, *The Inside Joke*, at the Upright Citizens Brigade in Los Angeles. After his father passed away, McDonald felt freer to explore publicly the trauma of his life with an alcoholic father — and his stories got big laughs from the UCB crowd. Craig Northey was the musical accompanist for *Hammy*'s twelve-show run in Montreal, backing McDonald on songs he'd written exclusively for the show.

"We joked about calling it a 'one-and-a-half man show' because of me," says Northey. "That festival was so good for them. I remember Paul Provenza had a talk show that they put on during the festival, and one night his guests were Eddie Izzard, Billy Connolly, Louis C.K., Lewis Black, Jim Jefferies, and Dave and Kevin. I was so proud seeing my buddies up there, holding their own with heavyweights who clearly respected the Kids. And then I reminded myself that the Kids were now among the heavyweights themselves."

In 2008, they followed up their triumphant run at Just for Laughs with a two-night stint closing out San Francisco's SF Sketchfest at the Palace of Fine Arts. Sketch comedians Janet Varney, Cole Stratton, and David Owen had founded Sketchfest around their shared appreciation for the Kids in the Hall, having followed the troupe since the beginning, sharing VHS cassettes with like-minded comedy nerds.

"They were fresh and interesting and funny and young," says Owen, "and we were just immediately smitten with them. Then, in college, I met Cole and Janet, and we all loved the Kids, so we started thinking about forming our own comedy troupe. In the 2000 tour program, there was a paragraph in the bio that said that Mark had once gone 'blind from unrequited desire,' after which Mark had added 'TOTALLY FALSE PEOPLE!' in all caps. So when we formed our sketch group, we named it Totally False People in their honour."

The double-night closing gala was a way of once again honouring the troupe that had inspired them in the first place. On the first night the troupe sat for a moderated interview followed by an audience Q&A, and closed the festival with a full performance. The two nights were such a rousing success that in April they commenced their first major North American tour in six years, featuring material drawn largely from the Montreal and San Francisco writing sessions, augmented by a few classics and some last-minute additions.

"There's always a point," says Foley, "where we are trying to figure out if it's too dark or too filthy. But that's something we've been asking ourselves before every show since the Rivoli. In the end, we also just have to say 'This is the best we could come up with.'"

The Live As We'll Ever Be tour hit thirty cities in the U.S. and Canada, including San Francisco again, this time at the War Memorial Opera House, a classic venue with a high stage and a deep orchestra pit. Their finale each night featured McKinney's Mr. Tyzik crushing the heads of random audience members and then finally each member of the troupe, with McKinney employing a handheld video camera to allow the audience to see his point-of-view, just like in the television series. "The audience could see themselves on the screen projection as Mr. Tyzik crushed their various heads," says Millan. "But what really made it work was the part where Mark turned the camera on the troupe and judged each of the Kids' career crimes, until eventually he had this schizophrenic moment where he had to crush his own head. The troupe always loved the idea that they were all dead at the end of the show."

In San Francisco, Mr. Tyzik had already successfully crushed the heads of Foley, McDonald, and McCulloch when it came time to put the pinch on Thompson. Hoping to add a little comedic pratfall to his head crush, Thompson thought it would be funny to roll off the stage. "We'd been having a hot night," remembers McKinney. "The crowd was there for us, and everybody was exhilarated, so it was kind of cool." In the excitement of the moment, Thompson forgot about the twenty-foot-deep orchestra pit in front of him, and when he rolled off the stage he hit the ground flat on his back with a resounding thud. It looked horrible, even from the audience's vantage point, but it felt even worse for Thompson, who, ever the trouper, somehow managed to crawl back onstage for his curtain call.

"I was in agony," recalls Thompson, "but I got to my feet to take my bow, damn it. The show must go on, after all."

Backstage, as the adrenalin of live performance began to wear off, Thompson doubled over in pain and an ambulance was called to rush him to a nearby hospital. While he would later joke that the most humiliating part of the ordeal was hearing the ambulance attendant repeating, 'We've got a forty-nine-year-old coming in,' over and over again on the radio, the worst part was learning firsthand about the insanely expensive American healthcare system.

"As a Canadian boy," says Thompson, "I was shocked that the ambulance was going to cost me $5,000, and to top it off, my credit card wouldn't go through."

Miraculously, Thompson managed to make it to the stage for their next show in Portland, and completed the tour, a little sore but more or less intact.

In June 2008, the Kids in the Hall were honoured with a star on Canada's Walk of Fame, alongside fellow luminaries as k.d. lang, Steve Nash, and James Cameron. Out on the red carpet, Kevin McDonald said the troupe was happy to be recognized as a part of Canadian entertainment history, and noted that their star was not far from the Rivoli, where it all began in 1984. To celebrate, the Kids staged a one-off reunion show at the old club on Queen Street West. "We called it our '24th Anniversary of the Rivoli,'" says McDonald, "because we couldn't wait to do the 25th Anniversary."

That night, the troupe performed mostly old material from their earliest days, including what Dave Foley says was the first sketch Scott Thompson ever pitched to the Kids: "The Rectum-Vagina Challenge." "We all hated it," remembers Foley. "Scott thought it was because we were homophobic, but we all said, 'No, Scott, it's because it's a TV commercial parody, you idiot.' Pretty much any kind of parody was frowned upon in our troupe."

"It was based on one of those ads where they're comparing two different types of detergent," adds Paul Bellini, "only they were asking 'Rectum or vagina?' It was just so appalling. You couldn't believe what you were seeing. When I first saw them do it twenty years ago, I thought, 'Oh my god, these guys will go far.' They threw the sketch out pretty fast, and Scott wasn't allowed to perform it again until the reunion."

The Rivoli's Carson Foster was back for the reunion show and admits he often found himself laughing for all the wrong reasons. "The best part for me was the way they were forgetting their lines," says Foster. "Meanwhile, I pretty much knew the whole show back to front from having watched it so many times from behind the bar."

At year's end, Himelfarb left the troupe on a high note, pleased that during his time with them they had all come to realize the importance of being the Kids in the Hall, no matter what else they had going on in their own lives. "That 2008 tour did remarkably well considering their age and everything else," says Himelfarb. "They were older, and they all had responsibilities, but it's always nice for them to come back to the comfort of their comedy buddies. My tenure with them ended in 2008, but I'm still friendly with everybody."

On the heels of the Walk of Fame ceremony, Telefilm Canada announced that *The Kids in the Hall* would be returning to television for an eight-episode miniseries that would debut on the CBC in 2010. "We still want to do stuff together," Foley told the *National Post*'s Vanessa Farquharson, "because we still have this knowledge of each other and comfort with each other in terms of comedy that we don't have anywhere else." Spirits in the troupe were once again high, with Foley even speculating that, if all went well, they might take a second stab at a feature film. But first, he joked, they would have to wait "until everyone who ever saw *Brain Candy* is dead."

TWENTY

Death Comes to Town

Apart from the short "Carfuckers" sketch projected for audiences on their Live As We'll Ever Be tour, there had been no new original filmed content from the Kids in the Hall since *Brain Candy*. Since 1999, when the troupe sporadically began touring again, each of the Kids had worked steadily on their own television and movie projects. Scott Thompson was a series regular on *Providence* and *Further Tales of the City*, in addition to doing voice-over work and guest starring on series such as *Grounded for Life*, *Touched by an Angel*, and *Aqua Teen Hunger Force*, and taking a role in the feature film *The Pacifier*. Mark McKinney had been a cast member and writer on Aaron Sorkin's *Studio 60 on the Sunset Strip*, and had cocreated the critically acclaimed series *Slings and Arrows*. Additionally, he'd made appearances on Canadian television in series such as *Hatching, Matching, and Dispatching*; *The Rick Mercer Report*; *Robson Arms*; and their old friend Brent

Butt's hit series, *Corner Gas*. After *NewsRadio*, Foley had written a star-studded, Gemini-nominated CBC holiday program, *The True Meaning of Christmas Specials*, guest starring a few of his friends, including Kevin McDonald, Jason Priestley, Andy Richter, Tom Green, Joe Flaherty, Dave Thomas, and Mike Myers, and had made regular guest appearances on hit shows like *The King of Queens*, *Just Shoot Me*, *Scrubs*, and *Will & Grace*, in addition to the Canadian feature films *Whitecoats* (also known as *Intern Academy*), directed by *SCTV*'s Dave Thomas, and *Childstar*, directed by Don McKellar. Kevin McDonald was a recurring cast member on *That '70s Show* and had appeared on *Arrested Development*; *Corner Gas*; *Yes, Dear*; *Grounded for Life*; and *According to Jim*; and had worked extensively as a voice actor for animations such as the *Lilo & Stitch* series. Finally, Bruce McCulloch directed the feature films *Stealing Harvard* and *Comeback Season*, and was the creator of the short-lived ABC sitcom *Carpoolers*, while appearing as an actor on television programs such as *Further Tales of the City*, *Twitch City*, and *Gilmore Girls*. Their visibility as solo actors and their frequent tours had kept their names and brand of comedy alive, and a whole new generation of fans revered their work.

Their Live As We'll Ever Be tour had packed houses all over North America, and perhaps more importantly, it had proven to the troupe that they could still generate fresh and strong new material. While on that tour, Bruce McCulloch was struck by a familiar urgency; it was time to make some more television as the Kids in the Hall. "I was like, 'We have to do something now,'" says McCulloch. "It was another one of those times where I took out the booster cables and I put them on our hearts and said, 'Follow me, boys.'"

Ever since the Rivoli days, McCulloch had been the "work pig" of the group, a fact which original Kids member Luc Casimiri attested to when recalling an early writing session in Mark McKinney's cramped apartment. "Bruce was on a mattress on the floor, with crayons everywhere and a typewriter," recalls Casimiri. "Mark opened a file folder of ideas. Bruce would type out everything — his stand-up sets, sketches, everything. Mark turned to me and said, 'This is why Bruce is going to be famous.' He was very disciplined. And you can still see it in the makeup of the group. In my opinion, none of their projects happen unless it's Bruce that's driving them."

Even while the tour was still on the road, McCulloch was brainstorming ideas for a new television series. His strongest idea was an episodic murder mystery set in a fictional Northern Ontario town with a secret. Shuckton, as he called the town, would be a small and unassuming Canadian community imbued with a supernatural darkness, populated by a cast of typically eccentric and obsessive Kids in the Hall characters.

McCulloch's plot for *Death Comes to Town* involves the murder of a small-town mayor, a morbidly obese former teen hockey star, a bitter rivalry between competing local television news anchors, a disturbed child, and a supernaturally inclined Indigenous man who receives a visit from the Grim Reaper (a leather-clad biker with few discernible life skills). In other words, this was fertile comic ground for the Kids in the Hall.

By 2009, the Kids in the Hall brand was solid and the troupe was a beloved Canadian comedy institution. While it had been years since Ivan Fecan, their old defender at the CBC, had left the Corporation, such was their reputation that the CBC's Fred Fuchs agreed with very little discussion to commit the network to an eight-part Kids in the Hall miniseries. Once they had a green light, McCulloch and producer Susan Cavan assembled a crew that included former *Brain Candy* director Kelly Makin. "The troupe hadn't really shot anything together in years," says Cavan, "but this seemed like a fantastic project and they were all really determined to make it happen."

Meanwhile in Winnipeg, Mark McKinney continued his work as head writer and showrunner on the television series *Less Than Kind*. "I was really busy, so I was happy to let Bruce quarterback the enterprise," says McKinney. "I could only intermittently chime in from Winnipeg, but ultimately, we all ended up writing on it."

McCulloch saw the massive project as his way of saying thank-you to his fellow Kids for putting up with him over the years. "I wanted to be really great and generous about it, and that included accommodating everybody's schedules and making sure everybody was comfortable with the characters they wanted to play."

Absent from their usual writing team this time was Norm Hiscock, who was busy with other projects, including *Corner Gas* and *Parks and Recreation*. However, Garry Campbell returned, joining McCulloch, McDonald, and Thompson at Hollywood's Steve Allen Theater to break down the storyline for the series.

The story begins as the tiny town of Shuckton's bid for the 2028 Summer Olympics has been — of course — rejected. Shortly after this news breaks, Shuckton's Mayor Larry Bowman (McCulloch) is killed, and a local drifter, a one-sixteenth Ojibwe man named Crim Hollingsworth (Thompson) is found with incriminating evidence on him and charged with the crime. But local former hockey hopeful Ricky Jarvis (McCulloch in a fat suit) believes that Crim is innocent, and with a woman named Marnie (McDonald), he sets about uncovering the identity of the real killer. Meanwhile, Death (McKinney) checks into the town's seedy motel like a leather-vested travelling salesman with a quota of souls to collect. There follows a courtroom drama evocative of *To Kill a Mockingbird*, and several intertwined subplots that reveal Shuckton to be a town with a secret, worthy of David Lynch's *Twin Peaks*. Two rival newscasters, Corrinda Gablechuck (McKinney) and Heather Weather (Thompson), fight over their coverage of the story, while the town's bald and eccentric coroner, Dusty Diamond (Thompson), tries to conceal his secret love for Mayor Bowman, which he has taken to necrophilic proportions. Meanwhile the Mayor's adopted son, Rampop (Landon Reynolds-Trudel), who sees all the local townspeople as animated butterflies, is the only person in Shuckton who can see and communicate with Death.

There's a lot going on, and hilarity, as they say, ensues. But with a plot so convoluted, and with this being the Kids in the Hall, an inevitable battle also ensued over the script. "We all knew that the plot needed to be strong if we were going to stretch it over eight episodes," says Campbell. "And we did argue a lot about it, but we were really lucky to have Mark and Dave giving their best ideas, because Dave, in particular, is a great punch-up guy, and he is always concerned about finding the funny. In the end, the balance between all five of them is why it worked."

In March, a few weeks into the writing process, Scott Thompson began to complain that he was feeling anxious and nauseous. He put it down to a recent incident that occurred near the tiny apartment he rented in a not-so-great part of Los Angeles. Gangs frequented the area, and Thompson often fell asleep to the sound of distant gunfire. But on one recent evening, the gunfire no longer seemed distant. In fact, says Thompson, the shots sounded uncomfortably close. "I heard nine or ten gunshots, right outside my door, and I went into shock. I spent the night huddled against the thickest wall I could find, so the bullets couldn't come through."

For Thompson, the sounds and smells of gunfire triggered traumatic memories of the 1975 school shooting he had lived through as a teenager in Brampton, Ontario. Having internalized this trauma for most of his life, he was now aware of a pain deep in his abdomen. "The next morning I woke up on the floor clutching my belly. I had been cowering on the floor all night, trying to stay low."

When he arrived at work later that morning, Thompson tried to laugh off the previous night's gunplay. After cracking a few jokes about it, he realized that Campbell and McCulloch weren't laughing. "I couldn't figure out why their eyes were misting and they were crying," says Thompson, "and then, finally, Bruce just said, 'Scott, you can't live there anymore. Get out of there; it's not good.' And I remember thinking he was right; it *wasn't* funny. After that, my stomach kept hurting; the pain never went away."

In the first week of April, Thompson's doctor informed him that he was suffering from non-Hodgkin's lymphoma, a cancer of the immune system that had manifested in his stomach. Upon leaving his doctor's office, Thompson notified the other Kids about his cancer, which he remains convinced was the product of internalized trauma. "When I told Bruce I had cancer, he said one of the funniest things he's ever said to me. He said, 'Are you kidding me? You mean you don't have AIDS? What kind of a world is this that you don't have AIDS?'"

"I remember when Scott told us," says McCulloch. "Suddenly, the project had gone from 'It's going to be fun to do something again' to 'Is Scott going to be able to do this or not?' I knew it probably meant the most to Scott for us to do this thing, but as an executive producer, I had to make a decision: 'OK, we have to say we're doing it, and if Scott has to do less, then he has to do less.'"

Immediately after his diagnosis, Thompson began chemotherapy at Cedars-Sinai in Los Angeles, all the while continuing to write the series until his Screen Actors Guild health insurance ran out, whereupon he was forced to return to Toronto to complete his treatments. With Thompson burdened by his medical crisis, Paul Bellini was invited back to reprise his earliest role as the "Scott wrangler."

"Scott was fucking falling apart," says Bellini, matter-of-factly, "but they all wanted to keep him in the show because he was well enough to work. Still, you can imagine the hormonal mess he was every day, crying over everything. I was mostly his babysitter, but we did end up basically rewriting most of his scenes and characters together, although I was uncredited."

The entire troupe eventually regrouped back in Toronto to develop the shooting script for *Death Comes to Town* at the Factory Theatre. Director Kelly Makin returned from Winnipeg, where he and McKinney had been working together on *Less Than Kind*, and says it was great to see the troupe in such unity, in stark contrast to the bitter infighting he had witnessed during the *Brain Candy* sessions. "Each day, we'd go up to the top floor of the theatre and read through the scripts as a troupe, rewriting and getting everybody's input," says Makin. "Scott was in radiation treatments at the time, so he would come in and work for as long as he could. The Kids could be known to fight sometimes, but now they were loving brothers, rallying around Scott, supporting him and working the shooting schedule around his treatments. Nobody knew at the time what would happen to him, but once they got together and started riffing, the magic came back."

McCulloch says that more than any other project he has worked on, with or without the Kids, *Death Comes to Town* was a simple matter of the troupe following where their premise took them. "I would say to the others, 'Let's just follow the fun. Let's just follow the water.' That's how we came up with backstories like Mayor Larry Bowman being a draft dodger, or how 'Doc' Porterhouse was the town abortionist, and all of the stories that could happen in a place like Shuckton, like having somebody be bludgeoned to death by a TV remote."

Thompson's cancer treatments stretched well into August, when *Death Comes to Town* commenced principal photography in North Bay, Ontario. News of his condition was kept under wraps, and only key members of the production team were aware of the serious challenges he faced. Producer Susan Cavan was impressed by the troupe's stoic solidarity. "They really pulled together. It was wonderful to see the magic that they can create in comedy when they're all together. It was so smart to isolate the whole troupe up in North Bay for the entire eight-week shoot. They were all held captive and it gave them a singular purpose."

For Thompson, that sense of solidarity was a shining beacon in an otherwise dark time. While his doctors were wary of signing off on his participation in the project, Thompson insisted upon joining his comedy brothers and getting to play characters in front of the cameras again. "My doctors weren't sure I could do this, but I told them 'I'm doing it. There's nothing stopping me.' I wasn't used to taking a backseat, and I don't like being carried, but the other four guys were just wonderful on this project."

Converting a local high school into their production offices, Makin and his cinematographer, Paul Sarossy, a veteran of many of Atom Egoyan's films, worked out the visual language for *Death Comes to Town*, while back in Vancouver, Craig Northey composed the musical score, assisted by Toronto composer Jim McGrath. "Jim's a very strong orchestral composer," says Northey, "and while I have a knowledge of theory and those basic ideas, I don't come from the same place as him. I mostly worked remotely from Vancouver, but I would visit the set to get feedback from Bruce and Kevin, and it was great to hang out with the guys, and check in with Kelly to make sure I was on the right track."

After knowing and working with the Kids for nearly two decades, Northey had become a member of the family, and his intimacy with the troupe afforded him profound insights into their dynamic on the set.

"Scott's situation brought on a truly profound understanding of what everybody contributes to the group," says Northey. "Scott is an actor with pure heart, who reminds everybody that a scene has to have an emotional centre. Dave can look at a scene that was already uproariously funny, and then throw in a better joke that takes it up another notch. Bruce is an unstoppable 'Type A' creative force who is just naturally funny with a soulful darkness. Mark is a great character actor, like a rocket scientist of character development, but with a brilliant understanding of dialect. And Kevin is such a natural performer and an improviser with so much heart; he's the rascally innocent who's always causing problems."

When Thompson's chemotherapy treatments caused his hair to fall out, he chose to play Dusty Diamond, the town coroner who is secretly in love with the Mayor, as a bald man. "I thought it was such a funny and weird choice," says McCulloch. "That was the moment when I realized that *Death Comes to Town* was going to be fine, because Scott had created this brand-new, hilarious character that he could do tirelessly. You know, he didn't seem to have cancer when he was improvising as Dusty."

Thompson created a backstory for Diamond that explained his baldness as alopecia, but another, more pressing motivation was that he was finding it painful to wear wigs, costumes, or even face makeup. "I already had Heather Weather and Crim in these big full wigs," says Thompson, "so I made sure that Dusty had none of that. I was willing to do the first two because they were great characters, and besides, there was a chance that this might be the last job I would ever do. But I could really only handle three characters, so I worked hard to make them all indelible, and you know, I also think I wanted just one of my characters to be a document of the real me at this time in my life — so that when I was older, I could look back and go, 'Wow, there I was, truly sick as a dog, but still shining.'"

McCulloch came to regret volunteering to play the role of Shuckton's morbidly obese and disgraced former local hockey star, Ricky Jarvis, for which he was required to wear uncomfortable prosthetics under the hot lights for hours at a time. "Playing Ricky was probably one of the low points of my whole life," says McCulloch, laughing ruefully. "We didn't have the money for those big-budget fat suits they have in Hollywood movies, and we couldn't really spare the overtime to let me out of the suit for breaks. On top of it all, the way we organized the production, we'd shoot people out so they could leave to go do other work, which left only Kevin, and me in the fat suit, in fuckin' North Bay. If there were one single analogy for *Death Comes to Town*, it would be me alone in a fat suit when everyone else had gone home. It really was one of the grimmest performances I've ever had to endure. At the end of the day, I'd rip off my fat face and down an entire beer."

Makeup designer Geri Wraith also spent two hours transforming Mark McKinney into the lead role of Death. Each shoot day, McKinney's face and body were airbrushed a pale grey, after which Wraith applied three scars and three tattoos, painted-on veins, a fake upper tooth, black nails, and contact lenses. "Mark was amazing in that role," says McCulloch, "and once he gets into the character, he can physicalize anything, which was perfect because, as Death, he's obviously the centre of the whole miniseries."

McKinney portrayed Death as part biker, part debt col-lector, who enters the sleepy town of Shuckton like some travelling salesman of eternal sleep. While McKinney notes that the role, tricked out with his leathers and greasy long hair, bore certain similarities to his character from "Bobby and the Devil," he identifies a few stark differences. "Death was sort of a slower character than the Devil, and this guy was like a recent bachelor who hasn't been on the dating scene in a while, a bit of a lost man who hangs out at a bar after work. And he's a little bitter, because he hasn't been assigned the best region with the more exciting deaths, you know?"

With so many distinctive characters to create, and so little time and money, Wraith was forced to work even more economically than usual. "On one day, Mark might have to shoot scenes as Death in the morning, but then in the afternoon, he'd also have to play The Judge, with these fake bushy brows and simple straight makeup. Then, he'd do a bit as Chicken Lady, which involved a prosthetic beaked nose, white/yellow skin, lashes, and eye shadow. Somehow, we got through it all, though, and Mark was a trouper."

Despite Thompson's health concerns, Bellini says the atmosphere on set was the happiest he'd ever witnessed. There were times, however, when Thompson needed to let it all out.

"Scott was all over the board emotionally," says Bellini. "I remember one time he came home crying his eyes out and saying, 'Paul, it's terrible, most of my characters in the show die.' Still, I know that I helped keep Scott on track, and I even reprised my role as the 'Man in the Towel,' which was fun to shoot. Everybody treated me very special on set."

Given his condition, Thompson found playing the role of Heather Weather, which required him to wear high heels, to be the most demanding part of the shoot. To add insult to injury, he got hurt while rehearsing a scene where Heather has an altercation with McKinney's rival newscaster, Corrinda Gablechuck. "Mark was supposed to crash into me and knock me down," says Thompson, "but as I went down, I tore my left calf muscle in half. It was a nightmarish injury on top of everything else that was going on. So, for the rest of the shoot, I'd be in a wheelchair as soon as I could get off camera. I was on crutches because I couldn't really walk. I also had a lot of water buildup in my legs, which is a common side effect of chemotherapy, but combined with my calf injury, my leg was the size of an elephant's. To be honest, it actually took me a year to fully heal."

On five different occasions during the shoot, Thompson had to be rushed to the hospital with a high fever, and he still becomes emotional when he recalls just how much his fellows Kids cared for him during this terrible chapter in his life. "I love them so much," says Thompson. "I mean, sometimes we hate each other, and we've done the worst things on earth to each other, yet in a fight, no one's going to hurt my brother. I come from a family of five brothers, so I understand the power of teamwork. I remember thinking I would try to do everything I could, but I knew I couldn't be 100 percent; they were just going to have to carry me. Sometimes I'd cry, and Bruce would come over and lie with me. It was sweet."

The troupe's morale was the polar opposite of what it had been on *Brain Candy*, largely because, this time, they turned toward each other for support instead of away. "I think it was because we all really wanted to get Scott through this thing," says McCulloch. "It was just as tough to make this series, but for some reason it was also really fun."

One night during the shoot in North Bay, Thompson had a fever dream about crows pecking at his cabin, trying to get at him. He awoke in a cold sweat, convinced that Death had come for him in the night. The next day, he began sobbing uncontrollably on set, hallucinating that McKinney truly was the Devil, and had to be rushed back to his trailer until he recovered. "I just couldn't stop crying," says Thompson. "I kept seeing Mark morph in and out as Death and the Devil. Still, I was convinced I was going to beat him, because in the script, my character Crim beats Death in the end.'"

Thompson's chemotherapy ended just as production was wrapping, and not a moment too soon. Depleted, he says he didn't have much left to give and barely made it over the finish line. "They finished shooting all my stuff about a week before the other guys. My doctor had told me that the cancer was gone but I still had to do radiation, because there could have been microscopic traces left. I was dressed as Heather Weather, Bruce was dressed as the Mayor, and we were doing the scene when Heather and the Mayor are in the bus that goes to hell. Bruce and I sat in the back, and he held my hand, and I put my head on his shoulder. We weren't Scott and Bruce; we were Heather and the Mayor, really. It's a memory I'll always remember. It was very, very special for me. They carried me. And I love them for it."

Thompson collapsed at the wrap party, and was back in Toronto the next morning to begin his radiation treatments at Princess Margaret Hospital. "There was no way I could have shot even one more day, because my whole system went to war against me and I just fell apart. My leg was so fat and swollen that it became completely useless, and the radiation took me to a very terrible place. I had no energy and had to sleep eighteen hours a day. I got shingles, my whole body got rashes, I grew breasts, and I had to have a double mastectomy. It was an awful, awful thing." But just as Crim had beaten Death, Thompson survived the ordeal.

Death Comes to Town debuted on January 13, 2010. The plan was to run the series over eight consecutive weeks, but after five episodes they were pre-empted when CBC realized that most of their potential viewers would be tuned in to the rival CTV network for their coverage of the Winter Olympics, held that year in Vancouver. "It was a classic CBC move," says Bellini. "You can't take a two-week break from a difficult-to-follow, serialized mystery and expect to hold an audience. They destroyed it, as usual, and in our last three weeks, our ratings were almost zero. But you know, in Canada, there's just no competing with hockey. What are you going to do? We can't all be Rick Mercer."

In America, *Death Comes to Town* got a second chance late in the summer when it aired on the IFC network. An ardent Kids in the Hall fan, Dan Pasternack was IFC's incoming president of development and production at the time and picked up the U.S. rights to the miniseries sight unseen. "IFC then asked me to sit down and watch *Death Comes to Town* and tell them what I thought," says Pasternack. "After bingeing the entire miniseries in one sitting, I told them, frankly, that it was not for everybody, and that plenty of people wouldn't get it. But I also told them that in my considered opinion the Kids in the Hall were Canada's Monty Python, and an essential sketch comedy troupe. So IFC went for it."

Pasternack's instincts about the selective appeal of *Death Comes to Town* proved correct. The series made very little impact south of the border, drawing mixed reactions from fans and critics alike. But Kelly Makin feels it was just business as usual for the Kids, who had historically sided with their own instincts over the lure of broader commercial appeal. "Maybe it's a Canadian thing," says Makin. "I don't know if, down in the States, you'd get people embracing a film about depression, or a miniseries about the grim reaper visiting a small Ontario town. I think sometimes the Kids just tend to find humour in those uncomfortable places where projects like *Brain Candy* or *Death Comes to Town* live."

McKinney holds a minority opinion within the troupe that *Death Comes to Town* never fully realized its potential. "I had concerns going in that the scripts weren't fully cooked," says McKinney. "Just like with *Brain Candy*, we picked an ambitious subject that needed to be very intricate plot-wise in order to pull it off. But I know we're all divided on that. I think I'm the only one who sort of goes 'Well, it was OK, but I'm not sure it was our best.'"

On the other hand, friend and fan of the troupe Paul Feig insists that he saw the old magic. "We were immediately hooked and devoured all the episodes," says Feig. "They are geniuses, and no matter how much time passes, they always seem to be able to recapture that chemistry." In the end, the troupe's collective ability to face down the darkness may have been the key to their continued survival both as humans and as comedians. According to McCulloch, the whole troupe believed that if they could just prop up Thompson and carry him to the finish line, *Death Comes to Town* might just save his life. "And looking back," adds McCulloch, "I'm pretty sure it did."

Thompson himself concurs, adding that their collective journey as the Kids in the Hall is the living embodiment of Lenny Bruce's old adage that "comedy is tragedy plus time."

"All five of us come from deep wounding," says Thompson. "I think all artists do. There are certain parts of your narrative that you can't really get over so you just keep scratching at them, and you make art out of it. One of my greatest thrills is to go onstage with a joke that people said couldn't be done and score with it. Maybe the next thing we do, we'll be branded as awful or reactionary, but who cares? Ten years later, perhaps we'll be in a different social place and praised. Everything changes, but it's so exhilarating to just survive. Nothing touches survival. Nothing."

TWENTY-ONE

We're Not Quitting

As the great Ottawa Valley bluesman Mississippi Gary might have said: "If the blues don't kill you, they'll only make you stronger." After suffering the outrageous slings and arrows of a life in show business, surviving internal squabbles, health scares, and the assorted pitfalls of growing up in public, the Kids in the Hall have emerged stronger and more resilient than ever. Death literally came to town and together they crushed its head.

The Kids' hard-fought brotherhood has come with a shared realization that they no longer need to quarrel over every little thing the way they used to. "Mark and I were savages in the beginning," says McCulloch. "I mean we thought we were in the Buzzcocks or the Sex Pistols, fighting to get our songs into the set. I was a jackhammer, and Mark was a bag of flies; you'd never know what he was thinking. He's a mysterious, weird fucker, but he's my comedy brother. Then, when we first met Dave and Kevin, they were elegant and quite gentle, and they would slowly decide on what they should do and if someone really wanted to do something, well, then you would let them do it. Our personalities were set early on, and this is also the great thing about life — we're basically all the same weirdos in our fifties."

These middle-aged men are still in the hall, and have adapted and grown over their three decades in the troupe. Today, McCulloch jokingly considers bringing back his hipster dude from "He's Hip, He's Cool, He's 45" for a future tour — only this time, he jokes, "He's hip, he's cool, and he *wishes* he was still 45."

Kevin McDonald, the self-described "King of Empty Promises," admits that he is far less passive-aggressive today than he was in the troupe's early days, and owes at least some part of this evolution to his time with the Kids. "Would I have been aware of that side of myself if the guys hadn't called me on it all the time? Would I be that smart? I don't know. I can still be passive-aggressive sometimes, but hopefully not as much as the others have mythologized about me."

While each of the Kids has had to work to become a more functional adult, Dave Foley insists that the chemistry within the troupe feels exactly as it did thirty years ago, provided that "there isn't a mirror in the room to remind us all of how old we are. Frankly, I think we all hated being in the group a lot of the time. But I still feel this special energy when all five of us are in a room. When we work together, I know I'm on stage with the four funniest guys I've ever met in my life, and they're making me funnier as a result. The audience is just electrified and we're sharing this whole experience."

Since *Death Comes to Town*, the Kids have continued to pursue their individual careers, with varying degrees of success and disappointment. McCulloch says it is now understood that they will always have the troupe to come home to. "We've all tasted victory at various times," says McCulloch, "but we've also known crushing defeat, so we come by our humility naturally."

Immediately after his successful battle with cancer, Scott Thompson revisited an unproduced Danny Husk screenplay he'd written ten years earlier and, with the help of Stephan Nilson and Kyle Morton at Frozen Beach Studios, he transformed it into a graphic novel. "I hope you like it," Thompson wrote in the introduction to *Husk: The Hollow Planet*, "but just remember that if you don't, you must hate life and love cancer."

After completing a sequel, *Husk Vol. 2: A Crack In It*, in 2013, Thompson took the role of Jimmy Price in Bryan Fuller's NBC drama series, *Hannibal*. A cult hit, *Hannibal* attracted large crowds to a cast meet-and-greet at San Diego Comic-Con in 2014, but NBC nevertheless cancelled the series in 2015, despite a vigorous letter-writing campaign from its small but loyal fan base.

Mark McKinney created a niche for himself on the stage and on Canadian television. *Slings and Arrows*, created with Susan Coyne and Bob Martin, ran on The Movie Network from 2003 to 2006, earning him a Gemini Award for Best Performance by an Actor in a Continuing Leading Dramatic Role for his portrayal of New Burbage Festival theatre manager Richard Smith-Jones. He enjoyed further success with HBO Canada's *Less Than Kind*, racking up numerous awards for writing, directing, and producing, and remained showrunner until the series ended in 2013. And in January 2014, he portrayed politician George Quimby in the six-part CBC miniseries *The Best Laid Plans*, before joining the cast of Simon Rich's FXX series, *Man Seeking Woman*, alongside Jay Baruchel and Eric Andre.

From September 2011 to June 2012, Dave Foley appeared as Jerry Dunham on CBS's short-lived *How to Be a Gentleman*, before moving on to the final three seasons in the role of Detective Bob Moore on the TV Land sitcom *Hot in Cleveland*. After returning to stand-up for his Showtime comedy special (and album) *Relatively Well* in 2013, Foley returned to Canadian television the following year, portraying public relations boss Dave Lyons in the CTV sitcom *Spun Out*. That series was cancelled in 2015 after criminal charges were filed against another cast member, though thankfully Foley was not involved in the case.

That same year, Kevin McDonald released his first stand-up comedy album, *Making Faces*, in which he explores the time-honoured clash between sketch and stand-up, and relates some autobiographical stories, such as "Masturbation Fire" about his time as Scott Thompson's roommate during the Kids' New York boot camp. McDonald also included a few of his songs like "Sugar-Free Sugar Daddy" and his confessional folk song, "Passive Aggressive." The following year, he launched a podcast, *Kevin McDonald's Kevin McDonald Show*, on the Forever Dog Podcast Network, where his guests have included Rachel Dratch, Gin

Blossoms, Dana Gould, Ted Leo, Wallace Shawn, Mike Myers, and of course, Foley and Thompson.

Similarly, Bruce McCulloch has created a few autobiographical works, including his memoir, *Let's Start a Riot*, published in 2014, and a one-man show that later became a TV series, *Young Drunk Punk*, directed by One Yellow Rabbit's Blake Brooker. Combining stand-up, live music, and autobiographical insights, *Young Drunk Punk* recounted his journey from Calgary punk to '90s Toronto hipster to a "pyjama-clad dad" living with a family in the Hollywood Hills. He even brought in his oldest living friend from the Calgary days, Brian Connelly, as musical director. For McCulloch, the process was all part of opening up and "letting the love I've always felt out of my body. It's so easy to be attracted to all the bad things that happen to you, but it's also nice sometimes to go, 'Oh, I learned something there. That was kind of sweet.' But just for a second because, as a comedian, it gets creepy if you stay there too long."

Besides launching solo careers for each of the Kids, the television series also launched the careers of their writers. Paul Bellini spent time at CBC's *This Hour Has 22 Minutes*, and Brian Hartt has thrived at *Mad TV* and *The Tonight Show with Jay Leno*. Garry Campbell also worked at *MAD TV*, in addition to *Less Than Kind*, and he was a co-producer, with McKinney, of the short-lived series from the Canadian sketch troupe Picnicface, for the Comedy Network. However, it is Norm Hiscock who has emerged as the most successful of them all. After two years at *SNL*,

Hiscock has won multiple awards as a writer and producer on hit series like *King of the Hill*, *Parks and Recreation*, and most recently, *Brooklyn Nine-Nine*. "We had a lot of freedom on *The Kids in the Hall*," says Hiscock. "For us it was just about hanging out with like-minded people, and I know that Andy Samberg told me that's what he and his friends also have in The Lonely Island. I loved those Digital Shorts they did on *SNL*, and those guys say they watched *The Kids in the Hall* and were big fans, so that's pretty awesome."

Twenty years after its disappointing theatrical release, *Brain Candy* found a second life as a cult classic. After participating in a live table read of David Wain's *Wet Hot American Summer*, Bruce McCulloch thought it would be fun to do one for *Brain Candy,* so in March 2014, the Kids and Craig Northey staged the first-ever live table read of *Brain Candy* at Toronto's Queen Elizabeth Theatre. Northey's house band included members of Sloan and the Skydiggers, and Gord Downie came in to perform "Butts Wigglin'," the film's unofficial theme song.

The following year, the Kids launched a massive twenty-six-city tour. Beginning in Toronto on April 23, the tour concluded in Denver, Colorado, on June 6. Mark McKinney says that, these days, the troupe is adamant about writing brand-new material for every tour. "We do our hits too, but I think it's neat that we still try to take a risk and generate at least 50 percent new material. I've seen a bunch of tours go up lately, and almost all of the people who are in our position are doing nostalgia or greatest-hits tours. I still believe we are a great live act."

As writing and rehearsals began for the tour, both

Dave Foley and Mark McKinney awaited news about their respective sitcom pilots. Foley had been cast in Ken Jeong's short-lived ABC sitcom *Dr. Ken*, while McKinney had taken a role on NBC's *Superstore*. "Before the tour," says McKinney, "I had been working on a bunch of stuff, including shooting the pilot. It wasn't until May, when we were playing a show in Durham, North Carolina, that I heard NBC had picked up *Superstore*. Then, later that same night, Dave found out that ABC had picked up *Dr. Ken*."

Returning for the 2015 tour, Jim Millan noted a new directness in the troupe's creative discussions. "They all work now at making each other better," says Millan. "Sure, they still get heated sometimes during the writing, challenging each other over where a scene needs to get cut, but they are great self-editors. I've seen them sacrifice good jokes of their own just to get better laughs later in a scene."

Mark McKinney says that beyond the usual behind-the-scenes back-and-forth, the shows themselves were creatively fulfilling and each of them experienced a sense of gratitude toward the fans who have stuck it out with them all these years. "It's amazing that we were still selling out the 2,000-seaters in some places, and that it was still really fun to work together. Until we went on stage, I don't think we even noticed how quickly that particular show graduated to being largely original new material. That old shorthand of writing together was still intact. Rock bands tour all the time, but when you're in comedy, you don't often get to go back and do it again, let alone to go 'Wow, I'm fifty and I get to sell out a 1,500-seater with my comedy troupe.'"

Bruce McCulloch says that humility not only comes easier to them now, it informs them of their own mortality, and having Mr. Tyzik crushing all of their heads is a symbolic finale, flattening out their various egos.

"In a sense, failure makes you who you are," says McCulloch, "and success makes you who you think you are or want to be. I'd say we succeeded maybe 51 percent of the time, and we've failed 49 percent of the time, maybe even more. Of course, adversity only makes us closer; it becomes a spark for our gasoline engine. We no longer character-assassinate each other the way we used to as younger men."

Today, Bruce McCulloch, Dave Foley, Mark McKinney, and Scott Thompson are all based in Los Angeles, and while Kevin McDonald currently calls Winnipeg home, he is constantly out on the road, working in Hollywood, or teaching comedy workshops all over the continent. Kids in the Hall tours are typically the only way all five of them ever see each other en masse, but according to McCulloch, the state of their union is strong, and although they may never fill arenas, they can still pack out a soft-seater like The Warfield and know that every member of the audience is on their wavelength.

"We're kind of the leaders of the outsiders, which is where I want to be," says McCulloch. "I didn't understand that before, but Kids in the Hall fans are just like us, with their weird points of view, their weird childhoods, their weird daddy issues, and their weird take on society." McCulloch also believes that one reason their audience still has warm feelings for them is that they never got so big that they became targets for derision. "My wife says that everything we touch turns to cult. "Like, *Brain Candy* is a cool movie but we never thought, 'Oh, let's just do a satirical movie with none of our characters that we've ever done before in it!' I don't smell money there."

And as for the present and future, Thompson says he welcomes any new Kids project that might come along, adding that their continued ability to collaborate on projects gives him optimism for the future, while reconciling him with their collective past. "I've made peace with a lot of things that used to bug me. At various points in the troupe's history, we've all been through tough times, but it's all in the past and we somehow worked through it all. By and large, we've always been there for each other."

While McKinney admits to having little enthusiasm about mounting another *Kids in the Hall* TV series, an uphill battle requiring the solving of a myriad of logistical problems, he says his "ears always perk up" at the idea of doing another tour. "I think it brings out the best in everyone, creatively. And of course, it's amazing and gratifying that the audience still comes out, which always make us want to do it again."

Dana Gould is still a fan and friend of the troupe, and believes that continuing to create fresh and live comedy is one of the reasons the Kids are still here. "Performing live as the Kids in the Hall is the nuclear rod that powers all of their outside endeavours. It fuels Bruce so he can go make a movie, or Dave and Mark so they can be in sitcoms. If you don't destroy your instrument or your brain with drugs and alcohol, you can't hide thirty years of experience. And you know, it's funny, because now my daughter loves *Superstore*, so she's laughing at Mark McKinney and I'm sitting there smiling because I know him from his other work. While I didn't tell her I know him, it's so great to watch a thirteen-year-old kid laugh at Mark McKinney in a completely different context. It's like knowing Paul McCartney, but from Wings."

The opening moment of the 2015 tour featured all five Kids decked out in white bridal gowns, a living metaphor for five guys married to a legacy, renewing their vows by merely remembering their lines. For all involved, it is their longest-surviving marriage, and they've made it work, for better or worse, for richer or poorer, in sickness and in health. And judging by the standing ovations after each show, the consensus is that their union is stronger than ever.

David Handelman, in the audience on the 2015 tour, says he was impressed that the Kids have remained "a living organism" instead of becoming a vaudeville sideshow, even if they have outlived their youthful moniker. "As they feared long ago," says Handelman, "they are now stuck with a slightly ironic name. Though compared to Mel Brooks and Carl Reiner, I guess they're doing okay!"

Backstage in San Francisco, Kevin McDonald waxed philosophical and seemed cautiously optimistic about the future of the troupe. "Every time we get together, and sometimes it's four or five years between these things, I think, 'Oh, will we still have that chemistry?' But we haven't lost it yet, and it's sort of come full circle. We're having so much fun on tour this time around. It's good to be back in San Francisco, which is like a second home to us."

"Of course, we're in L.A. tomorrow night," added Thompson, playfully, "so *that* will be like home to us too."

In the audience at the Theatre at Ace Hotel in L.A. were the Kids' old comedy colleagues Paul and Jackie Harris Greenberg. Now living in Los Angeles, both go back all the way to the troupe's earliest days in Toronto. Paul Greenberg's comedy troupe, The Vacant Lot, with Vito Viscomi, Rob Gfroerer, and Mark's brother, Nick McKinney, were direct beneficiaries of the comedy gold rush along Queen Street in the wake of the Kids' success, earning a sizable local following and even bagging their own short-lived, Lorne Michaels–produced television series. Paul also made the odd cameo in the Kids' TV series, while Jackie played the role of Natalie in *Brain Candy*. Paul says that the couple could barely believe the Kids were still putting up new material at the Ace Hotel "like it was still 1987. They probably didn't have to but I could tell that they didn't want to be like an '80s tribute band."

Jay Kogen was also at that show, and while he always felt that the Kids represented a wildly smart and fresh point of view in the 1990s, he was surprised by how vital they remained in 2015. "They brought sharp, energetic sketches, and remarkably, all-new material," says Kogen. "I left the theatre after feeling thrilled and inspired; they remain my comedic heroes."

According to Foley, the Kids in the Hall are mindful of becoming a wax museum of comedy, and he insists it is up to others to assess their place in the annals of comedy history. Humility aside, though, he readily acknowledges their influence on certain contemporary comedy. "I loved the *Key & Peele* series," says Foley, "and I think they definitely picked up on our film thing and our thing of approaching sketch comedy as serious acting, which was one of the things the Kids in the Hall did more than anyone before us."

Key & Peele director Peter Atencio confirmed this influence in a 2012 interview with *Splitsider's* Natasha Vargas-Cooper. "I was always drawn to comedy that looked exactly like the thing it was making fun of," said Atencio. "*Kids in the Hall* taught me that comedy could be really daring, and try things just for the hell of it—films like the 'Head Crusher' segments—those were my favourites. My senior project in a high-school film class was a blatant rip-off of the 'My Pen!' sketch."

Former *SNL* cast member and ubiquitous comedy presence Fred Armisen was already a competent professional drummer when he discovered the series, and he openly admits that *The Kids in the Hall* was a direct influence on *Portlandia*. "Carrie and I definitely took ideas from them," says Armisen, "and I'm always a little starstruck when I see them. I know I've said out loud, 'How would the Kids in the Hall end this sketch? How would they do it?' I remember being impressed with how cool it was that, when they did drag, they really played it real and didn't change their voices, and I have straight up copied that style and use them as a model of a way to act in drag. I also loved how different each of them were from each other, and how cool they all are. In a way, they remind me of Talking Heads; they dressed really normal but they were actually very subversive. It's also a big deal for me that Lorne Michaels produced both *The Kids in the Hall* and *Portlandia*. Both shows are from the same part of Lorne's consciousness, and I know that Lorne holds the Kids in the Hall close to his heart; their show still means so much to him."

Back home in Canada, the Kids' influence is still being felt. In June 2016, the CBC debuted the critically acclaimed *Baroness von Sketch Show,* an all-female sketch show earning frequent comparisons to *The Kids in the Hall. Baroness* member Jennifer Whalen grew up watching the Kids in Mississauga, Ontario, and recalls being amazed to see her own Canadian suburbs on a TV show. "It felt like they came from the same place that I did and that opened my eyes to using my own experiences as material," says Whalen, who readily admits that one of *Baroness von Sketch*'s most popular features, "Moms Say Hello," is an homage to the Kids' "30 Helens Agree."

"'30 Helens' was the first time I was aware of how a camera could be used to tell a joke," says Whalen. "It's a very elegant sketch. You get in, get a good laugh, and get out. That economy of joke, to me, is a beautiful thing."

Similarly, young Canadian comic and writer Amanda Brooke Perrin says the troupe made it OK to be weird and different. "They not only set the bar high for Canadian comedy," says Perrin, "but for young weirdos who wanted to create something unique."

If Bob Odenkirk were managing the troupe, he says he would have them produce a new series every two years, the way he and David Cross did with their Netflix comeback series *W/ Bob & David*. "Sure, you're older, so you could do a show about five dads, and then, maybe two years later, do something about five politicians," says Odenkirk. "Just write six episodes of something, spend a month shooting it, and you're done."

Today, musical director Craig Northey remains close to all five Kids, frequently backing them in their solo projects or as a troupe. There is now a palpable understanding between them that time is precious, and a collective admiration for the one dumb guy they are as a whole. "Everybody loves everybody," says Northey, "and each of them understands the value of the other four. Today, when I'm working with them, they seem to be drinking in every minute of it, and at the end, there's always the question 'When is the next time we get to do this?'"

In January 2017, Northey joined the Kids in the Hall for another live table read of *Brain Candy* before a sold-out crowd at SF Sketchfest. As always, Scott Thompson, the one Kid who has looked death in the face, was philosophical about the group's chances for survival. "I hope we'll all do something else again soon, because the last tours have been a lot of fun. I love to do sketch comedy. For me, it's the most fulfilling thing to do in comedy. Once you're on stage, everything—all your anger, all your pain—just disappears. Life is very tough, but it's very survivable. To me, I think there's nothing we can't defeat if we all work together."

Conan announcer Andy Richter has been a fan and friend of the Kids in the Hall since the late 1980s, and believes he knows the secret to their longevity. "They all began by having a kind of a crush on each other's minds," says Richter, "and amazingly, they've somehow held it together all these years. Back in Chicago, I was in improv groups that couldn't hold it together for two weeks, and here they've done it thirty years."

Back in 2015, Jim Millan reckoned the tour was their best yet. "They were absolutely in their prime," he says, "and firing on all cylinders. The fans loved it but I think it also reminded people in their profession what a unique and powerful group they still are."

On the 2015 tour, Kevin McDonald summed up the troupe with the following ode:

For those of you who just don't know,
Think I will explain the show.
We're the Kids in the Hall.
Maybe you're here because of rain.
So I think I will explain,
The Kids in the Hall.
We never really got bigger than cult.
Dave Foley says it's Scott Thompson's fault
For being a comic, sexual prophet.
A gay Che Guevara,
Or Cher Guevara.
I knew Dave and Scott and Mark.
When Bruce came, things got a little dark.
We're the Kids in the Hall.
We played at a club called the Rivoli.
Lorne Michaels discovered us but didn't like three
Of the Kids in the Hall.

Bruce and Mark were hired to write for *SNL*,
Live on Saturday nights.
The Anthony Michael Hall year
Speaks for itself.
But they soon were fired.
The five of us were hired to do
A moderately successful sketch show.
Let's go back to 1990,
Our TV show's very first year.
Had a Nielsen rating of about half of a half of,
A half of a half of,
A share.
Somehow we lasted five long seasons.
Guess "Head crusher" came in handy.
Then we made our eighty-eight minute epic,
Brain Candy.
Cost eight million, grossed three million,
We lost five million dollars!
Thought I had to get my old job back,
Middle-aged movie usher.
I hope you enjoy your big night out.
We're the show that your grandpas told you about.
Ageing Kids in the Hall.
We're not quitting.
We're not quitting.
We're not quitting
'Til one of us dies.
Probably Dave.

"I've had three families in my life," says Bruce McCulloch. "The really shitty one I was born into, then the Kids in the Hall, my other weird family who I see all the time, and finally the one I created."

As McDonald says, the Kids in the Hall are not likely to pack it in until one of them leaves the troupe or dies, and with the rise of individualized niche content providers such as Netflix, Hulu, and Amazon, the future of the troupe is whatever all five of them decide they want it to be. "We're probably always going to get that feeling when the five of us take a script that one of us wrote and by doing our magic spritzing thing the whole thing gets better," says McDonald. "There's something that still surprises me all the time. But it can't last forever; even Mick Jagger says it can't last forever."

As of this writing, the Rolling Stones are still together, and so too are the Kids in the Hall.

ACKNOWLEDGEMENTS

I 'd like to thank my father, Eric Robert Myers, for laughing so uproariously at Monty Python and *The Goon Show*, and in so doing, demonstrating to me and my brothers, Peter and Mike, that comedy was a virtuous art form. And to Kevin, Dave, Bruce, Scott, and Mark for manning "the laff boats" on all those cold nights in Toronto, and for allowing me to document their achievements in these pages.

Additional kudos to David Johnston and Janice Zawerbny for bringing this to House of Anansi, Douglas Richmond and Maria Golikova at Anansi for making me a better writer, Jody Beth LaFosse for transcription excellence and creative discussion, and Tavie Phillips for invaluable assistance.

SOURCES

The lion's share of this book comes from the author's own interviews with the five members of the Kids in the Hall: Dave Foley, Bruce McCulloch, Kevin McDonald, Mark McKinney, and Scott Thompson. Additional material was gleaned from interviews with Judd Apatow, Fred Armisen, Samantha Bee, Paul Bellini, Michael Ian Black, Brent Butt, Garry Campbell, Luciano Casimiri, Susan Cavan, Rob Cohen, Frank Conniff, David Cross, Ivan Fecan, Paul Feig, Diane Flacks, Joe Forristal, Carson Foster, Bobcat Goldthwait, Dana Gould, Jackie Harris Greenberg, Paul Greenberg, Allan Guttman, David Handelman, Dorian Hannaway, Brian Hartt, David Anthony Higgins, Steve Higgins, David Himelfarb, Norm Hiscock, Jay Kogen, Thomas Lennon, Kelly Makin, Nick McKinney, Seth Meyers, Lorne Michaels, Jim Millan, Chris Murphy, Mike Myers, Briane Nasimok, Kliph Nesteroff, Craig Northey, Bob Odenkirk, David Owen,

Cindy Park, Dan Pasternack, Gary Pearson, Amanda Brooke Perrin, Octavia "Tavie" Phillips, Don Pyle, Jonah Ray, Dan Redican, Andy Richter, Jeff Ross, Sandra Shamas, Garry Shandling, Jessica Shiffman (the "It's a Fact!" girl), David Steinberg, Scott Stewart, Carolyn Strauss, George Stroumboulopoulos, Pamela Thomas, Janet Varney, Jennifer Whalen, and Geralyn "Geri" Wraith.

ARTICLES AND BOOKS

Conlogue, Ray. "*The Kids in the Hall* talented, inventive." *Globe and Mail*, August 23, 1985.

Douwsma, Ben. "*Kids in the Hall*: The Lost Sketches." *Splitsider*, June 13, 2012, http://splitsider.com/2012/06/kids-in-the-hall-the-lost-sketches/.

Hardwick, Chris. April 2012. "The Nerdist Channel Presents *the Kids in the Hall*," YouTube videos. April 2012. https://www.youtube.com/watch?v=YhItXFBRk_Y&feature=youtu.be

Handelman, David. "Is America Ready for the Kids in the Hall?" *Rolling Stone*, May 1988.

Lyall, Sarah. "The Real Not-Ready-For-Prime-Time Players," *New York Times*, January 16, 1994.

Maslin, Janet. "Cross-Dressing and Happiness Pills," *New York Times*, April 12, 1996.

McCulloch, Bruce. *Let's Start a Riot: How a Young Drunk Punk Became a Hollywood Dad*. Toronto: HarperCollins, 2014.

O'Connor, John J. "Comedies from Sports and Canada," *New York Times*, October 19, 1988.

Rabin, Nathan. "Happy Happy, Joy Joy Case File #134: *Kids In The Hall: Brain Candy*," *AV Club*, April 1, 2009, https://film.avclub.com/happy-happy-joy-joy-case-file-134-kids-in-the-hall-1798216226.

Schneller, Johanna. "Kids Who Kill," *GQ*, July 1990.

Semley, John. *This Is a Book about the Kids in the Hall*. Toronto: ECW Press, 2016.

Tannenbaum, Rob. "Kids Stuff," *Details*, March 1993.

Yablon, Alex. "The Strange and Lasting Comedy Genius of *the Kids in the Hall*," *Vulture*, May 1, 2015, http://www.vulture.com/2015/05/weird-comedy-genius-of-the-kids-in-the-hall.html.

INDEX

PAUL MYERS is a Canadian writer and musician living in Berkeley, California. His previous books include the critically acclaimed *A Wizard a True Star: Todd Rundgren in the Studio; It Ain't Easy: Long John Baldry and the Birth of the British Blues;* and *Barenaked Ladies: Public Stunts, Private Stories.*